MAKING LAW FOR FAMIL

Oñati International Series in Law and Society

A SERIES PUBLISHED FOR THE OÑATI INSTITUTE
FOR THE SOCIOLOGY OF LAW

General Editors

Professor William L.F. Felstiner
Professor Eve Darian-Smith

Board of General Editors

Johannes Feest
Peter Fitzpatrick
Hazel Genn
Eliane Junqueira
Hubert Rottleuthner
Ronen Shamir

Titles in this Series

Emerging Legal Certainty: Empirical Studies on the Globalization of Law
Edited by Volkmar Gessner and Ali Cem Budak

Totalitarian and Post-Totalitarian Law
Edited by Adam Podgorecki and Vittorio Olgiati

Family Law and Family Policy in the New Europe
Edited by Jacek Kurczewski and Mavis Maclean

Foreign Courts: Civil Litigation in Foreign Legal Cultures
Edited by Volkmar Gessner

Procedural Justice
Edited by Klaus F. Röhl and Stefan Machura

(ALL THE ABOVE TITLES PUBLISHED BY ASHGATE)

Criminal Policy in Transition
Edited by Penny Green and Andrew Rutherford

Social Dynamics of Crime and Control
New Theories for a World in Transition
Edited by Susanne Karstedt and Kai-D Bussmann

Law and Poverty
Edited by ASbjorn Eide and Peter Robson

(PUBLISHED BY HART PUBLISHING)

Making Law for Families

Edited by
MAVIS MACLEAN

Oñati International Series in Law and Society

A SERIES PUBLISHED FOR THE OÑATI INSTITUTE
FOR THE SOCIOLOGY OF LAW

·HART·
PUBLISHING
OXFORD – PORTLAND
2000

Hart Publishing
Oxford and Portland, Oregon

Published in North America (US and Canada) by
Hart Publishing c/o
International Specialized Book Services
5804 NE Hassalo Street
Portland, Oregon
97213-3644
USA

Distributed in the Netherlands, Belgium and Luxembourg by
Intersentia, Churchillaan 108
B2900 Schoten
Antwerpen
Belgium

Hart Publishing is a specialist legal publisher based in Oxford, England.
To order further copies of this book or to request a list of other
publications please write to:

Hart Publishing Ltd, Salter's Boatyard,
Folly Bridge, Abingdon Road, Oxford OX1 4LB
Telephone: +44 (0)1865 245533 or Fax: +44 (0)1865 794882
e-mail: mail@hartpub.co.uk
WEBSITE: http//www.hartpub.co.uk

British Library Cataloguing in Publication Data
Data Available
ISBN 1–84113–205–5 (hardback)
1–84113–206–3 (paperback)

Typeset by Hope Services (Abingdon) Ltd.
Printed and bound in Great Britain on acid-free paper by
Biddles Ltd, www.biddles.co.uk

Foreword

Making Law for Families reanalyzes the concept of the family in the context of increasing challenges and questions raised by multicultural societies in ever more complicated international and transnational legal contexts. How is the family defined across cultural and national divides? To what extent and under what conditions should any particular state intervene? Is it possible to reconcile family law, which is grounded in the interpersonal obligations within a family unit, with legislation based on human rights discourse that is primarily concerned with an individual's obligations to the state? The essays in this volume seek to answer these and other difficult questions through grounded empirical research and insightful appreciation of how political systems practically function in various countries. An underlying concern is to explore to what extent and under what terms will the family unit will endure in the future as a basic unit of social management and control. Making Law for Families is the result of a workshop organized by Mavis Maclean and held between May 26 and June 2nd, 1999, at the International Institute for the Sociology of Law (IISL) in Onati, Spain.

The IISL is a partnership between the Research Committee on the Sociology of Law and the Basque Government. For more than a decade it has conducted an international master's programme in the sociology of law and hosted hundreds of workshops devoted to sociolegal studies. It maintains an extensive sociolegal library open to scholars from any country and any relevant discipline. Detailed information about the IISL can be found at www.iisj.es. This book is the most recent publication in the Onati International Series in Law and Society, a series that publishes the best manuscripts produced from Onati workshops conducted in English. A similar series, Coleccion Onati: Derecho Y Sociedad, is published in Spanish.

William L. F. Felstiner
Eve Darian-Smith

For Jacek Kurczewski,
whose involvement in legislative process
and dedication to its analysis
inspired this enterprise

Acknowledgements

This volume reflects the views of the chapter authors, but is also deeply enriched by the activity of the Oñati Workshop as an entity. We gratefully acknowledge the contribution of Jacek Kurczewski, Jean van Houtte, Teresa Piconto Novales, Fareda Banda, Valeria Mazzotta, Geoffrey Shannon, Sarah Tyerman, and Barbara Willenbacher.

We would also like to express our gratitude to the IISL in Oñati, particularly Malen Gordoa the Workshop Administrator, and to Eve Darian Smith for taking charge of us on behalf of the Editorial Board.

Contents

Section 3: The Rights Agenda: Rhetoric and Reality

Contributors

Dr Claire Archbold is a member of the Northern Irish Office of Law Reform, Belfast.

Dr Benoit Bastard is Directeur de Recherche at the COS, CNRS, Paris.

John Dewar is Professor of Law at Griffiths University, Brisbane, and a member of the Family Law Council for Australia.

John Eekelaar is a Fellow of Pembroke College, Oxford and Reader in Law at the University of Oxford.

Dr hab. Malgorzata Fuszara is Director of the INSS, Institute for Applied Social Studies at the University of Warsaw.

Dr Anne Griffiths is a Reader in the Faculty of Law at the University of Edinburgh.

Randy Kandel is an Adjunct Associate Professor in the Department of Anthropology, John Jay College of Criminal Justice, City University of New York.

Dr Beata Laciak is Deputy Director of the INSS, Institute for Applied Social Studies at the University of Warsaw.

Mavis Maclean is a Senior Research Fellow in the Faculty of Law in the University of Oxford. She is a member of the Governing Board of the IISL, and past president of the RCSL.

Encarna Roca is Professor of Civil Law at the Catedratica de Dret Civil, Barcelona.

Marty Slaughter is Reader in Law at the University of Kent at Canterbury, and former faculty member of the Cardozo Law School in the Yeshiva University, New York.

Dr Velina Todorova is Senior Researcher at the Institute for State and Law, University of Sofia.

1

Introduction: Making Law for Families: Studies in the Legislative Process

MAVIS MACLEAN

MAKING LAW IS an activity that requires not only academic argument and philosophical analysis, but also the skills of legal policy analysts and craftsmen operating in the world of politics. The contributors to this volume are a remarkable group of academic sociologists of law who through their energy and expertise have found themselves drawn into the world of law making, not only as expert advisers, but also as draftsmen, and as politicians and legislators in their own right. This experience led us to realise that the sociology of law has said little about this process in recent years. Our work in the field of family law has been concerned with arguing for and against various proposals for change, examining the implementation of legislative changes, pointing up adverse consequences, traditionally quick to criticise and slow to investigate and understand the business of law making. We felt that it was time to turn again to our original skills of reflection and analysis, in order to develop understanding of the conceptual framing of family law, the politique of making law for the family and finally the detail of the crafting process. Our aim is to develop the theory of the legislative process in a grounded way, through sharing the experiences described in this volume from colleagues in Europe (Western, Southern, Central and Eastern), Australia and the United States.

FRAMING LAW FOR THE FAMILY

The volume begins by asking the question "what do we seek from the law for the family?". How do we frame the concept of a regulatory system for interpersonal behaviour? As convenor and editor, I came to the project with a view of family law, located in my own base discipline, as an instrument of social policy. My starting point is to set up a number of policy models for regulating the relationship between individual, family and the state, organised around the aim of the activity. These ideal types would include a residual model for family law, which would aim to keep law out of family life and do no more than protect personal safety. Such a function might be covered sufficiently by the criminal law, though even the strictest limits placed on legislative intervention within the family tend to favour a special role for child protection. The family is often conceptualised as a "Black Box", and in a residualist approach the walls of this box are both strong and opaque. The family is "trusted" by society with self-regulation—an approach that thrives in a cohesive and stable society with well understood norms and values, such as a traditional Catholic society, or where the state is committed to liberal non-intervention, as under the recent Thatcher administration in the UK. Such a model tends to favour the status quo and therefore to be unacceptable to reformers, including feminists, concerned to counter patriarchal hegemony. At the other extreme on the continuum lies the instrumentalist model of family law, where the walls of the Black Box are transparent and permeable. Here the state uses the law to direct family life in a particular direction—whether seeking to impose a religious regime as in Israel, or a political regime as in Central and Eastern Europe between the Second World War and 1990. Extreme communitarianism may lead to a similar approach, as, for example, in the close legal control over discipline for children in Scandinavia. A "third way" may be found in what I would describe as a facilitative rights-based model, which sits well with increasing experience of multiculturalism in a global society. Here the law aims to provide a framework within which individual choice is maximised, but within the constraints of protecting human rights. For example, different ways of raising children according to religious beliefs are acceptable only up to the point at which a child's health and safety might be put at risk.

The normative issues are explored from contrasting standpoints in Part 1. John Eekelaar begins by confronting the question that has been avoided so far in this brief introduction, of the need to define what is meant by a family. He suggests that we should move on from this stumbling block to reframe family law as the law of personal obligation. Just as the law of contract and tort is becoming redefined in civil law as the law of obligation, so family law could benefit from being re-conceptualised as the law which regulates the obligations which we hold not in a commercial setting, but as a direct result of our personal relationships. The relationship between legal regulation and social norms in this view is a complex and dynamic one, whereby the law may act to incorporate developing social norms, or to strengthen a weakening social norm, or to withdraw support from an outdated or unacceptable norm. The economic dimension, which rests on the assumption of economic rationality, suggesting that family law can be used to regulate and alter the economic incentives for interpersonal behaviour, is addressed by Marty Slaughter. For women, marriage is a more specific investment of their time and energy and less portable than investment in the labour market by men. The law, therefore, might be held to act as a kind of block contract, which can adjust the individual imbalances experienced by those whose marriages end in separation. Although the legal framework is often held to provide protection for the individual rather than further a broader social policy agenda, the economic approach to family law indicates how regulation of the individual case impacts on a wider social policy agenda.

THE POLITIQUE OF THE LAW-MAKING VENTURE

Our second question asks what brings a topic to the top of the legislator's list of projects at a particular time and with a particular approach? Why, for example, have we seen in family law a global epidemic of legislation concerning the rights of children? Children Acts were passed in England and Wales in 1989, in Australia in 1995, in Scotland in 1995 and in Spain in 1987. In Bulgaria legislation is at the drafting stage and in Italy is under discussion at the time of writing. The content varies, from the English version pioneering the concept of parental responsibilities rather than rights, to the Italian version that is considering the right to play sports. But the legislative area is constant. Similarly, why do we see the regulation of same-sex partnerships in Sweden and in the Spanish Autonomias of Catalonia and the Pays Basque? To consider the question of both the policy and the political factors underlying these legislative reforms, we have used the French term which eloquently embraces both concepts as the "politique" of family law making.

We have identified three policy agendas underlying family law reform across jurisdictional boundaries. The first is a concern to take family matters out of the hands of courts and lawyers. John Dewar, drawing on his experience as a member of the Family Law Council of Australia, describes how the technocratic style of law making of the 1970s has been replaced by more political discussion in the preparation for reform of the Australian law concerning property and superannuation after divorce. There has been marked dissension between the judiciary and the government, and a reduced interest in using the empirical work of the socio-legal scholars. Dewar attributes the change to the aim of keeping people out of courts, and points up the essential difference between bargaining in the shadow of the law and bargaining where no such shadow is available. Benoit Bastard finds a similar political imperative in France to keep people out of courts. He describes the recent rise and fall of a campaign, supported by experts, to make divorce into an administrative procedure, which would mirror the administrative character of the procedure for entering a marriage. But professional groups were opposed, public opinion was not interested and the initiative has failed. The analysis demonstrates the need for either a broad or a powerful base of support for such an initiative to succeed, and it demonstrates how quickly family law reform can lose its base in socio-legal expert advice and become politicised.

Our second agenda is the more overtly political interest of the various political parties in family law reform, and we have examples from both state, or macro, and party, or micro, levels. The macro political element is evident in Encarna Roca's account of the regulation of registered same-sex partnerships in the Spanish Autonomias of Catalonia and Pays Basque. The desire of these Autonomias to use to the full their regional independence from the central government of Spain in Madrid has been demonstrated in legislative activity on as broad a front as possible. The competency of the Autonomia extends to regulating private, but not public matters, and therefore, although unable to legislate on divorce, which is held to be a public matter, the regional government can regulate cohabitation, which is a private matter. Thus to regulate same-sex cohabitation not only demonstrates the legislative capacity of the Autonomia to its fullest extent, but by covering a new and rather radical topic, demonstrates to the outside world the progressive and forward thinking character of that government, aligning it with the progressive regimes of Scandinavia.

The political influences described above have been brought into play by governments. But political activity in each country is not uniform; there are many parties with different views. The chapter from Poland by Beata Laciak and Malgorzata Fuszara addresses the family law policy agenda published by each of the new political parties of government and opposition. It focuses on the current drafts on cohabitation and divorce reform where debate centres on the various conceptions of the shape of the family, the autonomy of its members and their freedom to establish or dissolve a family. In Bulgaria, political difficulties arose when Velina Todorova attempted without success to involve foreign experts in the drafting of the Bulgarian Children Act. She and her colleagues are convinced of the need for child protection legislation in Bulgaria, and have made contact with experts in countries that have recently passed such legislation, who have visited the country putting on seminars explaining the support for the proposals. The politicians, however, were both anxious about the need to limit public expenditure, and cautious, as in Poland, about any move to expand the activity of the state, even with child protection as the objective. But the issue also arose of reluctance to embrace the influence of international networks of experts in the internal affairs of Bulgarian family law reform.

Our third and last agenda for the law-making venture demonstrates the need to transcend both party and national politics and looks to a universal concern with human rights, but also the practical difficulty of drafting rules and devising procedures to facilitate implementation. The penultimate chapter addresses the very particular concern with the rights of children to be heard in matters relating to their welfare; and the final chapter discusses the grand design of bringing family law for an entire common law (and thus uncodified) jurisdiction into line with the requirements of the European Convention on Human Rights. Both chapters are distinguished examples of the contribution that the socio-legal enterprise can make to the law-making venture in that they not only argue a case, but also do so from a position grounded in empirical study. In the first of these two chapters, Anne Griffiths and Randy Kandel address a common theme pervading the epidemic of legislation for children, that is the need to make the voice of the child heard. They give a detailed account of how this was addressed in the Scottish Act, and of how difficult it is in practice to achieve this aim even though it is widely accepted with enthusiasm. The final chapter links the theory of law-making with the technique of law-making.

We began in Part 1 with consideration of the grand designs for family law, how it is framed and what we want from legal intervention in this strange institution "the family", however we define it, and whatever we seek from it. When faced with the need to devise an appropriate justice system for multicultural societies, we have turned to a broad view of human rights as the baseline from which to work. Our final chapter on the process of law making brings home the problems we face here. Claire Archbold, now at the Northern Ireland Law Commission, has responsibility for bringing family law in the Province into line with the requirements of the European Convention on Human Rights. This task is sometimes described as "Strasbourg-proofing", using the analogy of "fire-proofing" or "weatherproofing", in order to avoid the necessity for cases to be brought before the Court of Human Rights in Strasbourg. In this chapter, the author describes how her day-to-day attempts to accomplish this task have led her to the uncomfortable conclusion that Human Rights do not sit well with family law. She argues that the conceptualisation of human rights comes from concern about the relationship between the individual and the state. In family law, on the other hand, the requirement is to balance the obligations and rights of individual, family and state, and of the individual as a member of a family, not only now but in the future. It is no surprise to be told how difficult this is. Our aim, nevertheless, is to take forward and develop our understanding of the underlying aims and parameters, of the skills of politique and technique, and to contribute both empirical data and analytical expertise to the complex task of making law for families. Our preferred solution seems to raise as many questions as it answers.

PART ONE

Framing Family Law: The Normative Aspects

2

Uncovering Social Obligations: Family Law and the Responsible Citizen

JOHN EEKELAAR

INTRODUCTION

I T IS OFTEN pointed out that social security law, and related areas of family law, tend to operate on the basis of *assumptions* about how people behave. Hence the British social security system designed by Beveridge in the 1940s assumed that most women would marry and provide domestic support to a male breadwinner. Accordingly national insurance-related benefits were structured around contributions made from a man who was earning a "family wage".[1] Similarly the payment of child benefit to mothers assumes that mothers will use this added resource for the benefit of children, and indeed it is assumed parents will generally distribute their resources throughout their family. Another common assumption is that a man who lives, unmarried, with a woman, will actually support her, and accordingly such a woman will lose entitlement to individual social security benefits even though she has no *legal* rights to support from her partner.

All this is well known. Indeed, such instances can be multiplied. Yet the fact that the law operates on the basis of various assumptions demands closer analysis. I wish to argue that these examples provide a glimpse into a very significant relationship between the legal and the social which could affect the way we think about law, and which can explain certain features of contemporary family law. First I will explore further the nature of the law's assumptions. I will then develop the implications this has for the relationship between social and legal norms. Finally, I will consider how some of this might affect thinking about family law.

---

[1] Fox Harding (1996: 137, 191).

THE LAW'S ASSUMPTIONS

I want to distinguish between three kinds of assumptions which can underlie the area of law characterised as family law. The first are assumptions that, by and large, a certain pattern of behaviour (or even a particular action) will, or is likely to, occur: I will call these predictive assumptions. The second are assumptions that people, by and large, believe that certain patterns of behaviour (or even a particular action) *ought to* occur: I will call these normative assumptions, because they make assumptions about social norms. The third are assumptions made by the law and policy makers about what forms of behaviour are appropriate: these may be called value assumptions. The third type differ from the second in that the second refers to assumptions made by the legislator or judiciary about what *people* think is proper behaviour, whereas the third refers only to what *legislators* (or judges) think is good or appropriate. Although these types of assumption can be distinguished theoretically, they may be difficult to separate in practice, and it is quite possible for all to be made simultaneously with respect to a single issue.

An example will illustrate the difference between the first two types of assumption, which are the main focus of this discussion. A government might decide to withdraw state funding of its railway system. Such action does not, of course, demonstrate a decision that the railways should stop running. The government will predict that the private sector will move in to take over running the railways. Such predictions are not, of course, always easily realised, as the British government's experiences with the Channel Tunnel or the coal industry demonstrate. No one, however, believes that the private sector is under any kind of *obligation* to invest in former state-sector activity. Its involvement is purely a matter of prediction. Compare this to the decision (taken many years ago) to allow testamentary freedom. Unlike some other systems, English law had no rule that a property owner must leave all or any proportion of his/her wealth to his/her spouse or children. But this did not mean that parents were not expected to provide for their children.[2] That there was a social norm encompassing such an expectation is clear from the Inheritance (Family Provision) Act 1938, which for the first time gave courts the power to make an award from a deceased's estate if the deceased had failed "to make reasonable provision for the maintenance" of the applicant (this included, in those days, a son who had not reached majority and an unmarried daughter of any age).[3] The reference to "reasonable provision" assumes the pre-existence of norms according to which a judgement can be made about what a person "should" do. It is not merely a matter of prediction. We can anticipate that many people will make charitable bequests, but we do not think they have an obligation to do this in the way we think that

---

[2] See Finch et al. (1996, 21–3).

[3] See now Inheritance (Provision for Family and Dependants) Act 1975; Succession Law Reform Act 1995. For a recent example, see *In re Pearce* [1998] 2 FLR 705.

people should make provision for their children in their wills. In 1938 there may have been no norm that an unmarried cohabitant should make some provision for the survivor of the relationship, but such a norm may have existed in 1975, when the law was extended to allow application to be made by a person who was dependent on the deceased at his death, but only for provision for maintenance.[4] This provision was broadened by the Succession Law Reform Act in 1995 to allow a claim by someone who had been living unmarried, but "as husband or wife" of the deceased for two or more years before the death, but the claim is still limited to an amount which is "reasonable" for the claimant's maintenance. Nevertheless, it is now possible to talk about it being reasonable for an unmarried cohabitant to provide for the maintenance of the other after death, and it may very well be that social norms go further and would expect a very long-term cohabitant to make provision going beyond maintenance (as is the case between spouses). The 1995 Act does not, however, go that far. So some social norms have been recognised by the law; others have not.

The same phenomena occur in other areas of the law where behaviour is judged according to "expectations", not simply of what is likely to happen, but of what *should* happen. So, when the Consumer Protection Act 1987, in section 3, defines a defect as being present when "the safety of a product is not such as persons are generally entitled to expect", the word "entitled" refers not simply to a "predictive" expectation, but to a "normative" expectation. When imposing liability for negligence, one of the steps taken by a court is to decide whether the defendant has failed to take "reasonable" care: has the defendant failed to comply with reasonable expectations of behaviour? Cane (1997) argues that tort law is a set of ethical rules of personal responsibility. To the extent that this is true, some of these ethical rules are found, or have their origin in, the kind of social rules to which I am referring. The failure of certain defendants to comply with the standards which social rules demand may lead to liability. However the fact that a defendant has breached a recognised standard of behaviour will not *necessarily* lead to tort liability, for the "law" needs to be satisfied that it is "just and reasonable" to impose a duty to compensate the plaintiff.[5] There may be other ways in which the breach of the norm could be addressed. Of course, it is the judges who enunciate these social rules. They are unlikely to do so on the basis of empirical investigation. More likely they just guess at what they are. Sometimes they will explicitly diverge from them. An example is the standard of care applied to the medical profession in *Bolam* v. *Freiern Hospital Management Committee*[6] according to which the standard of care of doctors was to be judged according to the standards prevailing in the medical profession at the time: in other words, what doctors "ought" to do was judged by other doctors, and not on some wider basis which might embrace community expectations.

---

[4] For a discussion of the evidence on which the law reformers based their assumptions about what people thought should happen to their property on death, see Cretney (1995; 1998: ch.10).

[5] *Caparo Industries* v. *Dickman* [1990] 2 AC 205; *Stovin* v. *Wise* [1996] 3 All ER 801.

[6] [1957] 1 WLR 582.

But that has been a reason for criticism of the "test", which is now moving more closely to a broader, community-based, standard.[7]

Two further examples move us back to family law. The first concerns the difference between English and New Zealand law on the question of whether a long-term unmarried cohabitant can legally acquire an interest in the property of the other cohabitant on breakdown of the relationship. In *Gillies* v. *Keogh*[8] Richardson J said:

> "Whatever the position in other countries, it seems to me that social attitudes in New Zealand readily lead to expectations, by those with apparently stable, enduring de facto relationships, that family assets are ordinarily shared, not the exclusive property of one or the other, unless it is agreed otherwise. . ."

The New Zealand Court of Appeal interpreted this as a normative expectation (i.e. in the sense that such assets "should" be shared) and was willing to give it legal effect. No evidence was offered to demonstrate the empirical truth of this assumption. Whether or not such an assumption might be made in England, the English courts have not been prepared to develop their legal doctrine into a position in which they might make it. If such an expectation does exist in England, there would be a disjuncture between the social norm about what should happen and the legal system's willingness, or capacity, to enforce the norm. The second demonstrates an explicit recognition of how judges draw on (their perception of) social norms in applying their discretion to make property and financial orders after divorce. Lord Hoffmann described the process in this way:

> "It is one of the functions of the Court of Appeal to lay down general guidelines on the relative weights to be given to various factors in different circumstances. . . These guidelines, not expressly stated by Parliament, are derived by the courts from values about family life which it considers [sic] would be widely accepted in the community."[9]

Were we not to recognise normative assumptions, but to treat all assumptions as being predictive only, our view of law and society would be a dualistic one consisting on the one hand of legal prescriptions, identified through their formal pedigree, and on the other, patterns of observable behaviour about which one could say no more than could the external observer in Hart's (1994) famous example: that some degree of prediction is possible. But if we accept that norms whose origin lies outside the legal system affect social behaviour, a huge segment of normative activity is revealed positioned, as it were, *between* the formal law and merely predictive behaviour. That this activity is normative—expressive of and guided by social rules—is a matter of great consequence for the operation of law and its scope for action.

---

[7] See Harvey Teff (1998).
[8] [1989] 2 NZLR 327 at 347.
[9] *Piglowska* v. *Piglowski* [1999] 3 All ER 632 at 644.

SOCIAL NORMS AND LEGAL NORMS

(a) Social norms

In view of the importance attached to social norms in this analysis, it is necessary to clarify the way they are distinguished from legal norms. For the moment
(we will return to the point) I will adopt the positivist criterion for law: that is,
that legal norms acquire their status as law by reason of their connection with
recognised sources. Social norms have no such connection and are therefore
more difficult to identify. Despite the importance of the distinction between predictive and normative behaviour, it is often difficult to identify whether people
are acting normatively or not. This is because the motivations for people's
behaviour are not always transparent. Sometimes it is clear enough. If a large
number of people collect to gaze upon some untoward event in a public street,
most of the onlookers will have gathered just because many others are there:
doing something because many other people are doing it is certainly one reason
for people's actions. But most people (in Britain, anyway) stand in queues for
buses, not just because others do this, but because most people think they ought
to do this. Someone who breaches that social convention will be disapproved of,
whereas someone who walks past the untoward event is not.

Yet there are clearly ambiguous situations. Perhaps tipping is an example. Is
this done (if at all) only because others do it, or because customers independently believe they ought to do it? This ambiguity has caused considerable theoretical difficulty. Hart's (1994, 255) "practice" theory of social rules stipulated
that social rules were constituted by the coincidence of a regular pattern of conduct "and a distinctive normative attitude to such patterns of conduct which I
have called 'acceptance' ". Dworkin (1977, 53) criticised this on the ground that
it failed to distinguish between concurrent and conventional morality. Applying
that distinction to an example given by Finch and Mason (1993), *concurrent*
morality refers to the situation where most people agree that they ought to support their elderly parents, but do not "count the fact of that agreement as an
essential part of their grounds for asserting that rule", whereas if they believe
they would not have that duty were it not for the "social practice", that would
be a case of *conventional* morality. Dworkin (1977, 57) argues, first, that Hart's
"acceptance" theory applies only in the second instance, and, even in that event,
that it applies poorly because people find it difficult to agree on the scope of the
conventions which they are accepting. He therefore suggests that people do
more than simply "accept" conventions; by following them they implicitly
endorse ("justify") them. Hart (1994, 255–7) later accepted that his theory was
an inadequate explanation for *morality*, and applied only to conventional social
rules: these existed where general conformity "is part of the reasons which its
individual members have for acceptance". There was, however, no reason, he
thought, that people should necessarily *endorse* the rules.

If one were to accept this, a person would be following a social rule only if one of the motivations for that person's action was based on an understanding that there was such a norm and this constituted part of the grounds for the action. But it is not clear that this formulation has much relevance to reality. As Finch (1989, 149, original emphasis) stated, "because many women *do* give up their jobs to care for a parent, it becomes easier for brothers, social workers and whoever else makes the intervention in a particular case, to say that a particular woman *should* do so". In other words, the basis for believing one has an obligation to do X may lie simply in the observation that others are actually doing X, whether or not it is perceived that there is an independent social norm that "one ought to do X". Dworkin's distinction between concurrent and conventional morality, although accepted by Hart, and Dworkin's insistence that acceptance implies justification (not accepted by Hart) seem of little importance when it is difficult to disentangle whether people think they should do something because there is a convention that they should do it or simply because other people do it. What is important in our context is the simple fact that a large proportion of people think that they themselves, and others, actually have certain obligations. What these obligations are can be discerned through empirical research. Finch and Mason (1993: 19, 166–9) showed that, in England, there was *no* general normative assumption that wider family members had obligations to support other members, though the case of parents and children was different, there being a majority view (but only of 58 percent of their respondents) that children do have an obligation to "look after their parents when they are old". They did however find that a sense of "responsibility" could arise through a process of "commitment" to certain family members which might develop over time (through interaction and reciprocal assistance). They suggest that the reason why the parent–child relationship is seen as the most likely context to raise a sense of obligation is that, by its nature, "commitments" are more likely to be invested in that relationship than in other kin relationships. But kin relationships do provide a framework in which such commitments might arise.

(b) Legal norms

Social norms have tended to be neglected in the positivist legal tradition. Even for Hart, they seem to have importance only as providing a basis for his explanation of the transition from the pre-legal to the legal world: once the union of primary and secondary rules is achieved, Hart's focus shifts to the problem of pedigree and the nature of secondary rules, especially the rule of recognition. Legal theorists closer to the work of sociologists and anthropologists such as Ehrlich and Malinowski have asserted that law can arise from social practices as well as formal institutions, and it is difficult to resist this from a study of family and kinship systems. But these claims have been criticised for ultimately failing to provide criteria to distinguish between law, morality, fashion, etiquette or even the rules of grammar. This has led Tamanaha (1997, 122) to advance the proposition that law "includes only those norms that are actually enforced by publicly approved coercive institutions, *and* only when the norms so enforced are also reflected in the actual behaviour of the group". Under this formulation, legal norms will also be social norms, though not all social norms will be legal norms. The problem with this solution, elegant though it is, is that it falls into the trap of most conceptualisations which seek a unified definition of law. There is no reason why propositions should not be characterised as legal if they satisfy the requirements of pedigree, even if they are not reflected in the behaviour of the group. On the other hand, mere conformity with pedigree requirements may not be all there is to an understanding of law.

The solution to the puzzle, it is suggested, is to recognise that what counts as "the law" can be perceived differently by a lawyer, advising on the status of the law and the legal obligations of the citizen at any one moment, and by a court, engaged in the formulation of the law. The lawyer's task is primarily descriptive; to identify the citizen's legal obligations by reference to propositions grounded in the accepted legal pedigree, perhaps making predictions of judicial or other official response in cases of uncertainty. The lawyer should be careful not to present his favoured interpretations of legal propositions as representing the law unless they are likely to coincide with those of the officials who have the authority (which the lawyer lacks) to make binding interpretations. The lawyer should also be careful not to confound the citizen's legal obligations with her social obligations. But when a judge decides what the law is in a case before him, he engages in a *normative* process, for he has authority to interpret, and thus re-constitute, the law. He is not describing or even following the law, but *applies* it and, in so doing, re-creates it. In this process, the judge may well draw on "actual behaviour" as manifested in social rules and incorporate them into legal formulations and decisions. For the judge, then, those social norms he chooses to incorporate into his reformulation of the law may be considered to be part of the "law", even if, before such incorporation, it was correct to describe those social norms as being outside the law.[10]

THE RELATIONSHIP BETWEEN SOCIAL AND LEGAL NORMS

Although from the individual citizen's point of view, social and legal rules are quite distinct, in practice social rules may be as significant as legal rules. They

[10] This analysis explains the puzzles of retrospectivity revealed in *Kleinwort Benson* v. *Lincoln City Council* [1998] 4 All ER 513. It was correct, *from the point of view of the court*, to hold that the new decision operated retrospectively, because the new interpretation represents not only what the courts believe properly to express the law *now*, but what it was on the earlier occasions, despite the contrary (and now overruled) earlier decision. *But it is also true* that, from the standpoint of the parties who had relied on the earlier (now overruled) decision, their legal rights and duties were *correctly* described according to that decision. It should therefore have followed that no mistake of law had been made, because *that* question should have been decided from the *parties'* standpoint, not that of the court.

may provide equal, or even more compelling, motives for action. Compared to legal rules, they may suffer the defects identified by Hart (1994, 92–4) in primary (i.e. "pre-legal") rules as uncertainty, staticity and inefficiency. But in this respect they may not be so different from very open-ended legal rules, especially of family law, which has been characterised by Dewar (1998) as being in a state of "normal chaos". Furthermore, as Lord Hoffmann indicated in the earlier quotation, they might at any moment be drawn upon by a court and incorporated into a legal decision. For the purposes of living his or her life, the citizen may not care to spend too much time distinguishing between "social" and the "legal" norms. The vagueness and indeterminacy of many social norms does not lessen their impact. Indeed, it may make their recognition and analysis more urgent.

On this view, therefore, there exists within society a network of social norms which is formally independent of the legal system, but which is in constant interaction with it. Formal law sometimes seeks to strengthen the social norms. Sometimes it allows them to serve its purposes without the necessity of direct intervention; sometimes it tries to weaken or destroy them and sometimes it withdraws from enforcement, not in an attempt to subvert them, but because countervailing values make conflicts better resolved outside the legal arena. It is time to take a closer look at this interaction.

(a) Abstention

Proponents of the public/private distinction have long pointed out that a failure of state intervention in family life may amount to as significant a statement of policy as intervention (Olsen, 1985; Gavison, 1992). Such non-intervention may be seen as tacit endorsement of the social norms applicable in various contexts. The reluctance of formal law to condemn marital violence has traditionally been seen as in effect conferring a licence on men to indulge in the unrestricted exercise of power over women. However, the position is probably more complicated, for that view ignores the possible presence of social norms which might limit the exercise of such power. Abstention does not necessarily imply endorsement of a norm-free area of activity. This may be demonstrated by the nature of the parent–child relationship. An historical examination of the legal structure of that relationship reveals a series of rules designed primarily to protect the father's interests in the person and property of the child as against outsiders (Eekelaar, 1986). The law did not proclaim either parent's duties towards their children, and indeed the transformation of the legal language of rights with respect to children to "responsibilities" in the Children Act 1989, was perceived as a revolutionary re-conceptualisation. However one should not be misled into believing that parents were "normatively free" to ignore their children's interests. Shaher's (1990: 112–17; 167–79) examination of childhood in the Middle Ages revealed much evidence of an appreciation of an obligation on parents to care for and educate children. It is true that this took place against a backdrop where corporal punishment was more widely accepted than it (probably) is now, and severe means were used in some contexts to instil religious virtue, but this was a reflection of pedagogical techniques rather than of indifference or deliberate cruelty. Shaher (1990, 179) quotes cases of legal proceedings taken by parents against teachers and masters of apprentices for ill-treatment of their children. Pollock (1983, 111–22), examining the post-medieval period, draws on private diaries to provide evidence of appreciation by parents of a duty to educate and provide for their children.[11] Puritan religious training could be harsh, and corporal punishment perhaps became more severe from the early nineteenth century (especially in schools), but she too found cases of public condemnation of parents for child cruelty in the nineteenth century. The most consistent theme in the parent–child relationship seems to have been the desire of parents (not always successfully achieved) to maintain parental *authority* over children. But it is equally evident that it was considered that such authority was necessary for promoting the interests of the children. The formal law, therefore, provided a framework for that authority, and if it did not expressly articulate a duty to exercise it favourably for children, this may have been because it was considered that it was sufficient and perhaps preferable to allow its regulation by social norms.

One reason why it may be thought preferable not to incorporate social norms into formal law could be that to do so would reveal and require express resolution of deep-seated political and social dilemmas. Parents are expected to love, or at least to show solicitude towards their children, not simply as a matter of prediction but as a matter of obligation. This may not be stated as a legal duty, although the social norm is indirectly incorporated into the law, because social workers may assess a child to be at unacceptable risk if they perceive that its parents are not looking after it in a "normal" way (Parton, Thorpe and Wattam, 1997). Here the law stands back from imposing a direct duty because of the conflict its enforcement would cause with the political values of family autonomy and non-intervention. Another example is found in the divorce law. Despite the divorce rate, there is still probably a social norm that marriage should be for life, at least unless strong reasons exist for bringing it to an end, and (despite actual behaviour) Jacqueline Scott (1999) has demonstrated that there is a strong social norm against marital infidelity.[12] But neither norm is any longer incorporated into the law. The withdrawal of these norms from the law cannot be taken necessarily to imply an attempt by the law to oppose them, but rather a recognition that their assumption of legal form would involve excessive intrusion into private and intimate behaviour.

[11] A telling comment was made by one Newcome in the seventeenth century, who hoped that: "I do not fall into reproach for not providing for my family (for this is now my constant fear lest I die and shall have nothing for my wife and children)." This indicates the expectation of "reproach" for such failure.

[12] British men and women have consistently maintained a high disapproval (between 85 and 90 percent) of sex outside marriage during the 1980s and 1990s.

(b) The move from abstention to incorporation

The absence of legal articulation of social norms does not, therefore, imply the absence of any obligation. Indeed, the implication may sometimes be the opposite: that the social obligations are so strong that their legal articulation is unnecessary. In such circumstances, legal intervention may indicate a weakening of the social obligations, since the most obvious way to try to strengthen them would normally seem to be by incorporating them into the formal law.[13] A straightforward example of the gradual legal recognition of social norms in family law occurred in the case of both the spousal support obligation and the parent–child support obligation. Even at the time of Blackstone (1765), the latter was seen as primarily a moral obligation, although it had become indirectly legally enforceable through the Poor Law. By this process, the community recovered from a liable parent the financial assistance it provided directly to, or for, the child. Such recovery is based on the premise that, in providing for the child, the community is discharging a (social) obligation of the parent. But this technique "legalises" the support obligation only to the extent that the state provides support for the child, which is limited. The social obligation may be wider. In 1844 unmarried women were allowed to make a direct claim on the child's behalf against the father, but this too was subject to a variety of procedural restrictions (as compared to claims on behalf of children of married women) until 1987. Now child maintenance claims are mostly covered by the Child Support Acts 1991 and 1995, which apply only where the parents are not living together (Eekelaar and Maclean: 1986, ch. 2; Maclean and Eekelaar: 1997, 38). In the case of married people, the obligation of a husband to support his wife was recognised indirectly through the agency of necessity (if he cast her out) and through separation orders made by ecclesiastical courts, which were obtainable only on the commission by the husband of certain offences. After 1878, the power to make such orders was extended to magistrates' courts, but again only if the husband had assaulted the wife. Yet from 1834 a husband's social obligation to support his wife was recognised indirectly through the Poor Law, when it allowed the support given to a wife by public funds to be treated as a loan recoverable from him (Eekelaar and Maclean: 1986, ch. 3; Maclean and Eekelaar: 1997, 27–32).

It is significant that in both cases the earliest examples of where the social obligation became, at least partly, incorporated into the formal law, arose where the community had incurred liabilities (either through the granting of credit or the payment of assistance) and in times of relatively high social instability. In that event the community was able to appeal to the father's (or hus-

---

[13] See the example of succession discussed by Janet Finch et al. (1996, 22–3) concluding that "this interpretation implies that legal intervention would become necessary only if testators began to bequeath their property outside the family on a large scale".

band's) socially recognised obligations as a way to recover at least some of its expenditures. But where those obligations are weakening, or are very weak, the community has to tread warily. Governments which try to exact tax from citizens to make payments towards causes with respect to which citizens have little sense of obligation, risk criticism. This could happen were they to try to compel contributions from relatives to offset state support for family members towards whom they felt no sense of obligation. It is an interesting reflection on the ambiguity of attitudes to the issue of post-divorce support in the United Kingdom that *the fact of having been married* to someone has never generated an obligation after divorce to repay the state for expenditures on a former partner. This is probably because divorce, on any meaningful scale, has arisen only relatively recently and there exists little or no sense of a social obligation of support between formerly married people (apart from child support, and even this is problematic), unless perhaps they had been married for a long time. The obligation arises mainly through the exercise of the discretionary adjustive jurisdiction of the courts, and the courts have found it difficult to draw on any background social obligation to underpin their orders, and the search for an underlying rationale for them remains illusive.

The recent history of the child support obligation is a strong example of an attempt to strengthen what was perceived to be the weakening of the social norm that fathers should pay for their children. Governments in recent years have latched on to the biological relationship as a basis for strengthening the obligation through the formal law. The difficulty is that this has not aligned perfectly with the underlying social obligation, especially as perceived by men. Maclean and Eekelaar (1997) found that, although fathers were willing to accept the existence of a social obligation to prioritise their first set of natural children as objects for their support after they had left them, they were much readier than mothers to qualify this when it came into competition with their social duties towards new sets of children. Indeed, the data showed that, characteristically, it was only when a father had built up a relationship with a child over time that the obligations towards that child survived the establishment of a new obligation to a later child. This is consistent with Finch and Mason's (1993) conclusion that, even in the case of parents and children, the sense of obligation was related more to the development of a commitment than to the biological fact itself. So the close legal identification of the obligation with biology has the appearance of a norm imposed, as Edwards et al. (1999) say, from "top down", reflecting more of a middle-class ethic than one widely diffused among the population. In terms of this analysis, it may reflect an assumption closer to the third type (of the values of the legislator itself) than of the second (of the norms of society).

Sometimes, however, the social obligation will be broader than the legal one. Parents may feel under an obligation to support their children for a longer period than the law requires. Grandparents may feel obliged to assist grandchildren, and children their parents, although these obligations were no longer subject to legal enforcement after 1948.[14] Where legal recognition is withdrawn from social obligations, what happens to the latter? This may depend on how the government treats them. When the Labour Government elected after the Second World War reduced the range of "liable relatives" against whom the state could have recourse when it gave assistance to a family member, it transferred in full the obligation to look after these family members from other family members to the community. No contribution was expected of other family members. It seems unlikely, however, that the sense of obligation which grandparents feel towards their grandchildren has diminished, though the evidence is sketchy, and the obligations felt by children towards their elderly parents remains strong.[15] On the other hand, withdrawal of the obligation may not be replaced by a communal obligation, and the state may rely on the strength of the underlying social obligation to endure for the benefit of the needy individuals. This policy has become more dominant since the 1980s. Thus the restrictions placed on the provision of income support benefits to individuals aged between 16 and 25 introduced in the late 1980s and early 1990s were implemented on the basis of an assumption that these young people would fall back on parental support.[16] Such support is not legally enforceable by the children against their parents unless the parents have separated.[17] More stringent criteria for the provision of local authority housing for the elderly by local authorities may force older people to have recourse to the social obligations felt by their children to safeguard their well-being.[18] A more long-standing example appears where social security benefits are withdrawn from an adult who cohabits without marrying with another who is earning. There again, neither cohabitant is legally bound to support the other, but it is assumed that there is a social obligation of support, probably applying only where the couple shares a residence.

The relationship between the legal and social obligations of a parent towards stepchildren is complex. There is evidence that stepfathers feel themselves under an obligation to support their stepchildren (Maclean and Eekelaar, 1997; Edwards et al., 1999), and English law does allow such an obligation to be enforced on behalf of a stepchild if a step-parent leaves the home, but only if the step-parent is married to the child's parent, and only to the extent that the step-

[14] National Assistance Act 1948, s. 42(1).

[15] See Finch (1989: 38–9, 43) referring to the prevalence of the "idea that the older generation in a three-generation family occupies the position of net giver of support, and that this is regarded as proper in the normative sense".

[16] Maclean and Eekelaar (1997, 43).

[17] Children Act 1989, s. 15(1), sched.1, para. 2(4).

[18] It may be that, if government wishes to transfer the cost of supporting individuals from itself to family members, it should make the obligation legally enforceable between family members, creating directly enforceable legal obligations of intra-familial support which coincide more closely with the social obligation, as is generally the case in European countries. Yet even when legally recognised, such obligations are not easy to enforce and it is not clear that making them legally enforceable by family members against one another necessarily strengthens their force. See generally Eekelaar (1997).

parent "assumed responsibility" for the child.[19] Furthermore, the obligation is enforceable only through the courts; it is ignored by the child support scheme. That scheme goes even further in its disdain for step-relationships, for no allowance is made, when assessing an absent parent's liability towards his/her biological children, of any "social" obligation towards stepchildren. In this, the UK (and Australian) schemes differ strongly from that in New Zealand. This might be seen as a case where legal obligations cut across possible social obligations in an attempt to weaken the latter. But the result seems to be more likely to destabilise the legal obligation towards the parent's natural children living in a different household rather than the social obligation towards the stepchildren and the government proposes to remove this feature of the scheme when it restructures it.[20]

SOCIAL NORMS AND THE DEPENDENCY OF WOMEN

The argument is sometimes made (Deech, 1977; Smart, 1984: 223, 227–8) that assumptions upon which legal support obligations are premised perpetuate or strengthen the economic dependency of women on men. The exposition above, however, has illustrated that there exists an intermediate layer of norms between the "law" and its subjects. There is therefore no simple, direct, relationship between the formal law and behaviour. Law operates upon, or through the agency of, these social norms. So if we are concerned about questions such as the dependency of women, or indeed, of children or of other social groups, it is necessary to consider the role of the law in the context of these social norms.

It seems clear that the social norms of family support were, at least originally, premised on a normative conception of sexual and generational roles. There may be some argument that they were based not on normative but predictive assumptions: i.e. that most wives would simply devote themselves to domestic matters and most husbands would earn the income. Nevertheless, the original restriction of the support duty to the husband, and indeed, the restriction of the support obligation to marriage, suggests a strong normative assumption that women who wished to have sexual relationships should marry and adopt a domestic role within marriage. Indeed, this could scarcely be denied in the face of historical and cultural evidence. The support obligation can indeed be viewed as an integral part of what may be called a social bargain: the wife should perform domestic functions, and in return she should receive protection and support from her husband.

Faced with these combined normative forces, one may ask what stance the law should adopt. We have suggested above that the law may abstain from "legalising" social norms where they are considered sufficiently strong to

[19] Matrimonial Causes Act 1973, s. 52(1).
[20] *A New Contract for Welfare: Children's Rights and Parents' Responsibilities* (The Stationery Office, 1999, Cm 4349).

operate independently, but that legalisation may be employed to provide more effective enforcement if they weaken, though any wide gap between the legal and social norms could cause difficulty. Therefore, as long as the foundational norm prevailed, (viz., that wives should mainly perform a domestic role) there was good reason for the law to reinforce the complementary norm (that husbands should support their wives) if it came under threat. Without such intervention, the social bargain could be broken. But such enforcement does not *in itself* assert any norm that women *should* adopt these roles; or even that they *usually do* adopt them. It assumes *that people think that they should adopt them*; that is, that there is an existing social norm to that effect. If the law's assumption is accurate, its intervention merely ensures that the existing normative arrangements are properly complied with. Objections against dependency should therefore be levelled against the foundational social norms, not the legal intervention with respect to support. However, the position becomes more difficult if the foundational norm begins to erode and the assumption becomes more predictive than normative. The second limb of the social bargain still holds (in the nature of a unilateral contract), so that where wives do in fact adopt a domestic role, the support obligation should apply. But it may require modification, to allow for cases where wives have not followed the domestic role. It should therefore become gender neutral, and sensitive to the actual economic circumstances of the parties. This indeed has occurred in UK law, where it is difficult to see how spousal and child support laws in themselves operate to impede the evolution of norms concerning family roles. And indeed, if it becomes acceptable that women might adopt those roles *without becoming wives*, the reciprocal obligations should be extended to cover those circumstances. This may have occurred in the UK with regard to the reciprocal *social* norm of support, but this has not been reflected in the law.

SOCIAL NORMS AND INCENTIVES

It is not difficult to see how fiscal policy may affect family life. Financial measures may be a clear expression of a wish to reward or deter certain behaviour patterns. These also operate against a backdrop of legal and social norms. Where there is a social norm that cohabiting adults "ought to" be married, for example, a tax allowance for married couples will support that norm. But failure to keep track of evolving norms can be self-defeating. For example, the "old" system whereby a husband and wife's incomes were aggregated for taxation purposes, the "married allowance" deducted and the tax levied on the husband, assumed that ordinarily the husband will have far greater income than the wife: that is, that the domestic role will be assumed by her. Indeed, it could be seen as a measure in support of a norm that she *should* assume that role because, if she had high earned or unearned income, depending on the size of any allowance permitted for the wife's earned income, the total tax liability would be greater than it would be if the couple were taxed separately (at lower rates). However, changes in the social norm that women should adopt the domestic role were too rapid and the application of that taxation regime began (at least theoretically) to threaten another social norm: that adults who cohabit should be married. For, if the woman's income was above a certain level, it would be financially better for the couple to live together without marrying and be taxed separately. That was the position in the UK until separate taxation was allowed for earned income in 1972, and for unearned income in 1990. However, there is no evidence that these factors affected the marriage rate, which declined steadily throughout that period, and although there is now a modest tax benefit to be obtained by marrying (soon to be removed), this seems to have done little (if anything) to arrest the decline in the marriage rate. Perhaps the experience of taxation and family life shows the relatively weak influence even fiscal measures can have when confronted by deep changes in social norms.

The basis of payment of social security benefits can also reveal assumptions about family living, and the British scheme as founded on the Beveridge Report, certainly did so. Thus a married man who paid national insurance contributions received additional benefits for a wife and children, whereas a married woman would only receive them if she could show her husband was not working as a result of some incapacity. Increases in unemployment and sickness benefit were payable only during a period in which "some female person" had care of a child of the beneficiary's family, and additions could be made to a retirement or invalidity pension if a "female person" caring for a child was residing with the beneficiary (Eekelaar, 1984: 202). These provisions, which were significantly modified in the 1980s, show a belief in the normative structure of a family founded on a male breadwinner and female carer, and might have caused little difficulty when this belief corresponded with such norms. By being tied closely to the performance of such roles, the provision of benefits appears (intentionally or otherwise) to reinforce them. However, the extent to which they acted as a brake upon the evolution of family roles is likely to have been limited. They could have had severe effects on couples who attempted complete role-reversal, for they would be substantially less well off than others. But there is nothing in the benefit structure to prevent individual married women from earning entitlement to benefits in their own right. In practice, however, women, especially those who have children, earn less than men and are less likely to have built up an uninterrupted contributions record and therefore it has been said that "a husband's financial support is in effect assumed" (Fox Harding, 1996: 193). The implication is that women should be supported by the state without regard to the presence of the husband's income. But that puts the matter too simply. What is assumed is that there is a social norm that couples who live together should share their resources, so that the partner with the lower income should, and will, benefit from the higher income of the other. This is the basis of the so-called "cohabitation" rule which denies social security benefits to non-earning individuals (not only women) who live with an income earner. Benefits can be paid on the basis of the contributions of the higher earner in the expectation that these, too, will be shared with the other partner. An attempt to treat cohabiting couples as if they were two single individuals could be seen either as undermining the sharing norm (for why should one partner share with the other if the other is assured of equivalent resources without such sharing?) or as excessive generosity to couples who comply with the sharing norm.

SOCIAL NORMS AND THE RESPONSIBLE CITIZEN

It might be wondered at this point if it matters whether the assumptions to which we have been referring are predictive or normative. After all, from the point of view of the state, when removing a communal duty to support family members, it may be enough simply to predict that other family members will move in to provide any assistance needed. Why does it matter whether this action is done as a matter of fact or under the perception of a social duty?

In fact it matters a good deal, for it allows the government to appeal to popular consciousness by urging people to adopt proper normative behaviour: in effect, to behave as Responsible Citizens. The government can therefore hold back from legislating, or incurring the costs of legal enforcement, while at the same time urging compliance. Indeed, when Tony Blair told the Labour Party Conference after the 1997 election that "a decent society is not based on rights. It is based on duty. On duty to each other" he probably had social duties in mind more than those arising under the law. The phenomenon of "naming and shaming" of individuals or corporations for transgression of apparent social norms is an example of direct appeal to the "responsible citizen".[21] The media can play its role in the process.[22]

The process is very evident in family policy. The movement of rhetoric in the Children Act 1989 from the language of parental "rights" to that of parental "responsibility" was far more than a technical change. The whole basis of the state's relationship to families was restructured. The Children Act of 1948 was revolutionary in the way it underwrote the new belief that deprived, and even abused children, should not simply be removed from their family environments, but that those environments could be assisted and even reconstituted through social casework, so children could be reintroduced into them, or even that their removal from them could be avoided. Yet this vision still saw a primary responsibility as lying on the state to sustain those families, and hence they retained the legal powers to do so. When the Children Act 1989 speaks of parental responsibility, however, it means that the primary responsibility lies with parents to care for their children; not with the state. The state's role is therefore pared back to

[21] This occurred when various insurance companies who had adopted unethical trading practices were reticent in making compensatory payments.

[22] Examples range from condemnation of "political sleaze" to securing the dismissal of the England football coach for apparent insensitivity towards the disabled.

cover only children "in need", and to intervene only where the risk assessment of the child suffering "significant harm" is too great. In typical vein, the Utting Report (1997) states:

> "Parents deciding to place a child away from home are . . . responsible for satisfying themselves that arrangements for keeping their child safe exist and are likely to prove effective . . . the decision about placement is ultimately their responsibility. In making it parents should possess all the information they need about the arrangements for keeping their children safe."

Although this rhetoric implies parental choice, the expectation is that the choice will be "responsibly" exercised on the basis of information and advice provided by the government. Thus the government has proposed the establishment of a National Family and Parenting Institute to, inter alia, "map and disseminate information and good practice: for example, on parenting and relationship support" (Home Office, 1998: 9). The Crime and Disorder Act 1998 permits courts to make a "parenting order" against a parent of a child who has been convicted of various offences, or who has been subject to an "anti-social behaviour order". Such orders may require the parent to "comply, for a period not exceeding twelve months" with any requirements in the order which the court thinks "desirable in the interests of preventing" repetition of the offence by the child or commission of any further offence. Furthermore, the parent may be required to attend counselling or guidance sessions.[23] Parents can be punished for failing to comply. Here the government uses both the criminal law and "persuasive" measures to reinforce what are held to be social norms (themselves not expressed in legislation) compelling parents properly to guide and control their children.

The government is also seeking to reinforce social norms which promote "responsible" attitudes to marriage. While the law itself has virtually withdrawn from the attempt to reinforce marriage through the application of the matrimonial offence doctrine, and, from the legal point of view, the –no-fault divorce scheme enacted in the Family Law Act 1996 would effectively[24] give married people a "right" to exit from a marriage which has broken down irretrievably, government policy seeks to reinforce whatever social norm remains that married people should not leave their marriages lightly. Hence the scheme included proposals for information meetings (subsequently held in abeyance), at which parties would be required "to consider whether their marriage really is over or whether it could be saved" and it is even suggested that Registrars of Marriages should provide couples who are contemplating marriage with "information about marriage" to give them a "clear idea of the rights and responsibilities they are taking on" (Home Office, 1998: paras. 4.29 and 4.13). The "responsible citizen" is expected to exercise his or her rights in a responsible way (see Eekelaar, 1999).

---

[23] Crime and Disorder Act 1998, s. 8(4) and (7).
[24] There may be some restrictions: for example, if the divorce would create "substantial" hardship for the other party. It is not known how this provision will be applied.

This appeal to the largely undefined concept of "responsibility (Piper, 1993, 1999), provides the opportunity for the further injection of "assumptions" into the application of the law. These may include value assumptions, those of the makers and administrators of the law, which may or may not coincide with the social norms of the community. There is a further problem. When Hart (1994) wrote about primary rules ("social norms") he seems to have imagined a largely homogeneous society, and even then he accepted the difficulty of identifying their content: that, indeed, was one reason for establishing legal institutions. But within pluralistic and multicultural societies they may vary between communal groups. What may be perceived of as responsible parenting, or as the responsibilities of marriage in one group, might be quite different in another. This is not the place to examine the problems multiculturalism poses for family law (see Freeman, 1998). The important point must be made, however, that the readiness of the law to permit the incorporation of social norms into its fabric gives scope for differential application of the law between groups. This may be considered as a virtue within a multicultural society. However, there is also the danger that lawmakers and administrators will apply the social norms pertinent to one group to a different group or even confuse their own values with a group's social norms. This, of course, is always a danger in any form of legislation, but in the case of the "legal" application of social norms it carries the added problem that, unlike in the case of legislation, the content of the norms being applied is not transparent; or, at least, not subject to the scrutiny of the legislative process. The activities of adjudicators and administrators therefore need to be carefully monitored to ensure that the consequences of their perceptions of social norms are understood and subject to discussion.

CONCLUSION: FAMILY LAW AS PERSONAL RIGHTS AND OBLIGATIONS

The preceding discussion has tried to demonstrate the thinness of a perception of family law which is confined to those norms which are articulated by formally recognised legal agents. Of course, such norms and those which await such articulation have a different legal status. But as far as the subjects of family law are concerned, their similarities and connections are more interesting, and more important, than their differences. Both sets of norms can be viewed as providing a source of obligations.

Legal rights and obligations tend to be defined by reference to formal definitional categories. Rights under the European Convention on Human Rights are linked to concepts such as "family life";[25] individuals may acquire rights as members of a "family",[26] or by virtue of holding legal parenthood or parental

[25] See *X, Y and Z* v. *UK* (1997) 24 EHRR 143 (could a transsexual in a relationship be experiencing "family life"?).

[26] See *Fitzpatrick* v. *Sterling Housing Association* [1998] 1 FLR 6 (did a same-sex couple constitute a "family"?).

responsibility. Legal rights to financial provision after cohabitation are dependent on the fact of formal marriage, even though the substance of the rights acquired and obligations imposed depends more on the fact and length of cohabitation than the formality of marriage. Consequently it is necessary to settle on a definition of those categories in order to mobilise the legal norms attached to them. But social norms, lacking the formulations of the law, operate much more flexibly. The question is only: does this individual have an obligation to that individual and, if so, what is its nature? We could say that all rights and obligations which arise out of individuals' *personal* lives, in the sense of their personal rather than commercial or "public" relationships, are relevant to "family" law. In fact, the term "family" law is itself too narrow, because it presupposes an a priori category ("the family") whether legally defined, or conceptualised in some other way, as being the location for such obligations. Thus one hears arguments, for example, that legal obligations should not be imposed between same-sex couples because this has nothing to do with "the family". Yet there may be felt to be some "personal" obligation between such couples as much as between heterosexual couples, married or unmarried.

If, as seems likely, the bulk of the material of family law is reducible to a network of personal rights and obligations, and these powers and obligations need not necessarily be seen as emanating from an entity designated as "the family", would it not be better to re-characterise the domain of family law as that of personal rights and obligations? And if these rights and obligations were to include social as well as legal ones, what a rich field would be opened up.

REFERENCES

Blackstone, Sir W. (1765) *Commentaries on the Laws of England* (Oxford: Oxford University Press).

Cane, P. (1997) *Anatomy of Tort Law* (Oxford: Hart Publishing).

Cretney, S.M. (1995) "Reform of intestacy: the best we can do", *Law Quarterly Review*, 111, 77.

—— (1998) *Law, Law Reform and the Family* (Oxford: Clarendon Press).

Deech, R. (1977) "The principles of maintenance", *Family Law*, 7, 229.

Dewar, J. (1998) "The normal chaos of family law", *Modern Law Review*, 61.

Dworkin, R. (1977) *Taking Rights Seriously* (London: Duckworth).

—— (1986) *Law's Empire* (London: Fontana).

Edwards, R., V. Gillies and J. Ribbens McCarthy (1999) "Biological parents and social families: legal discourses and everyday understandings of the position of step-parents", *International Journal of Law, Policy and the Family*, 13, 78–105.

Eekelaar, J. (1984) *Family Law and Social Policy* (London: Weidenfeld & Nicolson).

—— (1986) "The emergence of children's rights", *Oxford Journal of Legal Studies*, 6, 161.

—— (1997) "Family solidarity in English law", in D. Schwab and D. Henrich (eds) *Familiäre Solidarität* (Bielefeld: Gieseking).

28   *John Eekelaar*

Eekelaar, J. (forthcoming) "Family law: keeping us 'on message' ", *Child and Family Law Quarterly*.

Eekelaar, J. and M. Maclean (1986) *Maintenance after Divorce* (Oxford: Oxford University Press).

Finch, J. (1989) *Family Obligations and Social Change* (London: Polity Press).

Finch, J. and J. Mason (1993) *Negotiating Family Responsibilities* (London: Routledge).

Finch, J., J. Mason, J. Masson, L. Wallis and L. Hayes (1996) *Wills, Inheritance and Families* (Oxford: Oxford University Press).

Fox Harding, L. (1996) *Family, State and Social Policy* (London: Macmillan).

Freeman, M. (1998) "Cultural pluralism and the rights of the child", in J. Eekelaar and T. Nhlapo (eds) *The Changing Family: Family Forms and Family Law* (Oxford: Hart Publishing).

Gavison, R. (1992) "Feminism and the public-private distinction", *Stanford Law Review*, 45, 1.

Hart, H.L.A. (1994) *The Concept of Law*. 2nd edn (Oxford: Clarendon Press).

Home Office (1998) *Supporting Families: A Consultation Document* (London, Home Office).

—— (1999) *A New Contract for Welfare: Children's Rights and Parents' Responsibilities* (Stationery Office, Cm 4349).

Maclean, M. and J. Eekelaar (1997) *The Parental Obligation* (Oxford: Hart Publishing).

Olsen, F. (1985) "The myth of state intervention in the family", *Michigan University Journal of Law Reform*, 835.

Parton, N., D. Thorpe and C. Wattam (1997) *Child Protection: Risk and the Moral Order* (London: Macmillan).

Piper, C. (1993) *The Responsible Parent: A Study in Divorce Mediation* (London: Harvester Wheatsheaf).

—— (1999) "How do you define a family lawyer?", *Legal Studies*, 19, 93–111.

Pollock, L. (1983) *Forgotten Children: Parent-child Relations from 1500 to 1900* (Cambridge: Cambridge University Press).

Scott, J. (1999) "Family change: revolution or backlash in attitudes?", in Susan McRae (ed.) *Changing Britain: Families and Households in the 1990s* (Oxford: Oxford University Press).

Shaher, S. (1990) *Childhood in the Middle Ages* (London: Routledge).

Smart, C. (1984) *The Ties that Bind* (London: Routledge & Kegan Paul).

Tamanaha, B. (1997) *Realistic Socio-Legal Theory* (Oxford: Clarendon Press).

Teff, H. (1998) "The standard of care in medical negligence—moving on from *Bolam*", *Oxford Journal of Legal Studies*, 18, 473.

Utting Report (1997) *People Like Us* (London: Department of Health).

3

Marital Bargaining: Implications for Legal Policy

M.M. SLAUGHTER

INTRODUCTION

ECONOMIC ANALYSIS OF marriage has been popular in legal circles in the United States for the last ten years, in part due to the influence of the Nobel prize-winning economist Gary Becker whose *Treatise on the Family* (1981) provided the foundation. While Becker's theories have proved controversial, a point which I will discuss below, they provided the impetus for legal scholars to apply economic models to family law, particularly in issues of no-fault divorce and financial provision.[1] There is now a second wave of these studies, which introduces a more dynamic picture and explores marital bargaining or negotiation.[2] These studies apply to an area of economics called game theory.[3] A simple game, which I will discuss in this chapter, is called a zero sum game or "split the pie"; that is, if a surplus is produced by the efforts of two parties, bargaining theory asks how it will be distributed.

In this chapter I am going to discuss the insights game theory has to offer in analysing marital and familial behaviour. I am concerned with the fact that there is an overwhelming propensity for women to bear an unequal burden or cost of marriage and I will use bargaining theory to explore why this should be the case. Briefly, this is related to the fact that spouses bargain and make decisions in the shadow of the labour market and the marriage market. They also bargain in the shadow of the law—the law of marital contracts, divorce, custody and financial provision. The question is how these factors affect the dynamics of marital decision making and how they contribute to the structural

---

[1] American Law Institute (1997); Brinig and Crafton (1994); Carbone and Brinig (1991); Cohen (1987); Dnes (1997); Eekelaar (1998); Eekelaar and Maclean (1986); Ellman (1989); Estin (1993); Singer (1994).

[2] See the excellent and comprehensive article by Wax (1998). See also Mahony (1995); Guggenheimer (1998); Rose (1992).

[3] The standard reference is Baird et al. (1994). At this point it is sufficient to say that game theory simply models what choices two or more players will make in various circumstances, what the consequences of those choices are and the likelihood that a rational actor will make one of those choices.

inequality of women in marital bargains. Finally, I will explore how pre-marital contracting and/or changes in the law of divorce might change those dynamics.

I should add a word of caution. This analysis does not produce conclusions that have not been drawn before, especially by feminists who argue that marriage is an institution dominated by male power. Furthermore, the results often fall in line with what appears to be common sense or common knowledge. The virtue of the analysis is not that it produces new theories but rather that it provides a framework for formalising and systematising observations that have been made before.

ECONOMIC MODELS OF THE FAMILY

1. Common Preference Models

The current use of bargaining theory in analysing marriage is a response to earlier economic models, most notably that of Gary Becker.[4] A brief description of those models and issues is therefore in order. The original economic models of the family—first by Paul Samuelson and then more famously by Gary Becker—adopted a "common preference" model in which the household is treated as a unit that seeks to maximise utility: to put it colloquially, to maximise the marital pie.

Becker assumes that the family group consists of selfish "rotten kids" (dependants) and one altruistic parent (patriarch, dictator) who controls the resources and distributes benefits to the "kids". This person is "altruistic" in that his preferences reflect his concern for the welfare of the others and their utility or well-being is part and parcel of his preferences or satisfaction. The head will make decisions that maximise the family pie which in turn causes all the "rotten kids" in the family to act to similarly maximise. The bigger the pool of family resources the larger each person's individual share; each will then get a bigger slice of the surplus.[5] In this way, the family as a whole works as a single agent that maximises utility (the pie).

2. Challenges to Becker

Feminists and other economists challenged Becker's assumptions in a variety of ways. One of the most common critiques of Becker is that by assuming one head of the household who altruistically looks after the others, he assumed traditional gender models and subsumed the interests of the individual parties to the

---

[4] For an overview of models see Bergstrom (1997) and Behrman (1997).
[5] Lundberg and Pollack (1996, 142–3).

common unit of the family. Husband and wife are not treated as independent agents and the family is not recognised as having multiple decision-makers.[6]

A more telling point is that economic models of the family like Becker's tend to assume that the distribution of resources in a family is equal. By adopting such an altruistic head of the family, Becker's model is unable to take into account the way in which resources are distributed within the family and the processes by which such distribution are arrived at. Becker's model cannot predict what kinds of distributions are made. Thus it is unable to shed light on one of the most problematic aspects of modern marriage: the fact that all indicators show that in marriage women bear a disproportionate burden of its costs. A good case can (and has) been made showing that husband and wife shoulder unequal burdens and get unequal shares of the family resources. As a simple example, in families where both husband and wife work, wives do a disproportionate amount of the housekeeping and childcare; husbands garner a disproportionate share of leisure time.[7] Although the welfare of the family as a whole increases through the joint efforts of the members, this does not mean that welfare increases equally for all members or that the resources are distributed equally.

One bedrock assumption of bargaining models is that marriage is potentially a positive sum game: a person will enter marriage because he believes he will gain (in love, money, well-being, etc.) more than he would if he did not. Each party expects to be better off married than single or married to a different person. A different way of saying this is that this particular marriage produces a surplus, a degree of welfare above and beyond what would be achieved outside the marriage. A corollary of this is that given that actors act to maximise utility, they will enter or stay in marriage as long as it provides a surplus, or more welfare or utility than the alternative of going it alone (or with a different partner). In effect, in a bargaining theory the participants compare the costs and benefits of making the "deal" as opposed to other "deals" that are available to them.

Common preference models cannot make this relative cost-benefit analysis. Since the utilities of the individual members are subsumed into the family pool they cannot treat them as independent actors, and do not see them as comparing their costs and benefits with marriage with their costs and benefits outside of marriage.[8]

Many are offended by the concept of maximisation of utility when applied to a (supposedly) altruistic institution like marriage. The definition of utility is, however, broad enough to overcome these objections. This is an issue that has attracted considerable attention, but for purposes of this discussion it is sufficient to say that altruism and love are incorporated into, not excluded from the model. The most obvious form of utility is wealth, but that is not the only one. What one party considers good and what may give pleasure can include the love

---

[6] Wax (1998), n.36; Estin (1995); Lundberg and Pollack (1996, 140–6).
[7] A convenient and thorough survey with references can be found in Wax (1998, 516–25).
[8] Lundberg and Pollack (1996, 143).

and respect of the other and the good of providing happiness and welfare to the other.[9] It is quite possible that the agent derives pleasure from seeing the welfare of his or her family increase, and therefore one of his individual preferences is maximising this welfare. The "best possible outcome" of a negotiation or bargain can therefore include what is best for the bargainer's loved one.

Bargaining models also challenge another principle of consensus models like Becker's. The bedrock assumption of all economic models of the family is that it is comprised of rational actors who act to maximise utility. Bargaining models assume two rational actors or decision-makers who are interdependent but also independent. In terms of the family, they start from the premise that the household members (husband and wife) are dependent but distinct individuals who at some point have difference preferences and interests. As a result, in addition to having common interests, they sometimes have conflicting interests. Given that there is difference and potential conflict, they must negotiate or bargain to reach an acceptable decision.

Many are also offended by the assumption that husband and wife are independent actors with unique preferences who consider their own good or self interest, i.e. act to maximise their utility. Nevertheless, it seems safe to say that husband and wife repeatedly engage in decision-making in which each has preferences and desires. Unless they are clones (and then there's no point to the marriage)[10] or unless one party is a doormat, their tastes and preferences will diverge at some point, if only on whether to eat Chinese or Italian food or go to the mountains or seashore for their holidays.

Bargaining models or games explain the ways in which these differences are reconciled. The point of the game is to reach the most optimal outcome, i.e. the greatest amount of utility (the biggest pie) that the parties can agree to and still achieve satisfaction or a deal they can live with. That is what all compromises are: a point between the ideal and the intolerable.[11] The next section will review the factors that influence how these marital compromises or bargains are made and how it comes about that women systematically get an unequal portion of the surplus generated by marriage.

BARGAINING MODELS

There are no doubt many factors that contribute to these differences and what follows does not claim to be complete, although it does cover what have been identified as major factors. There are two components in bargaining. One is formal and the other behavioural (although there isn't necessarily a firm separation

---

[9] In this chapter, care of children is encompassed in the utility of the parents.

[10] For an interesting argument from a Hegelian perspective as to why this is the case, see Schroeder (1998).

[11] The ideal is a free ride—to get all the benefits with no cost, which amounts to getting your way all the time. The intolerable is to get less than you could get elsewhere.

between the two). The formal or structural elements are the different positions of the bargaining partners both intra-maritally and extra-maritally. These are related directly and indirectly to the labour market and the marriage market. These structural elements determine the bargaining set, that is, the range of acceptable bargains, and thus determine whether an acceptable bargain can be struck at all. The second set of factors refers to the parties' abilities to bargain. These abilities affect the precise terms or outcome of the bargaining and the distribution of the marital surplus.

1. Formal Elements

(a) Threat Points, Reservation Prices and BATNAs

Since divorce (or being single) is now an option to marriage, bargaining models posit decision-makers who compare the utility or advantages inside marriage with those outside marriage. Thus a critical feature of treating marriage as a bargaining game is reliance on the notion of a threat point. This is the point at which the individual says "I've had enough; I won't stand for another moment, or go a step further, or pay a penny more; it's not worth it." It is a point that describes the utility the individual will gain by staying in the arrangement and making the particular bargain compared to the cost of foregoing the agreement or arrangement.[12]

In the bargaining models of marriage, the threat point is the utility of the marriage as opposed to the utility of divorce (or remarriage).[13] It defines the point at which it is no longer worth it to go on with the marriage. When, for example, both spouses are working, there is continuous negotiation about the relative contributions of each to the household and childcare. If one of the parties feels especially overburdened and the other party refuses to do more of his or her share, the "threat point" is that the other will leaves. Or to take another example, marriage is an agreement to live monogamously. Each party agrees to commit himself exclusively and forego other sexual opportunities. For most, this generates a benefit of fidelity. If one of the parties does not do their share to contribute to this, i.e. if she commits adultery, the other party leaves. The "threat point," then, determines whether the marriage game will go on or will be called off.

In marriage, the bargaining game(s) encompasses all the daily decisions that are made about how to conduct family affairs—from who will do the dishes, to how childcare is to be arranged, to how to invest the family savings, to all kinds of emotional issues like warmth, admiration and sex. This game, therefore, guides the distribution of the resources or utilities between the marital parties.

---

[12] Lundberg and Pollack (1996; 1993).

[13] In the setting of pre-marital contracts, the threat point defines the point at which one would agree to the terms of the contract, or call the marriage off.

This is the "split the pie game". While the distribution is influenced by the threat points, it is not determined by them and there is no reason to assume that there will be equal sharing.[14]

The formal threat point, therefore, determines the range of payoffs the party is willing to accept from the bargain, not the final agreement. This is not unlike a seller who asks £200,000 for his home and a buyer who offers £150,000. The "bottom line" or lower limit is one's reservation price. The seller's reservation price may be £180,000; he will be willing to accept any offer of £180,000 or more. The buyer's reservation price may be £170,000; that is, he is willing to increase his £150,000 offer to this limit. These mark the threat points for each of the parties; if they do not receive their reservation prices the bargain is not worth it to them and the game or bargain will be called off.

The threat point or reservation price is determined by the BATNA (the best alternative(s) to a negotiated agreement).[15] The limit of a person's willingness to strike a bargain is a function of what they see as the alternatives to not reaching an agreement. The threat point for each of the parties to the bargain will depend on what their fall-back positions are. If they think they could do better outside this particular bargain they will not make the deal. Thus the buyer's reservation price is determined by his belief that he can find another house that is equally desirable for £170,000.

The person who has more and better alternatives is the person with the upper hand in the bargaining process. He has an "exit point" or threat point advantage. The person with more or better alternatives will not value this particular bargain as highly as the person who has fewer, worse or no alternatives. For example, in a buyer's market with a ready supply of affordable and desirable housing this will be the buyer. He can more credibly threaten the negotiations by being more willing to call off the bargaining game with the seller of a particular house. He can forego the agreement more willingly because the consequences for him are less serious and less costly than they are for the other. By the same token, the price of the bargain will be higher for the person with the fewer/worse alternatives. It will cost him/her more than it would cost the other.

If we translate this into the situation of marital bargaining, each of the parties has to calculate what their alternatives would be to not going forward with the marriage game. If they do not reach agreement, the marriage will be called off, they will lose this particular partner and may have to remain single. They have to calculate whether being single is better, and if not, what their alternatives are for making a different and better marriage.

What we will see is that *in general* the alternatives or fall-back positions are different for men and women. These differences add up to a situation in which *relatively speaking* women will be worse off than men if the marriage does not go on. As a result, women will value the marriage more than men and will be

---

[14] In fact unequal sharing in many cases is the only thing that will maximise the utilities of the couple. See Wax (1998, 560–5).

[15] Raiffa (1982); Mahony (1995).

more willing to make concessions or bear an unequal cost of the marriage (up to the point where their reservation price is reached). It is important to note that the claim here is not that men do not want marriage; the claim is that for a number of reasons women often want it more or want a more equitable arrangement. What matters is the relative strength of the partners' desire for marriage. The one with the greater desire for maintaining the marriage is the weaker bargaining partner. It is, therefore, important to look at the reasons why women might desire marriage more and thus be the weaker parties in marital bargaining.

(b) Extramarital Factors

(i) Labour Market

One of the most potent advantages men possess is that they have better alternatives in the labour market. By every available statistic men fare better than women in the labour market, even these days when women are making progress.[16] Men have more opportunity and reap greater monetary rewards. Many women are consigned to a pink-collar ghetto or to dead-end jobs. Many face glass ceilings or brick walls in their efforts to find meaning and empowerment in work, not to mention opportunity and equal remuneration. If one of the alternatives to marriage is work, for the most part men have the better alternatives. Or to turn this around, running a home and raising children may seem like much more rewarding work than that afforded to many women. Working at the jobs they can get is simply not as attractive an alternative to marriage for many women as it is for men.

Furthermore, many women gain financial comfort and security and a higher standard of living through marriage than through their own work in the labour market.[17] Their standard of living as a single person is often lower than it would be if they were married.[18] This can be the result of a number of factors. First, it is no coincidence that women are more likely to marry men who are either older and/or more well endowed (more educated, richer etc.) than themselves, rather than vice versa. I will discuss this more below, but it creates a situation in which in many instances women marry men who earn more money in the labour market than they themselves can earn, or at least than they earn at a given point in time. Second, the labour market discriminates against women in a variety of ways. Women who remain single and make their own way in the market are not as likely to go as far or make as much money as men.

[16] Wax (1998).

[17] This may decrease as women assume more important positions and are paid more. It also obviously depends on how much their spouses make and whether there are dependent children.

[18] Although Pahl (1989) reports that where men control the family budget and dole out a portion to the wife to provide for herself and the children, some divorced women report that they have a higher standard of living being single.

Second it has been suggested that as an alternative, men can either acquire or purchase more of their necessities than can women, e.g. financial support, prestige, power, a wide social circle, etc.[19] While it is not discussed very formally, women note that they lose out on social status, social life and the like by being single or divorced.[20]

(ii) Marriage Market

Each party's alternatives to a particular marriage depends not only on their alternatives in the labour market but probably more importantly on their "value" on the marriage market. This is a complicated area and I will try not to oversimplify so as to obviate all the problems, but once again, in general, men have the advantage.

(a) Fertility/attractiveness

As every woman of a certain age knows and as all statistics demonstrate, in terms of marriage "the best years" of a woman's life are her earlier ones.[21] This is related to a host of factors, the most important of which are her attractiveness and her fertility. (These may be related to one another and to other factors like vitality and health.) Both diminish or depreciate as she gets older. She becomes, as an accountant called it, a "wasting asset".

If the same were as equally true of men it would not affect the relative power of the parties in marital bargaining. Unfortunately (or fortunately, depending on your perspective), it is a fact of social life that it is not equally true of men. Men are more likely to be considered attractive well past the age that women are and the aspect of their extended fertility is obvious. It is common for men to begin (second) families well into middle age and beyond. It is not possible for older women to do so without the hardship and danger of reproductive technology, and when women in their fifties and sixties do have children they are treated as cases for moral and legal concern.

In terms of attractiveness, older men (can) look distinguished far more easily than older women (can), and with less time, money and effort. To be sure, much of this is due to cultural perceptions of beauty. Much of it, however, can also be attributable to the results of the disparity in the labour market. As men grow older they increase their earnings, status, power and wealth, which in turn increase their attractiveness. Money and power are sexy.

---

[19] Rousseau (1979) argued that as a result of these structural divisions of labour "men depend on the women only on account of their desires; the women on the men both on account of their desires and their necessities. We could subsist better without them than they without us."

[20] This is as true of wealthy women as it is of the less endowed. Recently a prestigious New York apartment building rejected the application of a grand dame of the fashion world because as a single woman she would be out in the evenings and limousines would be dropping her off late at night and making noise.

[21] Wax (1998, 549 and references therein).

These factors must be combined with recognition of the dominant cultural pattern of hypogamy.[22] That is, in general women marry men who are older then they are. By sheer numbers alone, as men grow older they have a larger number of possible (younger) mates. As women grow older they have fewer possible (older) mates.

These effects are increased if the woman has dependent children and/or has been a homemaker.[23] The rate of remarriage falls precipitously for women with dependent children, as does the labour market potential of women who spend time as homemakers and as a result have tenuous ties to the labour market.

(b) Desire for children

Women may value marriage more than men because they may have a greater desire to have children. The causes of this desire, if it exists, are of course, controversial. Certainly, however, their limited time of fertility makes the timing of marriage more urgent for women of childbearing age. This desire could also be seen as women's solution to their lack of position in the labour market. In the absence of more attractive alternatives, women can always work as mothers, a job with an immense amount of worth and satisfaction. The greater desire for children can also be seen as a result of a great deal of cultural conditioning that teaches that a woman is not really fulfilled or valued unless or until she becomes a mother. If women do have a greater desire for children, they may well value marriage in order to get a father, protector, provider and helpmate for their children.

(iii) Sunk Costs

One of the factors that will be taken into account in marital bargaining is the nature and extent of investment that has already been made in the relationship, i.e. the sunk costs. This is particularly true if there has been what Cohen (1987) calls "marriage specific capital" (and there usually is to some degree). This refers to the talents and efforts, the human capital, that is invested into homemaking and child rearing in a *particular* relationship. This is to be contrasted to the human capital invested in the labour market which consists of education, training, experience, seniority and the like. It differs from marriage-specific capital in that it is portable: it can be taken away, used and traded if the relationship (job) ends. Marriage-specific investment cannot. The problem, then, is that the partner who has made the most investment in the marriage—usually the woman— has less human capital to carry away from the marriage and take either to the labour market or to another marriage. This is compounded by the fact that in many instances, the current law on financial provision on divorce, particularly maintenance, offers women little protection against loss as a result of marriage-specific investment in that it more or less leaves the partners in the position they

---

[22] Cohen (1987).
[23] Wax (1998, 549 and references therein).

are in at the time of divorce. In a traditional role-divided marriage, the home-maker who has invested her capital in the marriage has few alternatives to mak-ing her own way outside the marriage and as a result can be less willing to exit the marriage. This is less true for women who work during marriage, but it is only a question of degree, not of principle.

(c) Intramarital Factors

The previous discussion assumes there are only two alternatives: agreement and harmony or divorce. But we know this does not characterise all marriages. There are some marriages that are not happy but neither do they come to an end. It may be that the parties cannot reach agreement, or not very much agree-ment. Rather, they exist in a constant state of non-co-operation or non-co-ordination, in what has been called the "burnt toast/harsh words" syndrome.[24] This must have particularly been the case when divorce was limited.

While these marriages do not as fully maximise the marital pie as co-operative marriages, there is not a complete absence of joint benefit as there is with divorce. Rather, there is still enough marital surplus that the parties are better off than they would be if they divorced. The threat points in this case are internal to the marriage. The point is for each to achieve some utility while inflicting misery or punishment on the other in order to get their way. In the absence of co-ordinated agreement the parties conduct their affairs separately, trying to maximise their individual welfare without overturning the marital boat. The wife, for example, may return to work to protect her future and shirk on her household tasks or withhold in emotional or sexual ways. The husband may withhold income or become abusive. It is likely, although not inevitable, that the person who supplies the domestic services is more likely to suffer more, if only because men seem to be able to tolerate a higher degree of domestic dis-order. Women's greater preference for a higher level of domestic comfort often is tied to their feeling that children need this.

2. Behavioural Aspects

If the negotiation set—the range of acceptable/possible solutions—is deter-mined by each partner's alternatives, what determines the precise distribution of the marital surplus? Assuming that the bargaining game is to go forward (since the alternatives are worse), what determines the distribution of the resources? Once the parties decide that this marital pie is bigger and better than any other available pie, what are the factors that determine the size of each party's slice? There is no guarantee in marriage that the slices will be equal. Indeed all the evi-dence points to the conclusion that they usually are not. The distribution of the

---

[24] Lundberg and Pollack (1994); Wax (1998, 552–5).

marital surplus will depend on the relative strength of each party's ability to drive a hard bargain, i.e. their ability to maximise their own utility.

(a) Credible Exit Threats

As I indicated in the section above, one of the most significant factors in determining the range of possible distributions is the availability of exit options. The specific terms within the possible set are in part a function of the relative strength and credibility of each party's exit threats. It is one thing to make a threat; it is another thing to have the ability to back the threat up with action, to make the threat credible. For example, a wife who has returned to university and gained qualifications has more credibility in threatening divorce than one who has been out of the labour force for many years. A two hundred-pound man has the credibility to make good his threat to beat his wife unless she gets the dinner on the table.

(b) Sense of Entitlement

The ability to drive a hard bargain also depends on how much each party values his and the other party's contributions to the marital surplus.[25] This is a question of valuation and perception rather than being an objective measurement (say, of time). Women are at a disadvantage here because women's unpaid domestic work is often considered to be of less value than work which commands (higher) wages in the market.

It should be pointed out that not only do men undervalue women's contributions but women often do also. They frequently undervalue themselves and have less of a sense of entitlement, for example, to demand a high price or a more egalitarian share of the marital surplus. If men think of their contribution as having superior value, they will think of themselves as having the superior entitlement in the bargain.

To a large extent this is a function of the fact that a homemaker and mother's work is unpaid and we have no agreed metric for valuing domestic work. The closest we come is the price paid for these services on the open market and this puts a low value on them. While these market values cannot not be immediately or perfectly translated into the family economy (a mother's care is priceless, etc.), it is clear that many homemakers fight a losing battle because the breadwinner is seen as contributing a greater share to the marital pool of resources. This can subtly result in the claim that the wife cannot demand more housekeeping time or effort from her husband because he is making a greater contribution by way of income. This can also be seen in the fact that the person who

[25] Wax (1998, 582–4).

makes the greater monetary contribution in a marriage wields greater control over the financial decision-making in the family.[26]

What, then, if a particular woman has a strong sense of her sense of entitlement and considers her worth to be more than current cultural norms or the law are willing to grant? What if a lawyer agreed to stop working to take care of the children but only if her husband were willing to agree to substantial reimbursement in the event of divorce? She can only get this bargain if her partner shares her sense of entitlement. Since these things are a matter of perception they are, of course, malleable and he may agree that she is right. But they are also the effect of strong cultural norms which can be difficult to change, particularly en masse. And it is more difficult for one woman to get a particularly good deal if most other women will settle for less.

Nevertheless, there is some evidence that when women's sense of entitlement is raised it causes them to walk away from what they perceive to be unfair bargains, including marriage, even if those bargains seem to be better than the next best alternative.[27] Even though the terms are better than what could be had otherwise, they are still not perceived as fair. This suggests that fairness might set a limit to the bargaining calculations or be a factor in the calculation of utility.

(c) Endowment Effects

The endowment effect determines the value that is placed on the resources that the bargainers are exchanging.[28] It pegs that value to a pre-existing measuring stick determined by culture and social norms. That measuring stick constitutes a baseline set of expectations, i.e. what each party sees himself as initially entitled to. To take an absurd example, if in a premarital contract a woman offered to have sexual relations as a result of the marriage, this would hardly be considered a "bargain" since the man no doubt considers that it goes without saying that (consensual) sex is a part of, or is an entitlement in marriage. He is unlikely to make any concessions for this term of the agreement. If the woman insists there will be no sex, then she must make concessions to get the man to give up his normal expectations about marital relations, that is, to buy his agreement.

The endowment effect holds particularly true for the expectations that parties bring to the agreement regarding the division of labour that has been associated with marriage. Suppose the wife expects her husband to be an ambitious, successful full-time breadwinner who will support her comfortably as a full-time homemaker. Suppose he wants to be a casual part-time worker in order to

---

[26] Pahl (1989). When women do contribute monetarily their income is considered to be supplementary rather than essential, to pay for "extras" like holidays and private schools, even though it is understood to be part of a common pool.

[27] Wax (1998, 590).

[28] Ibid., 584–6.

write poetry. He will have the weaker hand. He will have to purchase the concession (of working part-time) from his wife. Alternatively, if a man sees himself as entitled to a family with many children and a wife to do all the childminding but she wants to pursue a career, then she will have the weaker hand and will have to offer up concessions to get her way. (The concession is usually continuing to do all the housework in addition to working.)

Feminists originally envisioned that premarital contracts offered a way to alter these gender expectations in marriage.[29] Not only would they specify the terms to be applied on divorce or death, but they could also be used to regulate the conduct of the parties during an ongoing marriage. Thus a contract could provide that the man would contribute equally to child rearing or that a career woman would not be forced to move for the sake of her husband's career. Although courts will not enforce these kinds of terms and the subject is academic, the endowment effect helps to explain why women would have little leverage to dictate the terms they desire: they would be asking for terms that the social and cultural baseline does not recognise and this automatically places them in a weaker position in the negotiation.

(d) Risk Aversion

A risk averse person is one who will exchange something of value for a reduction of risk of loss; insurance is the classic example. It is an open question whether women are more risk averse than men are; or to put it another way, whether men are more willing to bear a greater risk of loss.[30] If they are, it affects bargaining: women will be more willing to settle for less than their preferred terms rather than risk the threat of divorce. It might also explain their (perceived) greater desire to marry or their unwillingness to put it off. They might be willing to accept the certainty of marriage to this particular partner rather than take the risk that a more desirable mate might not come along later.[31] For women, a bird in the hand might look better than one in the bush (and given what we have said about the marriage market, this might be a reasonable calculation), while men may think there are other fish in the sea (also reasonable). Once again the question is not the absolute degree of risk aversion or risk preference of men and women. What counts in the bargaining is the relative degree between the parties. The one who is more risk preferring is the stronger party.

---

[29] Weitzman (1981).
[30] Brinig (1995); Craver and Barnes (1999); Klein (1997). Furthermore, gender may not be an independent variable but it may combine with age in determining risk aversion.
[31] Brinig (1995).

One of the problems with marital bargaining is that it is continual. It consists of negotiations over a myriad of daily details throughout the course of the marriage. Even if there is an initial agreement, changes of circumstances can mean that there is constant renegotiation. If women are likely to lose out on bargaining, in a series of bargains they will continue to lose out, and with each loss their bargaining power for the next negotiation will be reduced. Thus they can enter a downward spiral in which they can ultimately end up worse off than when they started the marriage. The extreme case is domestic violence.

This problem is particularly poignant in that having and raising children is one of the circumstances that most often change a woman's bargaining power. This is true for a number of reasons. One is that having and raising children is a marriage-specific form of investment of human capital. That means that the woman is, of necessity, the first player in one of the major bargaining games of marriage.[32] If her investment in child rearing is greater than her husband's (and it usually is) the woman incurs greater sunk costs in the marriage. Another factor as Cohen (1987) points out is that this kind of investment is more likely to occur early in marriage. Men's investment in the family in the form of income tends to be greater in the later years of the marriage when he is benefiting from experience and seniority.

At the point where the woman's investment is greater than the husband's there is a chance for opportunistic behaviour on the part of the husband. This is particularly true in a regime of unilateral no-fault divorce. As Ellman (1989) has argued, he can leave the marriage taking more out of it than he has put in. And it is compounded by the fact that the law of financial provision on divorce is relatively mild compared to what it used to be. When there was a duty of lifelong alimony, early exit was expensive for husbands and acted as a deterrent to opportunistic defection. Now the "cost" is relatively low. Property is divided primarily to provide housing and support for the children. Excess property is divided but maintenance is rare. The law functions to leave the parties as close as possible to where they stand, but where they stand is often in an unequal relationship in terms of investments they have made in the marriage.

Another factor as Rose (1992) points out is that children function as "hostages" in the marital bargaining. A mother's responsibility for her children often makes her less willing to risk divorce. Being a single parent is difficult under the best of circumstances but it is even harder for the parent who must work, since it diminishes her chances to flourish in the workplace. Alternatively, the presence of (another man's) children greatly diminishes her chances in the (re)marriage market. Under these circumstances, and there are no doubt more, she has to make concessions to protect the "hostages", and threat of divorce

---

[32] Cohen (1987); Rose (1992); Wax (1998, 626–8).

becomes less credible. The less credible it becomes, the more the husband can raise his demands. The more she gives in to these demands, the less credible her threat of divorce becomes, until in the downward spiral she is pushed to her reservation point.

Rose (1992) and others have described women as having a taste for co-operation.[33] This is unfortunate terminology since it tends to internalise the differences between women and men rather than emphasise the structural effects that constrain their choices. Nevertheless, one can accept the characterisation of women as co-operators once it is realised that co-operation only works if there is a threat of retaliation behind it.[34] In that sense co-operation implies the existence of threat points. Game theory literature recognises that successful ventures require a "tit-for-tat" strategy.[35] They need co-operation to get them off the ground and to keep the game going. They also, however, need retaliation to keep opportunism and non-co-operation at bay. If the woman is the first player and is in general the more co-operative partner, what is there to enable her to "retaliate" in order to avoid opportunism? What can raise her threat point?

There are several points we might look to, both legal and non-legal. One possibility is obviously to change the distortions in the labour market in order to increase opportunities for women. Alternatively, a substitute for labour market income is government income in the form of welfare. Studies show that when moneys such as child benefit are paid directly to mothers, it increases the amount spent in the family on mothers and children.[36]

Another possibility is self-help, or self-insurance in order to raise the exit threat. Divorce is more costly and less desirable for women than it is for men. If women were to increase their levels of education and/or maintain their ties to the labour market more during marriage, the threat of divorce would not loom as large. This is not a panacea, however. It can result in a loss of domestic and child care services which can cause conflict, and it can be detrimental to the family surplus as a whole and thus to the woman herself and the children.

It has also been suggested that women marry younger or significantly older men, that is, less desirable men who do not have superior opportunities on the marriage market.[37] However, unless our culture changes substantially and all women adopt that strategy, this is unlikely to be a very successful solution.

In terms of law, some have proposed prenuptial agreements.[38] These proposals have taken two forms: those that agree to terms for settlement in the event

[33] Rose (1992).
[34] Ibid., 438.
[35] Ibid., 438.
[36] Lundberg and Pollack (1996).
[37] Mahony (1995); Wax (1998, 643–5).
[38] Bix (1998); Ertman (1998); Guggenheimer (1998); Weitzman (1981).

of divorce and more-encompassing agreements that govern the conduct of the parties during marriage. The former are enforceable in many if not most jurisdictions, and in England the Government is considering making them enforceable.[39] So far no jurisdiction will enforce agreements about marital conduct.

There are several problems with prenuptial contracts as a solution. The first is that it is difficult to specify terms adequately. As Scott and Scott (1998) have argued, marriage is a long-term relational contract in which the parties agree, implicitly at least, to put forth their best efforts in the common endeavour. The very nature of a relational contract is that it is meant to encompass a variety of contingent and changing situations. It is governed by general intentions and norms rather than explicit terms. It is difficult to specify in advance all the circumstances and contingencies that may occur in the course of marriage. I have yet to see a premarital agreement that includes arrangements if one of the spouses is disabled or if a disabled child requiring constant care is born.

Furthermore, it should be clear from what has gone before that whatever kind of marital agreement we are talking about, it is still a marital agreement, and that many of the disparities of bargaining power will be operative in making it. While it is true that the contract will be made because the terms are considered to be the best alternative to no agreement at all, those initial terms will simply incorporate the disparities.

Finally, private ordering is difficult because it is by its nature an individual solution for what is a collective problem. Feminists looked to premarital contracts as a means of securing better terms for women in marriage and divorce than current law provided. What they never spelled out was how women were supposed to acquire the leverage to command the superior terms to begin with. Bargaining models argue that in general they cannot gain that leverage. A man's alternative to making a prenuptial agreement with a woman who demands one is finding another mate and in a world where most women do not make such a demand (and probably could not be persuaded to give up their advantage by not doing so) it would be difficult to find willing men.

That leaves the collective solution of the laws regarding divorce. These, in effect, are the default rules to the marriage contract. They set the terms and therefore constrain the bargaining power of the parties. The first option is making divorce more difficult through waiting periods, spouse's agreement, etc., so that men's exit point advantage is weaker. The problem with this solution is that it makes women's exit point advantage weaker also. It can also trap women in unhappy marriages and is akin to throwing out the baby with the bath water.

Another solution has been to allow unilateral no-fault divorce but to raise its cost by re-imposing a regime of alimony—not necessarily lifelong alimony, but alimony sufficient to compensate women for their asymmetrical marriage-specific investment and subsequent disadvantage on the labour market. A number of schemes have been proposed and deserve careful attention.[40] The

[39] Home Office (1998).
[40] Ellman (1989); Singer (1994).

problem with these proposals, however, is that they conflict with the current ideology of clean break on marriage. Beneath this lies a deeper problem. If alimony were required not just of the rich but across the board, it would necessarily have to come out of the future income of the payer, usually the husband. Most importantly this would make many men unable to remarry and support second families. While I see nothing wrong with that, in that it might rectify inequities in the current law of divorce, it is not clear to me what the effects would be on women if a large number of divorced men were effectively taken out of the marriage market.

Wax (1998), however, makes the important point that if more equitable arrangements could be struck *ex ante*—before the marriage begins and children are born—either through private ordering or through the law's default rules, it would have one salutatory effect: it would solidify the wife's position at the beginning and stop the downward spiral that occurs because her bargaining power decreases if the marriage becomes more important to her than her husband, say, through the birth of children, ageing, the loss of fertility and loss of ties to the labour market.

CONCLUSION

The feminists have a good argument: marriage is an institution that inequitably favours men. That is not because they are less sensitive or more power hungry or because women are more co-operative or the weaker sex. For the most part it is because marriage as an institution operates in the wider field of culture and society, in particular in the shadow of the marriage and labour markets. Saying that there are structural inequalities in the public world which tend to create inequalities in the private world of the family is not meant to excuse them. The only problem presented in this brief description that cannot be overcome (easily) is that women are more limited in their fertility than men. All the other asymmetries can be addressed through individual or more realistically collective action, not least through law. If the asymmetries are understood as distortions of the marriage market, as creating an uneven playing field between the partners who come together in that most important of contracts, then there is no reason law and other social institutions cannot and should not make every effort to mitigate the distortions at whatever point they occur.

REFERENCES

American Law Institute (1997) *Principles of the Law of Family Dissolution*, Proposed Final Draft Pt. I.

Baird, D.G., R.H. Gertner, and R.C. Picker (1994) *Game Theory and the Law* (Cambridge: Harvard University Press).

Becker, G. (1981) *A Treatise on the Family* (Cambridge: Harvard University Press).

Behrman, J.R. (1997) "Intrahousehold distribution and the family", in M.R. Rosenzweig and O. Stark (eds), *Handbook of Population and Family Economics*, vol. 1A (Amsterdam: Elsevier).

Bergstrom, T.C. (1997) "A survey of theories of the family", in M.R. Rosenzweig and O. Stark (eds), *Handbook of Population and Family Economics*, vol. 1A (Amsterdam: Elsevier).

Bix, B. (1998) "Bargaining in the shadow of love: the enforcement of premarital agreements and how we think about marriage", *William and Mary Law Review* 40, 145–207.

Brinig, M.F. (1995) "Does mediation systematically disadvantage women?", *William and Mary Journal of Women and Law* 2, 1.

Brinig, M.F. and S. Crafton (1994) "Marriage and opportunism", *Journal of Legal Studies* 23, 869.

Carbone, J. and M. Brinig (1991) "Rethinking marriage: feminist ideology, economic change, and divorce reform", *Tulane Law Review* 953–1009.

Craver, C.B. and D.W. Barnes (1999) "Gender, risk taking, and negotiation performance", *Michigan Journal of Gender and Law* 5, 299–351.

Cohen, L. (1987) "Marriage, divorce, and quasi-rents; or, 'I gave him the best years of my life' ", *Journal of Legal Studies* 16, 267.

Dnes, A.W. (1997) *The Division of Marital Assets Following Divorce with Particular Reference to Pensions*. Lord Chancellor's Research Series No. 7/97 (The Stationery Office, London).

Eekelaar, J. (1998) *Financial Property Adjustment on Divorce* (University of Oxford: Centre for Socio-Legal Studies).

Eekelaar, J. and M. Maclean (1986) *Maintenance After Divorce* (Oxford: Clarendon Press).

Ellman, M. (1989) "The theory of alimony", *California Law Review* 77, 1–81.

Ertman, M.M. (1998) "Commercializing marriage: a proposal for valuing women's work through premarital security agreements", *Texas Law Review* 77, 17–112.

Estin, A.L. (1993) "Maintenance, alimony and the rehabilitation of family care", *North Carolina Law Review* 71, 721–803.

—— (1995) "Love and obligation: family law and the romance of economics", *William and Mary Law Review* 36, 989–1087.

Guggenheimer, L. (1998) "A modest proposal: the feminomics of drafting premarital agreements", *Women's Rights Law Reporter* 17, 147–208.

Hirshman, L.R. (1998) "Hard bargains: the politics of heterosexuality", *Washington and Lee Law Review* 55, 185–95.

Hirshman, L.R. and J.E. Larson (1998) *Hard Bargains: The Politics of Sex* (New York: Oxford University Press).

Home Office (1998) *Supporting Families: A Consultation Document* (Home Office, London).

Klein, D. (1997) "Distorted reasoning: gender, risk aversion and negligence law", *Suffolk University Law Review* 30, 629–70.

Lundberg, S. and R.A. Pollack (1993) "Separate spheres: bargaining and the marriage market", *Journal of Political Economy* 101, 988–1010.

—— (1994) "Non-co-operative bargaining models of marriage", *American Economic Review Papers and Proceedings* 84, 132–37.

—— (1996) "Bargaining and distribution in marriage", *Journal of Economic Perspectives* 10, 139–58.

Mahony, R. (1995) *Kidding Ourselves: Breadwinning, Babies, and Bargaining Power* (New York: Basic Books).

Pahl, J. (1989) *Money and Marriage* (London: Macmillan).

Raiffa, H. (1982) *The Art and Science of Negotiation* (Cambridge: Harvard University Press).

Rose, C.M. (1992) "Women and property: gaining and losing ground", *Virginia Law Review* 78, 421–59.

Rousseau, J.-J. [1762](1979) *Emile* (New York: Basic Books).

Scott, E.S. and R.E. Scott (1998) "Marriage as relational contract", *Virginia Law Review* 84, 1225–334.

Schroeder, J.L. (1998) *The Vestal and the Fasces: Hegel, Lacan, Property and the Feminine* (Berkeley: University of California Press).

Singer, J.B. (1994) "Alimony and efficiency: the gendered costs and benefits of the economic justification for alimony", *Georgetown Law Journal* 82, 2423–60.

Trebilcock, M.J. and R. Keshvani (1991) "The role of private ordering in family law: a law and economics perspective", *University of Toronto Law Journal* 41, 533–90.

Wax, A.L. (1998) "Bargaining in the shadow of the market: is there a future for egalitarian marriage?", *Virginia Law Review* 509–72.

Weitzman, L. (1981) *The Marriage Contract* (New York: Free Press).

PART TWO

THE POLITIQUE OF THE LAW-MAKING VENTURE

SECTION 1

THE OUT OF COURT AGENDA

4

Making Family Law New?
Property and Superannuation
Reform in Australia

JOHN DEWAR

INTRODUCTION

A USTRALIAN FAMILY LAW is undergoing its most radical overhaul since the current legislative framework was enacted in 1975. This chapter will concentrate on one aspect of the current debate, namely, reform of the law of distribution of property and superannuation on divorce. The chapter will begin by identifying the political context of the debate and will then go on to outline the themes informing the government's proposals, and then the proposals themselves. In doing so, it will argue that the proposals exemplify a new style of family law-making, which employs different techniques, seeks to attain different objectives and makes new assumptions from those we have been used to. In short, they exemplify a new political economy of family law. The final section seeks to identify some ways of making sense of this shift in the terms of debate around family law issues. While these observations are confined to developments in Australia, it is possible that there will be parallels in other jurisdictions.

THE POLITICAL CONTEXT OF FAMILY LAW REFORM
IN AUSTRALIA

The passage of the Family Law Act 1975 (Cth) gave Australia what many saw at the time as one of the most progressive and enlightened family law regimes in the world (Star, 1996). The legislative innovations were evident in the substance of the law, and in the means by which it was to be administered. For example, divorce under the 1975 Act was wholly no-fault, being based exclusively on twelve months' separation, and the attendant consequences of divorce were to be worked out without reference to fault. Instead, judges were given wideranging fact-finding powers and dispositive discretions, to be exercised in accordance with general principles and specific factors. A wholly new court, the Family Court of Australia, was created to administer and apply the new legislation. The Court was to place heavy emphasis on non-judicial techniques for settling disputes, and included a Court Counselling Service that was to act as a conciliation agency and as a source of therapeutic assistance for litigants. The Court's procedures were designed to promote settlement at any time before a final hearing. In short, the Court was to be a "caring court" that offered a wide range of dispute resolution and other services to its clientele. It was to offer a more humane approach to the resolution of family disputes than the fault-based regime that preceded it.

In summary, the 1975 Act was based on a "technocratic" vision of family law—that is, a vision according to which family problems could be addressed by careful design of specialist institutions and by investing experienced experts with wide-ranging powers over all aspects of family adjustment on divorce.[1]

The primary legislation has been amended many times since 1975, and other changes have profoundly influenced the way in which the Act and the Court have operated. The most significant changes to date have been:

- the extension of the Court's jurisdiction to include children of unmarried parents;[2]
- the introduction of the Child Support Scheme in 1989, which removed jurisdiction from the Court to make original orders for child support in most cases;[3] and
- a complete overhaul of Part VII of the Act, effective from mid-1996, which deals with parenting arrangements after divorce.[4]

The conservative (Liberal) government, which has been in power since 1996, is committed to an ambitious programme of legislative reform in the family law area. Government policy in this area is driven by a number of pressures and concerns:

---

[1] See Dewar (1997) for further explanation of this term.

[2] Under the Australian Constitution, the Federal Parliament has no authority to legislate with respect to children born outside marriage. The power to do so was achieved in 1987 when all the States (except Queensland and Western Australia) agreed to "refer" legislative power in this respect to the Commonwealth. This required matching State and Federal legislation: see the State Commonwealth Powers Acts and the Family Law Amendment Act 1987 (Cth). Queensland followed suit in 1990. Western Australia has its own separate Family Court and family law legislation. The States retain jurisdiction over adoption and child protection; and legislative power, once referred, can be revoked. The referral of powers over non-marital children also paved the way for the introduction of national child support legislation.

[3] The scheme applies to any child whose parents separated after 1 October 1989, or to a child born after that date, or to a child born before that date but with siblings born after it: ss.19–21 Child Support Assessment Act 1989 (Cth). The Court retains jurisdiction under the Family Law Act 1975 (Cth) to make orders for child maintenance with respect to other children.

[4] Family Law Reform Act 1995 (Cth). The legislation is similar, but not identical to, the English Children Act 1989: see Bailey-Harris and Dewar (1997) for a comparison.

- the effective lobbying of government members of parliament by men's groups who perceive the Family Law Act 1975, and the Family Court, as being "biased" against men (Kaye and Tolmie, 1998);
- a wish to reduce public expenditure on courts and legal aid; and
- a concern that the Family Court's pre-eminence as a provider of alternative (or "primary") dispute resolution services has drawn more people than necessary into the Court's litigation pathways and may have had the effect of increasing rather than reducing litigation (Attorney-General's Department, 1997).

These factors have led to the following changes that have either taken place recently, or are being debated:

- a proposal that the Court's counselling service be removed from the Court and placed in the community sector (Attorney General's Department, 1997). The case for this is that it would allow better co-ordination amongst all providers of alternative dispute resolution services. It would also, incidentally, decrease the importance (and budget) of the Family Court, and would reduce the Court to offering only one kind of service, namely, judicial resolution of disputes;
- consideration of legislation that will assist in the "enforcement" of contact orders (that is, assist contact parents to have contact in accordance with the terms of contact orders) (Family Law Council, 1998);[5]
- significant changes in the administration of legal aid, which has meant that legal aid for family law proceedings is much less widely available than previously, and that even when available is subject to "capping" or is available only for very limited forms of assistance, such as mediation or "conferencing" (see Dewar, Giddings and Parker, 1999). It is thought that one effect of this has been to increase significantly the numbers of unrepresented parties appearing in the Court—which has in turn further stretched the resources of the Court (Family Court of Australia, 1998). All of this has led to accusations being levelled at the government that it has created an uneven playing field in family law;
- the government has also announced that it intends to legislate to make prenuptial agreements binding, subject to some (as yet unspecified) safeguards.[6]

It can be argued that these proposals each reflect some of the pressures and concerns already discussed—a distrust of the Court, a sense that family law is biased against men and a wish to cut public spending.

It is against this background that the government released two sets of proposals—one in late 1998, the other in early 1999—for changes to the law on

---

[5] Attorney-General's press release, "Improved enforcement of parenting orders", 26 February 1999.

[6] Attorney-General's press release, "Greater certainty in family law property settlements", 19 February 1999.

superannuation on divorce, and changes to property distribution (Attorney-General's Department, 1998; 1999). In order to make sense of those proposals, we need to sketch in a brief description of the current law on these matters.

PROPERTY AND SUPERANNUATION: THE CURRENT LAW[7]

As in English law, there is no concept of matrimonial property in Australian law. This means that, on divorce, anything that is beneficially owned by the parties is available for distribution. Judges are empowered to make orders adjusting property ownership between the parties on the basis of two main factors—the parties' past contributions to the property and the family's welfare, and the parties' future needs.[8] The legislation leaves judges with a wide discretion to value property, to assess contributions to it and to make allowances for future needs. Early judicial attempts to introduce a presumption that spousal contributions were equal was halted by the High Court.[9] Spousal maintenance is separately available on proof of the applicant's need for it and the respondent's ability to pay it.[10]

A complex jurisprudence has built up over the years concerning the application of this framework. The most important developments have included:

- the development of special rules concerning property owned before the marriage,[11] and of business assets built up during it.[12] The jurisprudence uses the concept of contribution to exclude certain assets from distribution, or to reduce the non-contributing party's share of the overall pool;
- the re-emergence of a presumption or starting point of equality of contribution;[13]
- a growing emphasis on the so-called "s. 75(2) factors" (which concern the parties' needs and resources) such that it is not uncommon for an initial distribution based on equality of contributions to be adjusted by up to 25 percent in recognition of a disparity in the parties' future needs and capacity to provide for those needs;[14]
- the growing relevance of domestic violence to property distribution, largely on the basis that a spouse who makes contributions in circumstances of

[7] For detailed treatment, see Finlay, Bailey-Harris and Otlowski (1997), Ch. 6.
[8] s. 79 Family Law Act (FLA) 1975 (Cth).
[9] *Mallet* v. *Mallet* (1984) 9 Fam LR 449.
[10] ss. 72, 74 FLA 1975 (Cth).
[11] *In the marriage of Crawford* (1979) FLC 90–647; *In the marriage of Lee Steere* (1985) 10 Fam LR 431; *In the marriage of Money* (1994) 17 Fam LR; *In the marriage of Bremner* (1995) FLC 92–560, *In the marriage of Way* (1996) FLC 92–702; *In the marriage of MacGregor* (1996) 21 Fam LR 57; *In the marriage of Aleksowski* (1996) FLC 92–705.
[12] *In the marriage of Ferraro* (1992) 16 Fam LR 1.
[13] *In the marriage of McLay* (1995) 20 Fam LR 239.
[14] *In the marriage of Clauson* (1995) 18 Fam LR 693.

violence will have found it harder to make those contributions, which in turn means that the contributions s/he has made should count for more;[15]

- although there is evidence that spousal maintenance has fallen virtually into disuse (Behrens and Smyth, 1999), there has been a recent willingness to redefine the concept of need for the purposes of spousal maintenance as structural or systemic, rather than individual. Thus, the evidence suggesting that women generally experience significant drops in income, and suffer impaired earning capacity after divorce has been treated as relevant in assessing an individual applicant's need for maintenance.[16]

All these developments have been judge-made. Although they can all be justified in terms of the legislation, one effect is that it is very hard to see the connection between the words of the statute and the policies being pursued by the Court. This means that only the trained specialist is able to offer accurate predictions of what the outcome will be in any particular case.

Empirical studies of the operation of this matrimonial property regime have shown that women tend to get a larger share of the total asset pool than men (McDonald, 1986: 181–4; Bordow and Harrison, 1994). The figure of 60/40 is often cited, although much depends on how the total is calculated for this purpose. Research conducted by the Australian Institute of Family Studies in the early 1980s, and recently updated, suggests that if superannuation assets are added to the total, then the percentage going to women drops to about half, or slightly less (McDonald, 1986: 182; Dewar, Sheehan and Hughes, 1999: Table 6.1). Further, women seem to get a smaller percentage as the total value of assets rises (McDonald, 1986: 181–4).

There have been numerous reviews of the law of property distribution since 1975.[17] Almost all have expressed dissatisfaction with the uncertainty and unpredictability of the law, as well as with its seeming inability to prevent significant disparities in the post-divorce living standards of the parties.[18] Some, but not all, of these themes re-emerge in the latest proposals. A Bill was introduced into Parliament in 1995 that would have introduced a presumption of equal contributions, but this lapsed when the Labour Government lost the 1996 Federal election.

Superannuation is a more specific and technical issue, but no less important for that. At present, the Court can only deal with superannuation assets once they become beneficially owned by one of the parties. Generally speaking, this occurs only on retirement, which means that the value of superannuation

---

[15] *In the marriage of Kennon* (1997) 22 FLR 1.

[16] *In the marriage of Mitchell* (1995) 19 Fam LR 44, citing the Canadian case of *Moge* v. *Moge* (1993) 99 DLR (4th) 456.

[17] *Family Law in Australia*, Report of the Joint Select Committee on the Family Law Act (July 1980); P. McDonald (1986); Australian Law Reform Commission Report (1988); *The Family Law Act 1975: Aspects of its interpretation and operation*, Report of the Joint Select Committee on certain aspects on the operation and interpretation of the Family Law Act (1992).

[18] This emerged with particular force from the empirical work conducted by the Australian Institute of Family Studies: see McDonald (1986) and Funder, Harrison and Weston (1993).

during its accumulation phase (i.e. during the working life of the superannuant) cannot be dealt with directly by the Court. This is a significant limitation on the powers of the Court given that superannuation now accounts, on average, for 25 percent of divorcing couples' assets (Dewar, Sheehan and Hughes, 1999: 16–19). This would not be such a problem if superannuation entitlements were spread evenly between genders—but they are not. Instead, research shows that women's superannuation entitlements on divorce are far smaller than men's (Dewar and Hughes, 1999: 13–16). This is scarcely surprising given the earnings-related nature of superannuation, and the continued gender gap in earnings. This is not a problem so long as parties remain married, and so long as superannuation benefits are equitably shared between the parties; but divorce means that this will not be the case.

At present the Court cannot deal directly with superannuation assets on divorce, and is thus confined to one of three strategies: making off-setting transfers to the wife to compensate her for the loss of her husband's superannuation; postponing a wife's claim for property distribution until the superannuation benefits are in payment; or making an immediate order for payment of capital, but deferring its operation until the superannuation benefits are in payment.[19] None of these are satisfactory, and successive reports have identified "pension-splitting" as the fairest way forward, yet nothing has yet been achieved. There are two reasons why reform might be considered desirable. One is equity for divorced women, who are currently frozen out of what is a family asset of rapidly increasing significance. The other is a concern that unless divorced women receive a share of their husband's pension on divorce, they may enter retirement with little or no superannuation in their own name and will therefore be reliant on the means-tested state aged pension (AP)—an outcome that would run directly counter to current government retirement incomes policy (Attorney-General's Department, 1998: 34). Both factors push towards reform, though not necessarily the same sort of reform.

REFORMING PROPERTY AND SUPERANNUATION:
RECURRENT THEMES

Before looking at the reform proposals in detail, it is worth identifying some recurrent themes that run through the two papers. These themes shape the way in which the need for reform is identified, and foreshadow the form taken by the proposals for change. The recurrent themes are:

- that the current law is uncertain, so that cases are harder to settle (the efficiency argument);
- that the current law is not transparent, so that ordinary litigants do not understand what is happening and are likely to complain of bias (the justice argument);

[19] Finlay et al. (1997, 296–300).

• that demographic changes, and especially the growing participation of women in the workforce, have altered the nature of marriage so that marriage is now more an economic partnership with both parties making a financial contribution (the social change argument).

There is a subsidiary thread to both papers, which is that couples should be free as far as possible to make their own binding arrangements (the autonomy argument). The need for parties to be able to exercise choice is especially evident in the *Superannuation* paper. Indeed, as we shall see, the superannuation proposals are designed to promote party choice as the primary means of dealing with superannuation entitlements; but the notion of party choice (in the shape of binding prenuptial agreements) reappears in the *Property* paper as a way of "encouraging people to take responsibility for their own financial affairs, rather than relying on outside intervention" (Attorney-General's Department, 1999: 44).

The Efficiency Argument

This argument appears at numerous points in the *Property* paper. For example:

"There has been much criticism of the lack of certainty and transparency about how the Court approaches property division and suggestions that this has resulted in spouses being less able to agree property issues." (Attorney-General's Department, 1999: iii)

In discussion of the Options for reform, the *Property* paper argues that:

"a tighter and clearer framework [will make] the process of property settlement more transparent and easier to understand. This will enable people to predict more accurately the likely outcome of a property application and, therefore, assist them in their negotiations. It would also reduce the number of property disputes which need to go to the court for resolution." (Attorney-General's Department 1999: 39)

Similar arguments appear in the *Superannuation* paper, although there the focus is on the inconsistent treatment of superannuation by the Courts which "creates uncertainty, especially for those seeking to negotiate a settlement outside of Court" (Attorney-General's Department, 1998: 10). The paper states that "providing guidance for parties agreeing on solutions" is one of the policy objectives informing policy in this area (Attorney-General's Department, 1998: 32 and Ch.4).

The Justice Argument

The *Property* paper argues that part of current dissatisfaction with the current law stems from the "perception that decision-making by the court in property proceedings is arbitrary [which has] caused many to believe that decisions about property reallocation are biased towards one of the parties" (Attorney-General's Department, 1999: 2). The *Property* paper rehearses similar arguments made in previous reviews of the law of property distribution. The *Property* paper proposes to require a Court, when departing from a 50:50 split of property under any of the proposed models (see below), to describe the circumstances and evidence giving rise to the need to depart from equal sharing, and to detail clearly the basis on which the departure has been made. This is justified on the ground that it will avoid "the perceptions that decisions are not based on fact, are biased towards one of the parties and are arbitrary" (Attorney-General's Department, 1999: 44–5).

The justice argument appears in a more positive form in the *Superannuation* paper. Here, it is argued that the limit on the Court's power to deal directly with superannuation has created particular "difficulties" for non-superannuated spouses, because it is so frequently left out of account on divorce (and not even, it seems, taken into account in the limited ways possible under the existing law: see Dewar et al., 1999: 19–25). The paper aims explicitly for a "fairer" system that will ensure that superannuation is more likely to be taken into account. At the same time, the current system is presented as unfair to the superannuated spouse because its inflexibility means that "current property must often be traded away in exchange for [*sic*] an asset that may not be able to be realised for many years" (Attorney-General's Department, 1998: 9).

The Social Change Argument

This argument receives the most extensive treatment of all. In the *Property* paper, it first appears in the Attorney-General's Foreword:

> "Since 1976 [when the Family Law Act came into effect], the family unit and its social context have changed significantly. Importantly, the increased workforce participation by women before and during marriage has meant that marriage is becoming increasingly recognised as an economic partnership as well as a social relationship." (Attorney-General's Department, 1999: iii)

This argument is repeated in the Executive Summary, although here it is elaborated as "a growing recognition, and acceptance, that both parties to a marriage contribute equally to the acquisition, maintenance and improvement of the assets of the marriage either as income earner or as homemaker and/or child carer" (Attorney-General's Department, 1999: 1). To this is added the "facts" that couples are more likely now to live together before marrying, have children later and are both more likely to participate in the paid workforce. The paper adds that the introduction of child support legislation in 1989 means that day-to-day care of children need no longer be taken into account in property and spousal maintenance proceedings. Chapter 4 of the *Property* paper recites the statistical evidence to support these propositions, and concludes:

"This evidence supports the claim that, due to increased workforce participation, women are making an economic as well as a nurturing contribution to marriage. Moreover, empirical evidence suggests that couples are accumulating what may be regarded as 'matrimonial property' prior to marriage, due to the increased incidence of couples living in de facto relationships before marriage." (Attorney-General's Department 1999: 32)

The implication, in other words, is that marriage is increasingly a relationship of economically active, and equal, partners. There is no clear recognition of the long-term effects of parenting on the economic prospects of the primary carer of children. It is as if child support has dealt with that issue, leaving the adults more or less equal.

The social change argument also appears in the *Superannuation* paper. In this context, the relevant change is the growth in the incidence of superannuation throughout the workforce and its increased significance as a component of family wealth (Attorney-General's Department, 1998: 9).

ALL ROADS LEAD TO "EQUALITY"

In the *Property* paper, each of these three arguments, in different ways, anticipates the eventual conclusion: namely, that there should be a starting point of formal equality in the distribution of matrimonial property, subject to contracting out by the parties. In this context, equality serves a number of purposes simultaneously: it promotes efficiency by increasing the certainty of the law; it promotes justice because it provides the law with a coherent principle that is readily understood by ordinary people; and it brings law into line with the social "fact" that men and women are economically more equal.

Of course, what is striking about this is how much is left out of account. For example, there is no evidence to support the proposition that clear rules or principles assist in the settlement of disputes. This proposition assumes that the way legislation is drafted plays a big role in the negotiation and settlement of family law cases, but there is no evidence either way for this. Further, it is not obvious that simple notions of equality do accord with everyone's conceptions of justice in family matters. While it is certainly true that some lobby groups, and especially men's rights groups, have adopted the language of simple equality as synonymous with "justice" (Kaye and Tolmie, 1988), more sophisticated analyses recognise that achieving equality in this context is as much about outcomes as it is about starting points (e.g. Australian Law Reform Commission, 1988; Funder, 1992; Graycar, 1995). Finally, the social "facts" on which the proposals draw are remarkably selective: they draw exclusively on figures showing the incidence and length of premarital cohabitation, age specific birth rates and labour market participation rates, and ignore evidence about differentials in earnings between men and women, about vertical and horizontal gender segmentation of the labour force,[20] and about the long-term effects of divorce on men and women, such as that published by the Australian Institute of Family Studies (McDonald, 1986; Funder, Harrison and Weston, 1993). Although, as we shall see, the proposals do not adhere rigidly to an equal sharing model, conceptions of equality other than crude equal division receive only secondary consideration in the paper.

What is striking, in other words, is how speculative, or selective, are the assumptions on which the proposals are founded. This is not a style of family lawmaking that is concerned to be empirically informed, or statistically valid: instead, it is an overtly politicised discourse that espouses the virtues of certainty, efficiency and freedom of choice, which distrusts the intervention of state "experts" wielding wide-ranging adjustive powers, and which is premised on an individualised and decontextualised view of spouses as people whose economic prospects are relatively unaffected by the fact that they have been married or have had children. The close attention paid to the "social change" argument, and its lopsided presentation, suggests that the *Property* paper is playing especially to the gallery of the men's groups. This deliberate eschewing of statistical knowledge is one way in which the proposals exemplify what I have called a new style of family lawmaking. I will return to this point later.

The arguments for equality in the treatment of superannuation are slightly more elaborate. In addition to the efficiency, justice and social change arguments already discussed, equality is additionally justified on a number of grounds. The following passage, for example, suggests that there are three separate rationales supporting equal division of superannuation—contributions, expectations and needs:

"Superannuation interests built up during a marriage for retirement purposes should be equally shared. A superannuation interest in the name of one spouse is usually built up through the joint efforts of both spouses. If the parties had not separated they would have had a reasonable expectation that they would equally share in the proceeds of the superannuation at retirement. In retirement, both spouses are also generally likely to have similar needs as there are usually no dependent children and, in most cases, neither spouse expects to earn further income." (Attorney-General's Department 1998: 30–1)

Equality is also presented as being consistent with the "policy objectives" informing the proposals—specifically, "consistency with retirement incomes policy" and "ease of administration for superannuation schemes" (Attorney-General's Department, 1998: 34). Although it is not expressly stated, equality serves both purposes by ensuring that both spouses have at least some superannuation on retirement, thereby reducing eligibility for the state aged pension[21]

[20] The Property paper does acknowledge that while women's workforce participation has grown, the proportion of women in full-time work has declined (para. 4.10)—yet no weight is attached to this, nor is it seen as diminishing the weight that should be attached to bare participation rates.

[21] The aged pension is a means-tested benefit (combining tests of both income and assets), and may carry with it entitlement to other benefits such as rent assistance, which means that the government has a strong interest in promoting self-funded retirement.

and other state benefits, and by reducing administration costs for fund trustees and managers (who, presumably, will find equal division easier to manage than any other regime).

These rationales have been subjected to extensive criticism (Millbank, 1993; Dunn, 1999; Dewar, Sheehan and Hughes, 1999; Kingsford-Smith, 1999). For example, it has been pointed out that men and women are not equal in their retirement needs—instead, women have greater needs than men because (a) it is likely that their earnings between divorce and retirement will be lower so that they have a reduced capacity to provide for their own retirement, and (b) actuarial assumptions about life expectancy mean that annuities cost more for women than men, which in turn means that women need more capital than men to produce the same income in retirement. Similarly, a policy of requiring women to take a half share of superannuation is likely to reduce their chances of obtaining the family home on divorce, which in turn means that women will be more likely to rent and therefore to spend a larger proportion of their incomes on housing, which in turn means that they are more likely to be dependent on state benefits in retirement than if they had been awarded the home outright. It seems unlikely, however, that these arguments will have much effect—the principle of equality seems likely to exert too strong an appeal over the minds of legislators to be resisted by evidence alone.

THE PROPOSALS IN MORE DETAIL

We turn, then, to examine the proposals in more detail. There is a complex relationship between the two sets of proposals, in that the shape of the superannuation changes depends on what happens to the property proposals. We therefore begin with the property proposals.

Property

The Discussion Paper outlines two models for reform (termed Options 1 and 2), both of which draw heavily on equality as a starting point. Under Option 1, the current regime would be retained but with the addition of a statutory presumption that the spouses' contributions to property have been equal. This would lead to an equal division of all property beneficially owned by the parties, whether acquired before or during the marriage. This presumption of equal contributions would, however, be rebuttable in that the Courts would have a discretion to depart from equal sharing where the parties' contributions have clearly been unequal. The Courts would also have discretion to depart from equal sharing where there are disparities in the parties' future needs, with those needs to be assessed by reference to a checklist of factors similar to those contained in the current s. 75(2) Family Law Act 1975 (Cth).[22]

---

[22] Under Option 1, spousal maintenance would be retained, but the paper suggests that claims for maintenance may be best dealt with as adjustments to the 50:50 split. If periodical payments are

Option 2 is based on what the paper calls a "deferred community of property" regime—that is, only property acquired during the marriage would be subject to a presumption of equal division on divorce.[23] The chief advantage of this is that it removes "contributions" as the conceptual basis for property division, and instead treats equality as reflecting the underlying assumption that "marriage is an equal partnership, having both a social and economic dimension" (Attorney-General's Department, 1999: 39). This means that there would be no retrospective adjustment of equal shares to take account of unequal past contributions; but there would be a prospective adjustment. The Discussion Paper proposes two alternative forms of such adjustment. The first would be a "future needs" adjustment similar to Option 1.[24] The second would be aimed at addressing "the economic consequences of divorce and its breakdown". The following passage provides an example of how such an adjustment might work:

> "In a situation where both parties are in paid employment, and seem likely to remain so, there may be no economic consequences of the marriage that would require a 50/50 split of the communal assets. This would be the case even where each of the parties have different income earning capacities, unless the differences can be attributed to the marriage. If the differences are because one of the parties has greater skill and business acumen, the disparity would not have arisen as a consequence of the marriage. However, in the situation where one party—usually the wife—has sacrificed earning capacity in order to remain in the home, especially where there are children, while the other party has been in paid employment outside the home, there will be economic consequences of marriage and its breakdown that may require a departure." (Attorney-General's Department, 1999: 43)

In this form, the adjustment from 50:50 would be based on principles of compensation for losses arising from the marriage rather than being designed to meet future needs (see also Funder, 1992; American Law Institute, 1997: Ch. 5 for similar proposals).[25]

Turning to superannuation, everything depends on the outcome of the Property proposals. There are essentially two alternatives. If Option 1 is adopted, then legislation would be amended to allow superannuation to be split between the parties in the same way as other property would be split under that option (Attorney-General's Department, 1998: para 5.10). The paper offers no discussion, however, of the particular issues associated with "future needs" adjustments of superannuation as distinct from other assets.

ordered, the paper proposes that they should cease on the recipient acquiring a new de facto, as well as de jure, partner.

[23] The net increase during the marriage in the value of property acquired before the marriage would also be included: Attorney-General's Department (1999, para. 5.35).

[24] In the Paper, there would be one difference: that under Option 1, the future needs factors would include a reference to "any other fact or circumstance", as at present, whereas under Option 2 there would be no such "catch-all" factor. The reasons for this difference are not clear—there seems to be no intrinsic connection between the "community" idea and the more constrained adjustive factors.

[25] The role of spousal maintenance under Option 2 receives very little discussion.

If either variant of Option 2 were adopted, or if the law of property distribution were to remain unchanged, then the proposals in the *Superannuation* paper would prevail. Under these proposals, parties would be encouraged to agree their own split of superannuation entitlements, and legislation would be amended to allow agreements, once formalised in court, to have a binding effect on fund managers and trustees. Detailed mechanisms are proposed to enable a split of existing entitlements, either (depending on the type of scheme) by creating a new account in the name of the transferee, or by "flagging" the benefits to be split when they accrue. If the parties cannot make their own arrangements, then an application to Court will be necessary, and the Court will be required to split the superannuation interest referable to the period of cohabitation equally between the parties, subject to some specific exceptions. Equality would be a default position if the parties were unable to agree any other split, with the Courts having less leeway than the parties to depart from it.

If Option 2 were implemented, then there would be some consistency between the rules relating to superannuation and those relating to all other property—the same notional basis of "communal" property and a presumptive equal split would apply (although it is not clear how any future needs or compensatory adjustment would work in relation to superannuation, if at all). However, if the law of property distribution remains the same, then there would be a strange dissonance between the regime applicable to all property, and that applicable to superannuation—one would continue to be based on contributions, the other on notions of community. The results of this would be hard to predict (see Dewar, Sheehan and Hughes, 1999: 29–31, for an attempt).

RECONFIGURING FAMILY LAW?

I suggested at the outset that these proposals exemplify a new style of family lawmaking, or a new political economy of family law. The regime that has been in place since 1975 is based on certain assumptions, techniques and objectives that have been described as "technocratic"—that is, it exemplified a belief in the power of specialist institutions, official expertise and state-sanctioned discretion to deal with the problems of family adjustment to divorce. This has been associated with the liberal state's commitment to privacy, in the sense that reliance on discretion has enabled disagreements about the law's role in relation to families on divorce to remain hidden.

The changes being described here may be seen as a part of a broader shift in family law, away from this "technocratic" model towards something identifiably different. The proposals discussed here are consistent with, and form a part of, this shift, but are by no means its only components. How, then, can we grasp and make sense of that change? I suggest the following pointers.

(i) New Legal Norms: From Discretion to Rules

One change lies in the normative form increasingly assumed by family law legislation, and particularly the apparent rolling back of discretion and its replace-
ment by a more rule-like framework. I have made this argument, and defined
terms, at greater length elsewhere (Dewar, 1997), and suggested that the reasons
for this shift, exemplified by the proposals under discussion, can be traced to
two broad factors. The first is a more explicit concern with the cost of a family
justice system, both internal and external. By internal costs, I mean those associated with running courts and providing litigants with representation through
a legal aid system; by external costs, I mean the costs accruing to the state from
family members becoming dependent on state benefits following family breakdown. The second is a concern to offer a more clearly articulated basis for family law, resting on a clearer sense of family rights and responsibilities. The
impetus behind this second factor is complex, but stems from the increased
politicisation of family law in general, both in the sense that there is now more
organised lobbying around family law issues, and in the sense that politicians
seem increasingly concerned to convey certain messages about family obligations through family law (see further below).[26]

The current proposals exemplify these concerns to a large degree. Thus, we
have seen that "efficiency" arguments have been used to justify a more rule-like
basis for property division (i.e. to reduce internal costs), and that promotion of
government retirement incomes policy (i.e. reducing reliance on state benefits)
is an important part of the superannuation reforms. Similarly, arguments based
on perceptions of the justice, or lack of it, of the system have also led to a more
rule-like starting point. A significant aspect of this is a concern to clarify the conceptual basis of the law in ways that ordinary people can understand, and to
make judges more accountable to litigants for decisions they make.

(ii) New Sources of Norms: From Status to Contract

One of the assumptions of a technocratic family law was that legislators and
judges were of central importance in setting the terms of divorce. Although there
was encouragement of private ordering, this was thought of as taking place "in
the shadow" of legislative and judicial activity (Mnookin and Kornhauser,
1979). The terms on which divorce was to be granted were ultimately those dictated by the state and its agents, the judges. These consequences were not freely

---

[26] This is not to suggest that family law has not in the past been concerned with rights and
responsibilities, but that it is now more explicitly concerned with them and uses the language of
rights and responsibilities more freely. This partly explains the change in family law's normative
content. The more explicit use of "rights-talk" in a family law context may have unpredictable consequences: Dewar and Parker (1999, 75–6) and Archbold in this volume.

chosen by the parties themselves—they were a matter of status, of imposed norms, rather than contract.

An important thread running through the reform debate in Australia is the importance of encouraging and assisting parties to make their own binding arrangements before, during or after a marriage. This would represent a change to the current law, under which any agreement is merely a factor to be considered by a Court in the exercise of its discretion.[27] As we have seen, this change is presented as an opportunity for the parties to take "responsibility" for resolving their own disputes. Although the details are not yet known, it seems likely that parties will be free to make whatever arrangements they want subject only to certain procedural safeguards concerning consent, disclosure and, perhaps, change of circumstances. Of course, parties will negotiate against a backdrop of legislation—but that legislation is now presented as serving the primary purpose of facilitating the making of agreements, rather than overriding them, or constraining or dictating their content. In short, parties are free to create their own "proper law". An analogy can be drawn with the privatisation of government services. Where once the state was the service provider, now the state is the regulator of the provision of services by others, setting performance standards or benchmarks, but otherwise allowing service providers to discharge their functions as they see fit.

The implication of this is that there is no longer a single source of legal norms governing family relations. Instead, there are potentially as many sources as there are couples who are able to reach agreement. We return to this point later.

(iii) Changing Audiences for Legislation: the Art of Radiating Messages

Another shift, which is related to the two already discussed, concerns the assumed audiences for family law legislation. A feature of technocratic family law was that it was addressed primarily to the technicians—lawyers and judges. An increasing feature of modern family law is that it seeks to "speak" over the heads of the technicians to a broader audience, to "radiate messages" about how to divorce well (Dewar, 1998, citing Galanter, 1992). This is most evident in Australia, perhaps, in the area of child law, where statements of legislative "objects and principles" (and in particular the stated right of a child to contact with both parents[28]) have been found to have had a huge impact on public (and professional) perceptions of the likely effects of legal change (Dewar and Parker, 1999). But similar tendencies can be observed in the proposals discussed here.

There are a number of possible reasons for this new style of legislation. One is that legislators seek to use legislation to perform an overtly educative role, or to create the illusion that there exists a set of organically shared values around divorce and family life. This could be seen as a strategy characteristic of reflexive

---

[27] *In the marriage of Woodcock* (1997) 21 Fam LR 393.
[28] s. 60B Family Law Act 1975 (Cth).

modernity, in which traditionally authoritative cultural resources such as law are used self-consciously to create a sense of continuity with the past while at the same time accommodating significant social change (Beck, 1992; Strathern, 1992; Giddens, 1999). Law, in other words, is a vehicle for the "ideological retraditionalisation" (Geertz, 1964) of family life—in this case, of marriage as partnership, and in other contexts, of parenthood as a matter of "nature" that creates obligations "for life".

Another is that the new style of family law legislation is broadly consistent with the policy of facilitating agreement, so that the legislation states principles that operate as background noise, or tone-setting, rather than as conferring measurable entitlements. Either way, the style and objectives of the legislation is observably different from that which characterised the technocratic regime. In particular, the retreat into discretion characteristic of the technocratic regime has been reversed.

(iv) Death of a Metaphor? The Horizontalisation of Family Law

Finally, I want to suggest that the changes being reviewed here exemplify, and are a response to, a further shift in the nature of the family law "system". The nature of that shift is best understood by looking again at the idea that parties bargain with each other "in the shadow of the law". This phrase, derived from Mnookin and Kornhauser's seminal article on the subject (1979), has provided a powerful metaphor for understanding the relationship between law on the books and law in action. It suggests that there is a direct relationship between what legislation says, and what judges interpret legislation to mean in particular cases, and what parties will agree to in out of court negotiations. It implies that, because parties know that they can ultimately go to Court and obtain a ruling from a judge, this knowledge will constrain and direct parties' negotiations in private. It also implies a hierarchical image of law: that legislators create laws which then "trickle down" to the parties themselves, mediated only by the interpretations of those laws provided by judges and private practitioners. According to the metaphor, when legal advisers offer advice on a "settlement range", they are merely exercising a form of delegated decision-making, or are predicting what a judge would do in the known circumstances of a case. The metaphor also helps sustain the liberal self-image of a liberal legal system—that all are equal before the law, that the shadow it casts is the same for all.[29]

---

[29] Mnookin and Kornhauser identified five factors that influence the divorce bargaining process: parental preferences, bargaining endowments created by legal rules, the degree of uncertainty in the outcome if the parties went to court coupled with attitudes to risk, transaction costs and the parties' ability to bear them, and strategic behaviour (1979, 966). This remains an insightful way of understanding the process of out of court bargaining, but the point being made here is that it overstates the extent to which legal rules create clear bargaining endowments. Instead, the relationship between legal rules and bargaining endowments is contingent, complex and uneven.

Some writers have begun to question whether this metaphor remains useful as a way of making sense of how things work. Richard Ingleby, for example, has suggested that there are multiple shadows of law—and in particular, that "[n]egotiation between solicitors is a 'semi-autonomous' process which takes place in the shadows of, and itself casts shadows on, other such processes" (Ingleby, 1992: 155; see also Melli, Erlanger and Chambliss, 1988). Others, such as Jacob (1992), have suggested that whether law casts a shadow at all depends on a range of variables, one of which is the client's initial "framing" of their problem as one that does or does not require a legalistic resolution.

In a similar vein, Dewar and Parker (1999, 83–7) have suggested, on the basis of empirical research into new Australian child law legislation, that Australian family law has become "horizontalised"—that is, that there is no single authoritative source of legal meaning in the family law "system", but that instead the power to produce legal meaning has been dispersed, and that the different meaning-producing procedures operate on each other, side-by-side, with no single source having effective hierarchical superiority.[30] This is partly because of the autonomous nature of inter-lawyer negotiation, as Ingleby suggests, and because of initial "framing" and choice of "entry points", as Jacob suggests; but also because of the steady withdrawal of legal aid funding, which has meant that for some poorer litigants, the limited dispute resolution services offered by legal aid bodies and community legal services, or interim orders in the Family Court, are effectively the final forum for the resolution of disputes (see also Dewar, Giddings and Parker, 1998). The relationship between what happens in those fora and what would happen in a full-blown Court hearing may be very tenuous indeed. The only way for some litigants to get to Court is to represent themselves—and there is already substantial evidence that such litigants may be almost wholly unaware of what shadow law casts (Hunter, 1998).

All of this points to the fragmentation or horizontalisation of authority within a family law system, to the extent that the metaphor of law casting a single endowment-conferring shadow over all out of court activity is no longer descriptively true, and may instead be dangerously misleading. The current proposals for reforming property law may be seen as simultaneously exacerbating this trend and as a response to it. It exacerbates it by creating a further source of legal meaning, namely binding prenuptial agreements. Part of the rationale of such agreements is precisely that they enable parties to *escape* the rules that would otherwise apply. While it could be said that law here still casts a shadow in a negative sense, as something to be avoided, it cannot be said to be constraining decision-making in the positive sense that the original metaphor would have us believe.

But the proposals could also be seen a response to the phenomenon of fragmentation or horizontalisation. As we have seen, it is a frequently-repeated premise of the proposals that a clearer framework of principle, with clearer

[30] See also Murphy (1997), for a discussion of "horizontalisation".

rules and less reliance on opaque discretions, will make it easier for parties to settle their own disputes. In this respect, modern family law, as already noted, seeks to address itself to a wider audience than just judges and other technical specialists. This could be seen in another way, however, as an attempt to give law a more clear-cut shadow so that parties' negotiations are conducted in the *same shadow*, no matter in what forum that negotiation happens to be taking place. On this view, the power of family law legislation is such that it irons out differences in an individual litigant's ability to access the family law system, or to obtain advice on their case. In this respect, a more rule-like family law does more than merely make settlement easier: it also provides a guarantee that the outcome will be the same however it is arrived at. It seeks to re-create law as the source of a determinate shadow, and thus to make good the promise of equal treatment implicit in liberal legalism. Yet this is happening at the same time as the institutional structures once thought necessary to guarantee liberal equality before the law, especially legal aid, are being dismantled. Law still casts a shadow (and, it is hoped, a clearer shadow than before) but it is now disembodied or de-institutionalised—it is law as pure idea.

One might note in passing that there is an instructive contrast with child support. There, equality of treatment and consistency of result has been achieved by removing child support almost entirely from the legal system and shifting it to the realm of administration; here, consistency is sought by means of a conscious *dispersal* of decision-making throughout the legal system, under the umbrella of overarching principles and rules. Both trends entail the removal of courts and judges as the centrepiece of the "system". Instead, as we have seen, it is a deliberate aspect of government strategy to confine Courts to their role of "secondary dispute resolution"—that is, a last resort when all else has failed. This serves to underline the theme of "horizontalisation". As already noted, the only overarching reference point is the disembodied or de-institutionalised voice of law itself.

CONCLUSION

Family lawyers are found of announcing "transformations" in their discipline. It would be tempting to announce the coming of another such transformation in Australian family law on the basis of the evidence presented here. That temptation has been resisted, because the picture is not a clear one. Instead of neatly identifiable trends and smoothly linear patterns of development, we have instead a number of "emergent properties" that may not yet cohere around an identifiable set of themes. Yet, when taken together, these changes do seem to announce the uneasy arrival of a family law regime that is starting to look identifiably different from that inaugurated nearly a quarter of a century ago—a regime in which assumptions, objectives and techniques have been quietly and subtly transformed. In the particular context of matrimonial property and superannuation, that shift is evident in new normative types, new sources of norms, new audiences for legislation and a self-conscious attempt to address the fragmentation of the family law system.

REFERENCES

American Law Institute (1997) *Principles of the Law of Family Dissolution: Analysis and Recommendations, Proposed Final Draft Part 1* (Philadelphia: American Law Institute).
Attorney-General's Department (1997) *The Delivery of Primary Dispute Resolution Services in Family Law* (Canberra: Commonwealth of Australia).
—— (1998) *Property and Family Law, Options for Change: A Discussion Paper* (Canberra: Commonwealth of Australia).
—— (1999) *Superannuation and Family Law: A Position Paper* (Canberra: Commonwealth of Australia).
Australian Law Reform Commission (1988) *Matrimonial Property: Report No. 39* (Canberra: AGPS).
Bailey-Harris, Rebecca and John Dewar (1997) "Variations on a theme—child law reform in Australia", *Child and Family Law Quarterly* 9, 149–64.
Beck, Ulrich (1992) *Risk Society: Towards a New Modernity* (London: Sage).
Behrens, Juliet and Bruce Smyth (1999) *Spousal Support in Australia: a Study of Incidence and Attitudes*, AIFS Working Paper No. 18 (Melbourne: Australian Institute of Family Studies).
Bordow, Sophie and Margaret Harrison (1994) "Outcomes of matrimonial property litigation: an analysis of Family Court cases", *Australian Journal of Family Law* 8, 264–77.
Dewar, John (1997) "Reducing discretion in family law", *Australian Journal of Family Law* 11, 309–26.
—— (1998) "The normal chaos of family law", *Modern Law Review* 61, 467–85.
Dewar, John, Jeff Giddings and Stephen Parker (1999) "The impact of legal aid changes on the practice of family law", *Australian Journal of Family Law* 12, 33.
Dewar, John and Stephen Parker (1999) "Parenting, planning and partnership: a study of the impact of the Family Law Reform Act 1995", *Family Law Research Unit Working Paper No. 3* (available from http://www.gu.edu.au/centre/flru/ frameset2.html) (Brisbane: Family Law Research Unit).
Dewar, John, Grania Sheehan and Jody Hughes (1999) *Superannuation and Divorce in Australia*, AIFS Working Paper No. 18 (Melbourne: Australian Institute of Family Studies).
Dunn, Kristie (1999) "Splitting the difference: superannuation, equality and family law", *Australian Journal of Family Law* 12, 214–35.
Family Court of Australia (1998) *Study of the Effects of Legal Aid Cuts on the Family Court of Australia and its Litigants* (Canberra: FcoA).
Family Law Council (1998) *Child Contact Orders: Enforcement and Penalties* (Canberra: Commonwealth of Australia).
Finlay, H, Rebecca Bailey-Harris and Margaret Otlowski (1997) *Family Law in Australia*, 5th edn (Sydney: Butterworths).

Funder, Katherine (1992) "Australia: a proposal for reform", in L. Weitzman and M. Maclean (eds) *Economic Consequences of Divorce: An International Perspective* (Oxford: Oxford University Press).

Funder, Katherine, Margaret Harrison and Ruth Weston (1993) *Settling Down: Pathways of Parents after Divorce*, AIFS Monograph No. 13 (Melbourne: Australian Institute of Family Studies).

Galanter, Marc (1992) "Law abounding: Legalisation around the North Atlantic", *Modern Law Review* 55, 1–24.

Geertz, C. (1964) "Ideology as cultural system", in D. Apter (ed.) *Ideology and Discontent* (New York: Free Press).

Giddens, Anthony (1999) "Risk and responsibility", *Modern Law Review* 62, 1–10.

Graycar, Regina (1995) "Matrimonial property law reform and equality for women: discourses in discord?", *Victoria University of Wellington Law Review* 25, 9–30.

Hunter, Rosemary (1998) "Litigants in person in the Family Court", *Australian Journal of Family Law* 11, 171–78.

Ingleby, Richard (1992) *Solicitors and Divorce* (Oxford: Oxford University Press).

Jacob, Herbert (1992) "The elusive shadow of the law", *Law and Society Review* 26, 565–90.

Joint Select Committee on the Family Law Act (1980) *Family Law in Australia: Report on the Family Law Act* 00, 000–00.

—— (1992) *The Family Law Act 1975: Aspects of its interpretation and operation* 00, 000–00.

Kaye, Miranda and Julia Tolmie (1998) "Fathers' rights groups in Australia and their engagement with issues in family law", *Australian Journal of Family Law* 12, 19–67.

Kingsford-Smith, Dimity (1999) "False economies: women and superannuation", Paper delivered at FLAW Conference, Sydney.

McDonald, Peter (ed.) (1986) *Settling Up* (Melbourne: Prentice-Hall).

Melli, Marygold, Howard Erlanger and Elizabeth Chambliss (1988) "The process of negotiation: an exploratory investigation in the context of no-fault divorce", *Rutgers Law Review* 40, 1133–72.

Millbank, Jenni (1993) " 'Hey girls, have we got a super deal for you'. Reform of superannuation and matrimonial property", *Australian Journal of Family Law* 7, 104–20.

Mnookin, Robert and Lewis Kornhauser (1979) "Bargaining in the shadow of the law: the case of divorce", *Yale Law Journal* 88, 950–97.

Murphy, Tim (1997) *The Oldest Social Science? Configurations of Law and Modernity* (Oxford: Oxford University Press).

Neale, Bren and Carol Smart (1997) " 'Good' and 'bad' lawyers? Struggling in the shadow of the new law", *Journal of Social Welfare and Family Law* 19, 377–402.

Star, Leonie (1996) *Counsel of Perfection: The Family Court of Australia* (Sydney: Oxford University Press).

Strathern, Marilyn (1992) *After Nature: English Kinship in the Late Twentieth Century* (Cambridge: Cambridge University Press).

5

Administrative Divorce in France: A Controversy Over a Reform, that Never Reached the Statute Book

BENOIT BASTARD

URRENT CHANGES IN family law are taking many different directions, which do not appear to converge.[1] There is, on the one hand, a movement towards imposing formal structures in what was previously an informal situation. In particular, legal forms are being prescribed for relationships, which are different from marriage, such as *concubinage* and cohabitation. But at the same time, we are also witnessing a move away from formal structures to reduce rather than increase the dominion of the law, and consequently that of the legal system, over the ways in which couples function and organise themselves.[2] Among these moves towards the freeing up of formal structures, which sometimes go as far as complete separation from legal practice, there are certain changes concerning the divorce process which aim to put back into the hands of the couple themselves the way in which the consequences of divorce are handled. For example, we have seen the introduction of divorce by mutual consent, and the introduction, in law, of concepts, which are not clearly defined. These changes place upon the judge the burden of using his discretion in making a judgement about the circumstances to be taken into account when deciding upon the consequences of the divorce. The trend towards easing the formalities surrounding divorce—which goes hand in hand with the de-institutionalisation of marriage—has spread to most European countries during the last thirty years. In Great Britain, for example, this development can be seen even more clearly in the recent reforms which aim to give mediators an increasingly important role in the handling of divorces.[3]

The idea that a divorce decree may be handed down by a court at the request of the parties concerned is part of a trend towards giving more responsibility to the couple in an administrative process within the private sphere. This kind of

[1] I would like to thank Marie-Annick Mazoyer for her help, as well as the members of Typhaon Commission, which gave me the warmest of welcomes. This work is of a provisional nature.
[2] The notion of "deformalising" is used here in the sense that the philosopher and sociologist Jean de Munck gives it in *France: Les Révolutions Invisibles* (1999).
[3] Maclean (1996), pp. 299–316.

"divorce without a judge" is still relatively unknown in countries where law controls the ways in which people can have access to divorce, and offers guarantees concerning the outcome to the divorcing couple and to their children. In France, the idea of an administrative divorce procedure was recently mentioned by the Minister of Justice, Elizabeth Guigou, as a possibility for reform. But though the possibility was mentioned, the matter was not taken forward. No proposal for reform was drawn up, and there is no evidence of any move in this direction. Indeed, the Commission set up following recommendations made by Irène Théry, which is now in charge of the reform of family law, seems reluctant at the time of writing to go any further down this particular path.

The consequence is that, although it may be interesting to us as scholars to discuss this proposal to remove a part of the divorce process from the legal sphere in France, we are doing no more than considering an example of a projected legal reform which, while it forms part and parcel of the liberation of family affairs from the legal process, has not been adopted and is not, for the time being, on the statute book.

The questions, which we will ask, based on an analysis of this project, are thus concerned with its failure. How was this de-formalising of the divorce process envisaged in the outline proposals? Who supported these proposals? What kinds of opposition did these proposals provoke and why did they have such a decisive impact? Analysis of these proposals will also give us an opportunity to ask ourselves questions about the role of the sociologist and the position of the expert when facing the politicians involved in the making of the law. The proposed reform owes a great deal to the work of Irène Théry—who played a most important part in putting it into the policy arena.

These questions will be considered using information from two main sources: firstly a series of meetings with certain people who played key roles in the working out of the reforms, and secondly the articles which appeared in the press covering the different stages of the controversy. During the period which followed the announcement made by Madame Guigou in the autumn of 1997, the media had a hugely exaggerating effect on the debate surrounding the question. This interest has resulted in their making available to the public a particularly useful account of the particular points at issue. The different stages of this unsuccessful reform will now be described, and then the reasons for its failure examined.

A PARAGRAPH IN *LE DÉMARIAGE* (UNMARRIAGE)

Before the Minister of Justice became interested in non-judicial divorce, any discussion of such a change in the way that divorce could be initiated had only taken place in strictly limited circles. The possibility was first mentioned in 1993 in *Le Démariage*, where Irène Théry devoted a paragraph to the subject, and proposed that "the debate should be opened".

"One of the questions that has been least aired at the present time is the reason for the existence of judicial divorce. Should it be necessary to go to court in all cases, even where the separation does not involve any legal quarrel, or anything that might be prejudicial to public order? The question has been raised in other countries in the case of non-contested divorces where no children are involved and where it is difficult to see what need there is for judicial involvement. Could these divorces not be simply administrative, in the same way that marriage is? And other non-contested divorces? A debate should take place."[4]

AN ARTICLE IN *LIBÉRATION*, AND VARIOUS INITIATIVES TAKEN BY A GROUP OF JUDGES AND BARRISTERS

A second reference to the question was made in an article in the newspaper *Libération*, in February 1996.

"Today, the judge for family affairs looks after most of the problems linked to the family... But why should this be done by a judge?... In most cases [involving divorce], the role of the judge is no longer to allow or not allow the divorce as couples have already made the decision. Similarly, in most cases, the judge does little more than approve arrangements made by the two parties. When the length of the marriage has been short, or when there are no goods to be shared out, or when the married couple have been able to sort things out for themselves, the judicial process appears to be very cumbersome... In these cases, the judicial system loses some of its credibility and its symbolic force.

Marriage is not simply a contract between two married people... It cannot therefore be dissolved without some sort of formality. The state official who officiates at the marriage could equally well officiate in the case of divorce. A trial separation period of three to six months could be set, and the declaration of the divorce organised. A book could be given to each party, similar to that given when a marriage takes place, reminding them of their rights and their duties to the other partner, to any children ... These new arrangements could still allow people to go to court in cases where the two parties do not agree on the very principle of divorce and its consequences. The judicial debate would recover its *raison d'être*."[5]

Twelve people signed this article: five judges and seven barristers, of whom ten were women and two were men. It arose from the reflections of a small, informal working group, which was to set itself up later as an association under the name of Typhaon. A number of these magistrates and barristers had known one another for a long time. They had worked together for some time in the area of legislation concerning rented property, and had already been responsible for a number of critical proposals and had a reputation for a certain amount of militancy in their views.

---

[4] Théry (1993), p. 389.
[5] Various lawyers in *Libération*, 21 February 1996.

"We were a small group of professionals—former judges and barristers in the domain of rental law—we got to know one another 15 to 20 years ago. At that time, there was a great deal of debate on the subject of rental law. In 1982, 1983 and 1989 successive laws focused on this particular law. It was a political debate. A group of *juges d'instance* [judges of first instance] who were members of the Magistrates' Union took part in the debate. It got together on an informal basis and I took part in it. The group held discussions about rental law. And it brought into these discussions a number of barristers who were members of the Barristers' Union of France. We all worked together. Later, this area of law was no longer an area of contention: rents were controlled and the laws that were voted in by the right calmed things down. Everything went quiet. At the same time the judges left the courts of first instance." (A magistrate, Typhaon member)

But this collaborative work continued and was carried over into the areas of family law to which a number of judges had been assigned, and new members joined the group.[6]

"A number of us found ourselves working in the area of family affairs. We said to ourselves: 'What about thinking about what we are doing', and they once again set up SM [Le syndicat de la magistrature (a union of magistrats)] and SAF [Le syndicat des avocats de France (a union of lawyers)] group. As people had got older, and because we were not sectarian, the group got bigger. It welcomed barristers who were not from the SAF and magistrates who were not from the SM. All this was done on a friendly basis, and people were co-opted. We worked like that for a period of two years, meeting once a month. There were discussions and exchanges." (A judge, Typhaon member)

The debate about divorce led people to raise once again questions about the role of the judge and about the meaning of the current divorce procedure. This discussion led to the petition contained in the *Libération* article.

"We asked ourselves questions about the role of the judge in divorce cases, and we found that we were all in agreement: we were frustrated as judges, and they were frustrated as barristers. Divorce is an area which frustrates everyone. We are wasting time, and that's no use to anyone. Clients are also frustrated and disillusioned. Thus the question was how to rehabilitate the role of the judge in family affairs? In our debate, we raised in particular the problem of people who are able to work things out for themselves because they have no children and no worldly goods. This was how we came to publish the article in *Libération*." (A judge, Typhaon member)

It is remarkable that this intervention in February 1996 provoked so little reaction. In fact the group even had trouble in finding a press outlet to publish their point of view. Later on, its authors still had not come across any reaction to the article.

"We had a great deal of trouble in publishing this article. It didn't interest anyone. When it was published, it was very disappointing: nothing, no reactions, a complete flop." (A judge, Typhaon member)

[6] Irène Théry was associated with the Typhaon Commission as from this time.

Provisionally things stopped there as far as the "divorce without a judge" question was concerned.[7] The Typhaon group, given the small amount of interest that had been shown towards this first proposition, carried on with its discussions and began to work in the area of the exercise of parental authority. Members began to organise a colloquium on co-parenting in the summer of 1997. It was at this colloquium that the group formally established itself as an association and gave itself the name of Typhaeon.

"We said to ourselves that we were going to do something else, and we worked on the question of parental authority shared between two people. We organised a colloquium on co-parenting in June 1997. We set up this colloquium in order to do something concrete and in order to continue to work together on serious issues. It was at that time that we found the name Typhaon. The name was suggested by a friend who is a linguist. Typhaon is the name of one of the wives of Jupiter who, because she was dissatisfied with him, had a child all by herself. This child became a monster. Having children all by yourself turns children into monsters. The idea was to reaffirm the role of the father." (A judge, Typhaon commission member)[8]

The question of administrative divorce was no longer on the agenda during this period, but an alternative proposition concerning divorce was coming to the forefront. This proposition had come from a magistrate closely involved in the area of mediation. In an article which appeared in the *Gazette du Palais*, Danièle Ganancia did not take up the idea of de-judicialising divorce which had been clearly set out both in the *Liberation* article mentioned above, as well as in the initial proposal made by Irène Théry. Ganancia instead suggested a simplified form of divorce, known as a "statement of divorce", that was still to be dealt with by a family law judge, but the judge would be assisted where necessary by a mediator.[9] In this approach, legal reform would involve getting rid of divorce involving guilt, which "turns people into enemies who simply could not live together", but the magistrate would retain the powers that he now exercises in divorce-related matters. An announcement was made that a proposal for legal reform along these lines from the socialist deputies was imminent.[10]

At this time a number of other questions relating to the family were also giving rise to concern in judicial and government circles as well among the general public. In particular, questions relating to the "social union contract" first described in 1995 (which was to become the Pacte Civil de Solidarité (PACS), first presented for discussion in the National Assembly in October 1998) began to take centre stage in the media. The private questions about the nature of family life became both public and politicised. The PACS developed as a way of

[7] It can be noted, however, that in 1996 the report that Jean-Marie Coulon devoted to the reform of civil procedures rejected the transfer of responsibility for judicial handling to an administrative court, and retained an alternative that consisted in simplifying the procedure by mutual consent.

[8] The papers delivered at this colloquium, which was held on 12 June 1997, were published in *Dialogue*, no.1412 (1998), "Should divorce be more run of the mill?".

[9] Ganancia (1997), pp. 16 and 33–9.

[10] "Démarions-nous sans faute" ("Let's get unmarried but no-one's the guilty party"), *Libération*, 4 August 1997.

giving legal status to same-sex couples who had been ignored by the law until 1999. Following the ravages of AIDS there had been concern, for example, about the lack of protection from eviction from the home on the death of a partner. It was in relation to one of the many studies that marked the progress of consideration of the PACS debate about the legalisation of the private status of cohabitation, that another reference to the question of de-legalising the public act of divorce that interests us, is to be found. In one of the very important articles that she wrote during the development of this social contract union, which finally became law in October 1999, Irène Théry proposed once again a change in the way that divorce might be approached. With reference to the different ways in which this new type of contract could be dissolved she raised the question again, using the term "civil divorce".

> "It is difficult to understand why divorce should be judicial, particularly in cases where there is no legal dispute between the divorcing partners. Rather than approaching the problem indirectly with a social union contract that would in reality set up two different types of heterosexual marriage, why not set about in the longer term putting in place a reform that would introduce civil divorce, alongside the different judicial procedures which would of course be maintained?"[11]

A MINISTER'S STATEMENT SETS OFF A CONTROVERSY

The question of "divorce without a judge" acquired a national dimension with the announcement by Madame Elisabeth Guigou, following the Théry article quoted above published in October 1997, of her interest in this question and her desire to engage in a "broad debate" on the subject of divorce reform to provide for divorce by mutual consent. Madame Guigou made a number of remarks in the presence of journalists, the detail of which is not at our disposal. It appears, according to certain sources, that Madame Guigou may have made the proposal during a speech to "state officials", and that she may have referred to it again in an interview that appeared in *France-Soir*.

> "Many people are asking themselves whether, when a couple wishes to divorce by mutual consent, they could avoid having to appear in front of a judge. After all, they got married in the presence of the mayor, who is a state official. Could we not envisage dissolving the marriage in this manner as and when the two people involved have reached agreement?"[12]

The question of what prompted this remark remains open. Even if it is true that a memorandum of the Typhaon proposals was sent to the Minister of Justice's office, we cannot assume that it was by this means that she came to favour this idea. It is worthy of note, however, that this simple sentence prompted a number of reactions which turned into a controversy. The mention

[11] Théry (1997).
[12] *France-Soir*, 10 November 1997, quoted by *Le Point*, 13 December 1997.

of what was nothing more than a "consideration" was taken for an actual project for reform—despite the fact that, to our knowledge, no official document exists that put forward such a project. Very strong reactions came from all the professional groups who felt that they would be affected by a potential reform: mayors, magistrates, barristers, solicitors, and so on. The members of the Typhaon group were immediately asked to take part in this public debate because of the discussions that they had already had, though their relationship with the media had not always been particularly easy.

> "Elizabeth Guigou unveiled her project . . . and all the media were on our backs. As far as the judges were concerned, there were very few of us. That was very difficult with the television. One of us had an interview on Channel Deux, another on Channel Cinq. It was awful. We were set up. . . For all of us, it was a most unpleasant experience as far as the television was concerned, and rather less unpleasant with the written press." (A judge, member of the Typhaon group)

As academics, we are not, in this chapter, describing a formal "project", but a movement towards change, which did not come to fruition, but was nevertheless surrounded by controversy. We will therefore restate the arguments put forward by various people—or the arguments that various people attribute to one another—in order to support or to criticise the proposal that they believed was included in what the Minister had to say. At the same time, we will try to lay out the main issues that divided the protagonists.

Arguments in Favour of Civil Divorce

Among the different arguments put forward to justify or to lend support to the project, we find the idea, mentioned above, of reserving the intervention of the judge to situations where divergent interests are involved and a judgment must be made. By following this route, the project can also be taken to support the idea that the couple can thus avoid having useless and stigmatising procedures imposed upon them. At a more general level the project fits into the wider move towards privatisation that seeks to hand over the responsibility for their divorce to the two people involved. Equally, but in a less obvious manner, an argument emerges according to which the introduction of such a form of divorce could have economic consequences in reducing the costs for the couple, and for the public purse by reducing demands on the court system. These arguments will be referred to again when we go on to describe how they were put into practice during the weeks that followed the announcement made by Madame Guigou.

Keeping the Intervention of the Judge for Situations that Demand It

This first argument has often been repeated in support of the Minister's proposal. It was heard being used by members of the Typhaon Commission when they were in demand by the media. For example, Marie-Christine George, a magistrate, rehearsed the birth of the project in the following terms:

> "We had the impression that we weren't always being very useful and the rule of law was being discredited by adherence to a form of law that no longer had a *raison d'être*."[13]

Another judge was of the opinion that to restrict the intervention of a judge to situations where there was true conflict was an appropriate response to recent legislative changes.

> "Married partners are equal in law. Since 1993, even in the case of divorce, the two parents retain parental control. The judge no longer has to defend the interests of the 'weak'. He has to become a referee of disputes."[14]

How to Avoid to Procedures that Treat People like Children and Recognise the Responsibility of Divorcing Partners

Irène Théry once more described the characteristics of the situations that were being examined:

> "I would remind you that in one third of divorces, no child who is a minor is involved and that often there is no property at stake. Furthermore, there are cases where, even with children, people are in agreement. And it is the case that we are imposing long and costly procedures on such people, and where there is nothing at stake."[15]

The idea of "going along with" the privatisation of divorce can be found in the speeches of those people who were in favour of reform, as a corollary to the preceding argument. This idea is associated with the question of how to extend the private sphere within which the couple is able to take responsibility for its affairs.

> "Public and private spheres must be redefined. The judicial authorities must get involved in the link between the parents and the child. But one's emotional life is a private matter. You can't intervene under the pretext that there may be some sort of conflict in the future. Today a real evolution in attitudes can be observed . . . in 30–40% of divorce cases by mutual consent, the partners come to court after more than a year of separation. They have already got things perfectly well under control."[16]

> "Do people really need us when they are in agreement about everything and have already organised their separate existences? What possible reason can there be for the judge's intervention in their private lives? They can mourn their separation elsewhere."[17]

---

[13] *Le Figaro*, 26 December 1997.
[14] Marie-Christine George, magistrate, quoted by *L'Evénement du Jeudi*, 20–26 November 1997.
[15] Irène Théry, *Le Figaro*, 29 December 1997.
[16] Marie-Christine George, quoted by *L'Evénement du Jeudi*, 20–26 November 1997.
[17] Claudette Boccara, magistrate, quoted by *Le Figaro*, 26 December 1997.

We should note that the arguments in favour of civil divorce mentioned above were always linked with conditions and precautions. Nevertheless the dividing line was becoming more and more clearly defined between those who think it useful to add a non-judicial path to divorce—a solution that confirms and prolongs the "pluralism" of the 1975 law—and those who would like to see the concept of guilt disappear altogether from divorce. Irène Théry, the leader of the first group, has severely criticised the second position, which she describes, somewhat curiously, as "the logic of de-judicialisation":

"The argument picks up on an old theme, which was already around in 1975 at the time of the great divorce reform. Certain people said that it was wrong to keep, within French law, divorce through guilt, a type of divorce that was 'out of date', they said. I have already been critical of the sort of moralising ideology that stigmatises all types of disagreement, whereas the real question for justice is to distinguish between illegitimate disagreements and legitimate disagreements that exist and should be treated with respect. The other sort of argument, which I defend, is quite different. It is the one which incorporates the idea of a 'French type of pluralism' . . . [In 1975] it was the case that both divorce by mutual consent was legalised and the concept of divorce because of guilt was maintained. Time has vindicated this approach as this latter kind of divorce, which its detractors said was condemned by history, today accounts for 44% of cases. Why on earth try to do away with this reality?"[18]

"Along with the various conditions associated with the civil divorce project, it was made clear that the principle of divorce without court intervention should go hand in hand with maintaining the possibility of recourse to a judge, who would be available at all times, in case difficulties arose. In the same way, the alternative procedures suggested by various commentators included the possibility of an initial consultation with specialists who would help the couple put the structure of their legal separation in place. It was suggested that a statutory official could make the declaration of divorce. A probationary period of three to six months would follow during which the post divorce arrangements could be established with the help of a lawyer or a mediator."[19]

Finally, the idea of maintaining the serious nature of a "divorce ceremony" was taken up and developed.[20]

"As far as the form of the proceedings is concerned, it seems to me that the nature of the dissolution of every marriage should be a solemn one. Within the context of the Typhaon group, all the women members were in agreement [the female members outweighing the male members of the group] when we said that, even if there is no dispute, the ceremony should be of a serious nature. A ceremony must be thought up that would take place in the presence of a state appointed official, and at this ceremony the couple should be pronounced divorced, and they should be reminded of their duties."[21]

---

[18] Irène Théry, *Le Figaro*, 29 December 1997.
[19] Marie-Christine George, magistrate, quoted by *L'Evénement du Jeudi*, 20–26 November 1997.
[20] On the question of the serious nature of divorce, our analysis of the role of the judge during the proceedings should be consulted: Cardia-Vonèche, Liziard and Bastard (1996), pp. 277–98.
[21] Irène Théry, *Le Figaro*, 29 December 1997.

Freeing up the Courts

One final argument in support of the project remains to be discussed—the idea that the de-judicialisation of divorce would free up the courts and reduce congestion.

> "The separated couple would gain in terms of time and money. As far as the courts are concerned, things would improve considerably. Let us not forget that half of civil proceedings are divorces."[22]

> "A divorce that took place in the Town Hall would equally have the advantage of clearing away a whole pile of disputes and would allow us to devote more time to complicated cases."[23]

This argument was only offered as providing a secondary benefit to be derived from such a reform, and the arguments in favour of such change were linked, in the opinion of supporters, to an improvement in the quality of decisions taken by the courts and by the couples involved. Irène Théry stated in an interview that "One cannot decide upon such a reform in the name of judicial comings and goings."[24]

Arguments against Civil Divorce

Opposition to the relaxation of formal divorce processes arose in a way which exactly mirrors the arguments in favour described above. Those critical of the project were of the opinion that either this new approach to divorce would not take off because it would not find a "following", or that it could take off but with harmful effects for the couples who chose this path.

This Sort of Divorce would only Appeal to a Minority

The first argument appears as a counterpoint to the idea of a possible reduction of pressure on the courts. The argument suggests that the couples concerned—with no problems, no children, or whose situation would not raise judicial difficulties—are only a small proportion of the total.

> "Divorce in the presence of the mayor would only involve a very tiny minority of couples: peoples without problems, without children, and without worldly goods. In my opinion, these would amount to no more than 10% of cases."[25]

---

[22] Marie-Christine George, magistrate, quoted by *L'Evénement du Jeudi*, 20–26 November 1997.
[23] Claudette Boccara, magistrate, quoted by *Le Figaro*, 26 December 1997.
[24] *Le Figaro*, 29 December 1997.
[25] Danièle Ganancia, judge specialising in family matters, in an interview in *Le Figaro*, 26 December 1997.

In other words, there would only be a very slight freeing up of the courts as far as divorce cases were concerned.

The fall in the number of cases could moreover find itself reduced to nothing if one considers that divorce in the mayor's presence could in turn could bring about a new sort of post-divorce case. This argument was put forward by Jacqueline Rubellin-Devichi. As a professor of law, she had been highly critical of the project—which, according to her, amounted to "resurrecting the administrative divorce that is to be found in the former Soviet Union"—on the grounds that the "dispute, postponed until after the divorce had taken place, would not be made easier for all that".[26]

In the same way, those critical of the project advanced the point that the economic argument alone could not be put forward to justify the reform of divorce which, hypothetically, should primarily be directed towards improving the quality of judgments handed down, as well as the judgments given to those actually appearing in court.

To drive the point home, those who were frankly contemptuous of the project suggested that possible candidates for this simplified form of divorce probably do not exist. Basing their views on their own experience of divorce, several law professionals were of the opinion that a divorcing couple who cannot agree would be incapable of managing the overall effect of their separation.

"I am a little sceptical. As soon as children and worldly goods are at stake, things get difficult."[27]

"People who get divorced are certainly normal adults and—in most cases—responsible, but they are going through a major crisis. The majority of them, when they are getting divorced, no longer have the necessary logic to sort things out properly."[28]

De-judicialisation does Away with Procedural Guarantees and can give rise to Cases of Injustice

In the eyes of a considerable number of its critics, the project for the de-judicialisation of part of the divorce procedure carried with it a major risk: the loss of the guarantees that are assured by the legal process. Law professionals, both barristers and judges, rehearse this argument in different ways.

"Divorce that does not take place within the legal system must be refused in order to safeguard legal security."[29]

"If such a course of action is adopted, couples will be encouraged to minimise their differences in order to obtain a rapid decision."[30]

---

[26] *Le Point*, 13 December 1997.
[27] Sylvaine Courcelles, magistrate, quoted by *L'Evénement du Jeudi*, 20–26 November 1997.
[28] Sylvaine Courcelles, quoted by *Le Point*, 13 December 1997.
[29] A barrister, quoted by *Le Figaro*, 26 December 1997.
[30] Sylvaine Courcelles, magistrate, quoted by *L'Evénement du Jeudi*, 20–26 November 1997.

How can it be considered possible for the two parties involved to get through the procedures by themselves when these require expertise?

"It is a fiction to pretend that people who are in apparent agreement can do without the protection of the judge. Whatever their social status may be, in most cases, they know nothing about legal procedure. Their first contact with the legal system comes about thanks to their divorce."[31]

In the same way, it is pointed out that barristers and magistrates have experience of divorce that mayors do not have.

"Divorce is always a break, a maelstrom. In a word, it is a trauma that barristers and magistrates can help overcome, but not mayors."[32]

These same critics point out that people who want to lend their support to the de-judicialisation process are exaggerating when they point to the fact that the judicial system is log-jammed, when one can see for oneself that the higher level courts are managing perfectly well.

The argument that concerns legal guarantees raised by the legal handling of divorce assumes another dimension when critics of the proposed reform mention the idea of equality before the law.

"This formula runs the risk of never being accepted by the Constitutional Council because it creates inequality between citizens in the legal process."[33]

"The setting up of town-hall divorce would amount to creating, for certain people, a 'poor person's' divorce or a 'two speed' divorce. The danger would then exist that certain cases would be left unresolved because of the lack of appropriate help."[34]

The Position of Different Groups Affected by the Controversy

Having presented in outline the arguments of those who opposed the proposed reform and those in favour, it is now possible to offer a provisional synthesis of the position of those affected by the controversy. A number of mayors were in favour of the proposal, while others were concerned about the extra responsibilities that would fall upon them or the amount of work that would be passed on to them. Moreover, a number of mayors reacted at an ethical level by refusing to become "divorcers". Mayors, and particularly those in small villages, responded in this way when they thought about the difficulties that would be raised by the fact of having to divorce people who fell within their administrative charge.

[31] A barrister quoted by *Le Figaro*, 26 December 1997.

[32] A barrister quoted by *Le Figaro*, 26 December 1997.

[33] Danièle Ganancia, judge for family matters, in an interview in the newspaper, *Le Figaro*, 26 December 1997.

[34] Supporters of the proposed reform had anticipated this risk themselves. Irène Théry stated in an interview (*Le Figaro*, 29 December 1997) that "We must avoid civil divorce becoming the poor person's divorce or the divorce of the most favoured."

"In my position as mayor, I am delighted when I have to officiate at a marriage. But would we not be taking away its solemn character if we were also considered able to pronounce a divorce?"[35]

Lawyers, for their part, were expressing total opposition to the proposal. They were doing so for the sake of those going through the legal process, but they also pointed out that they knew that people would be accusing them of adopting this position in order to defend their interests in the divorce market, as happened in the 1970s when they fought to keep obligatory legal representation in divorce cases. "People will be accusing us of protecting our interests", a lawyer noted in *Le Monde*.[36] Organisations that represent the profession shared the same view of the matter. They emphasised the importance of the work carried out by their members in divorce cases, including those cases where the two parties end up by agreeing. The role of the lawyer was described as "to inform, to give advice about the consequences for the family, as well as the financial, inheritance and tax consequences of a divorce".[37] "For lawyers, de-judicialisation is not to be welcomed inasmuch as it would encourage the couple to do without advice."[38] The position of the French Lawyers' Union was outlined in an article in *La Croix*:

"Is it not the case that couples who have just divorced in an amicable manner are surprised by divorce procedures? Isn't it necessary to give the proper time to prepare the re-organisation of the family and the necessary financial decisions? Those in favour of the proposal are suggesting that giving better form to divorce procedures would necessitate looking again at the relationship between the couple and the different administrative processes and to reform the compensatory benefits—but there's no question of changing anything to do with the causes of divorce!"[39]

It has already been noted that the judges were divided in their reactions. Although a number of judges concerned with family matters in the Paris region were strongly supportive of a proposal which some of them had initiated,[40] it was still the case that a good many of the members of the bench, even amongst those who were in general in favour of the reform of divorce procedures, were not ready to relinquish their hold over the way in which family break-ups are handled. As Dean Carbonnier had said, the judges were "little inclined to let go of an area which they find difficult but which gives them the prestige of mediation and of policing the family".[41]

It appears that the Minister of Justice was not unaware of reactions within legal circles. She reacted immediately to the first article that appeared in

---

[35] Pierre Méhaignerie, deputy mayor of Vitré, quoted by *Le Figaro*, 26 December 1997.
[36] *Le Monde*, 3 December 1997.
[37] Ibid.
[38] Ibid.
[39] *La Croix*, 13 November 1997.
[40] One of the articles that appeared in *Le Figaro* (26 December 1997) attributes the parentage of the reform to an "active minority".
[41] Quoted by Théry (1998), p. 122.

Le Monde on the subject, which was entitled: "Mme Guigou envisages a divorce by mutual consent without barristers and judges". In a right to reply piece, which appeared in the same newspaper, the Minister pointed out:

> "To reduce this question, which deserves serious debate, and on a purely hypothetical basis, the different ways of making a decision, to this one statement, constitutes an error... Before reaching agreement, couples will need someone to advise them of their rights, and to tell them what is possible and what is not possible."[42]

Other players in the legal sphere were clearly in favour of the proposal. Thus it is the case that solicitors, as opposed to barristers, were delighted with the opportunities that would be given to them as a result of such a reform, and to see the work that they do with couples better recognised in the finalising of decisions relative to the economic and practical consequences of divorce. The National Union of Solicitors has proposed that its members should be responsible for a contract defining the terms of an "un-marriage" which would have the same validity as a divorce decree absolute.[43]

Other professional groups working within the legal sphere or its periphery were also interested in the idea of obtaining a more important role in the area of divorce as a result of this proposed reform. One thinks in particular of the mediators who could play a role at the stage of the preparation of this new type of divorce.

It remains for us to consider the positions of people working outside the professional sphere. It is a fact that while the media have highlighted the reactions of the specialists who are directly involved, they have given no space whatsoever to those men and women directly involved in divorce. From this point of view, it is well known that the associations that represent the interests of fathers are very much in favour of any reform of this nature and the question of the steps taken by these associations to support the idea of administrative divorce is worthy of examination.

> "Let's take divorce and its procedures concerning parental authority out of the legal sphere so as to leave the judges free to carry out their essential duty which is to 'speak the law'... We should no longer have to call on a judge in order to obtain a divorce."[44]

The French people as a whole are also in favour of simplifying divorce inasmuch as it could result in a reduction of the problems that arise in the case of marital breakdown. This position is confirmed by the results of public opinion polls on the question. A poll carried out immediately after the Ministerial announcement shows the extent to which public opinion was in favour of such a measure. The idea of a quick separation available through the Town Hall was "attractive" to 70 percent of the French. An even greater number—85 percent— felt that such a formula would be "less painful and less traumatic" (see Table 1).

[42] *Le Monde*, 7–8 December 1997.
[43] *Le Monde*, 3 December 1997.
[44] Fédération des mouvements de la condition paternelle (Fathers on the move), April 1998.

Table 1: IFOP Public Opinion Poll/*L'Evénement du Jeudi* (20–26 November 1997).
Would you be in favour of a mayor being able to pronounce a divorce when couples have reached agreement without appearing in front of a judge?

Yes, totally	42%
Yes, on the whole	28%
TOTAL	**70%**
Probably not	9%
No, not at all	19%
TOTAL	**28%**
No opinion	2%

The simplification of divorce procedures will make divorce less painful and less traumatic. Yes.

Overall: 85%   Married people: 86%   Divorced people: 89%

A few interviews in the press confirm the fact that a simpler process appears to correspond clearly with popular ideas for social reform.

"Finally we might treat people like adults! I think it's an excellent thing that people who are in agreement no longer depend on a court that has no business sticking its nose into what is a private matter."[45]

More recently, a poll on family matters brought up this question again, and the results show that the idea of making divorce into an administrative matter is supported by a majority of those questioned. It should be noted, however, that when considered in comparison with legal divorce, this new solution had a much less favourable reception (see Table 2).

Table 2: L'Express Public Opinion Poll (6 June 1999).
Do you feel that divorce should be put into effect

	Yes	No	No opinion
By a judge?	70%	27%	3%
By a civil servant, e.g. the mayor or his deputy?	53%	43%	4%

To conclude, I quote again the newspaper article about the position of the French people on the proposal.

"It would be foolish to put Elisabeth Guigou's proposal too quickly on the shelf along with other utopian ideas of the 1968 vintage. It does at least have the merit of giving expression to a growing collective preoccupation: rightly or wrongly, more and more

[45] Interview with Claire Gallois, writer, *L'Evénement du Jeudi*, 20–26 November 1997.

French people are trying to take over control of their private lives. I can get married if I want to and when I want to, and I can leave you without having to ask permission from anyone. If we can't agree about the flat or the children, then we'll go and see the judge. But only if this is the case."[46]

As a provisional conclusion concerning the positions adopted with regard to this reform, it is clear that there is less reference to the "ideological" question of the eventual effects of the reform on the future of the institution of the family than to the practical conditions in which divorce procedures are or should be handled. The reactions of the legal players, in particular, seem to be very clearly dictated by their position in the field of divorce. Lawyers and judges, while expressing their preoccupations concerning legal security for the parties involved and the need to safeguard the interests of weaker parties, have made it quite clear that they wish to remain in charge of these matters. On the other hand, other professional players with very different status—i.e. the solicitors or mediators—show themselves to be interested in the proposal for a change that would strengthen their position in the "divorce market-place".[47]

"COUPLE, FILIATION ET PARENTE AUJOURD'HUI": THE ROLE OF THE REPORT BY IRENE THÉRY IN THE WIDE-RANGING DISCUSSION

After the media interest that had been raised by Elisabeth Guigou's statements subsided, public interest in the administrative divorce question fell away. It was only later in the more general context of the Irène Théry report on the reform of family law that the question was raised once again. It is well known that this report forms part of a programme of work requested by the socialist government with the aim of underlining its concern for legislative reform and the modernisation of the French administration. The report requested from Irène Théry by the Ministers of Employment and Social Solidarity, as well as by the Minister of Justice, aimed at defining the reforms needed to take account of the many changes taking place in the area of family law. It was a matter of "putting down markers for a left wing family policy".[48]

Amongst the many proposals in the report—which describes the status quo in family matters and foresees law reform measures in the areas of cohabitation, filiation, parental authority and succession—we find the proposed reform for civil divorce at the head of the list. The proposal takes up seven pages of the report and gives a more precise outline to this form of divorce by integrating the various elements of the debate which have just been described. In effect, it anticipates a number of objections and takes up certain options for change.

In summarising the arguments that justify the reform proposal, we can see that the earlier discussion on the causes of divorce addressed in the 1975 law

---

[46] Jacqueline Rémy, *L'Express*, 11 December 1997.
[47] See further discussion in Bastard and Cardia-Vonèche (1995), pp. 275–85; and (1996).
[48] *Le Monde*, 15 May 1998.

foresaw every situation except one, that in which there was no disagreement between the divorcing persons.[49] But this situation now exists. In quite a number of couples, the married pair is very attached to the idea of defining for themselves the form of their separation and does not like having to put up with legal procedures. Such legal control belittles the two people concerned inasmuch as it amounts to putting their autonomy into question. It is similarly belittling for the law itself.

As a consequence, the introduction of a new way of getting divorced has been proposed. It can be justified "first of all by its necessity and significance, out of respect for individual wishes, and out of respect for justice".[50] The proposal made is for "divorce by means of a declaration made in common".[51] The divorce would be recorded simply by the acknowledgement of the couple's agreement to put an end to their marriage. It would not imply approval of any arrangements concerning the effects of the separation.

The wording of the proposal then mentions its practical implications and speaks in particular about the question of determining which body should be entrusted with the handling of this new form of divorce. Two possibilities are suggested: the Town Hall or the Clerk of a higher level court. The opening up of this second possibility is a testimony to the consideration given to opinions that were expressed during the controversy, which has already been described. Concerning entrusting the task to the mayors, Irène Théry makes clear that this solution seems preferable to her because of the symbolism attached to it and because it marks more clearly the difference from the way in which legal divorce is handled now (which would be less well assured in a situation where the Clerk of a court would be charged with receiving the declaration). At the same time, Irène Théry pays attention to the reservations expressed by the general public:

> "What will be the attitudes of a number of mayors who are hostile to divorce? Will we have to widen the geographical field of competence of Town Halls in order to facilitate the work of smaller communities and in order to reconcile appearing in front of a civil servant with the respect owed to people's private lives?"[52]

In response to reading the opposing views that have been described above, Irène Théry suggested a number of different precautions that could be taken. This new liberty would not mean that divorce, which is a solemn act that changes the legal situation of individuals, would in the least way be "fudged" or devalued. Amongst the precautions to be taken, we can include putting in place a period of reflection, allowing the two people involved "to show their ability to take charge themselves

---

[49] It is worth remembering that there are four types of divorce, unequally used according to legal areas: divorce because of guilt, divorce by common request (by mutual consent), divorce by accepted request and divorce through breakdown in the couple's family life.

[50] Théry (1998a).

[51] A third appellation following that of "administrative divorce" and "civil divorce". Irène Théry has written that this denomination corresponds to the desire "in no way to prejudice, at this stage in the debate, the authorities deemed apt to receive this declaration and to verify the agreement".

[52] Théry (1998a).

of the effects of their separation"; the possibility of legal consultation which, while not obligatory, could be "recommended"; the solemn character of such an action; and maintaining the possibility of an appeal to a judge in all circumstances.[53]

The reasons for putting forward the proposals for civil divorce have not changed. The practical implications have been specified. And a certain prudence in the way that the proposal is now expressed bears witness to the fact that its author is well aware of the opposition that the proposal has aroused.

> "It is in no way a question of taking divorce out of the legal sphere, as some people are saying in order to scare others, but simply of adding another possibility to the choice of means of different types of divorce on offer 'à la française', while at the same time respecting its character."[54]

When all is said and done, everything is happening as if Irène Théry was holding on to the essential points of her proposal as one of the elements of the overall reform that she is putting forward, while at the same time noting various types of opposition and being well aware of the fact that the future will present difficulties.

As soon as the Théry Report was submitted, the whole of the family law reform task was sent to a specialist commission. It does not appear that this commission is working towards the creation of non-judicial divorce. At the same time, professional organisations where lawyers gather together are maintaining their opposition to the proposal, with the result that that this attempt at simplifying divorce cannot be effected in the near future.

CONCLUSION

This account of a reform that did not take place may provoke different reactions. Three will be mentioned here:

- The question of the power struggle that led to the failure, at least for the time being, of this reform proposal.
- The question of the place of the expert and her relationship with the political sphere.
- Finally, there is the basic question raised by the introduction of divorce without a judge—the question of knowing what implications the evolution of contemporary ideas about marriage could or should have in the case of divorce, and in considering the autonomy of the couple.

Within the framework of the present chapter, I will limit myself to a few brief remarks about each of these questions.

---

[53] Théry (1998a), p. 126.
[54] Ibid., p. 125.

Professional Interests versus Political Will and Public Opinion

Why was this reform of the divorce process rejected even before detailed work on the proposal had taken place? To summarise, from the available evidence presented in this chapter, it appears that a small group of expert players involved in looking for ways of improving the way justice works in family matters launched this idea, which found itself caught up—without anyone knowing quite, how this happened—in a flurry of proposals put forward at the instigation of the government in order to demonstrate its interest in family matters and to prepare an innovative policy in this field.

Curiously enough, as soon as the proposal for a "mayor's divorce" was made public, the same type of debate that had taken place concerning other reforms in family law, such as the PACS, did not happen. In particular, we saw neither the same traditional division between left and right, nor the usual exchanges about the protection or the destruction of the institution of the family, nor the tensions between the conservative character associated with the law and the wish to align the judicial system with the evolution of custom and the demands of public opinion.[55] The absence of this sort of debate illustrates the fact that, if need be, it is possible to leave to one side traditional debates with regard to the family.

The tension that can be seen is to be found in a completely different area. In the professional field this tension is the result of opposition between groups adopting different positions concerning who should be in charge of the divorce process. The number of players taking part in this debate remains very small: there are a few participants—professionals and intellectuals—and opposition to the idea from organised resistance by different bodies, such as lawyers who are benefiting from support from the mayors. As soon as those in favour of the status quo as far as this question is concerned had won the argument, it is remarkable that this proposal to simplify the judicial process served purely and simply to throw into relief the very marked difference between the position of, on the one hand, the players in the judicial field and, on the other hand, the expectations of the public. The former—judges and lawyers in particular—made clear their opposition to any reform which would take away their control of the divorce process. Public opinion seems, on the other hand, to be totally reconciled to the creation of administrative divorce.

There is no common ground—and no debate—between the opposition expressed by professionals in the field and the expectations of the public. If the idea of "civil" divorce appears acceptable to those working in the social field, or as a change that moves in the direction of strengthening confidence placed in the private sphere, this point of view is not being taken into account by the

---

[55] Perhaps the sort of debate that usually occurs would have come to the front of the stage if the idea of administrative divorce had been more successful. It might have been the subject of parliamentary debate.

organisations or groups who are capable of promoting the interest of such a proposal. Contrary to what happened over the same length of time concerning the PACS, with the exception of the Typhaon, there was no militant lobbying organisation that supported the de-judicialising of divorce. This is why the proposal could not be defended in the face of the resistance based on the immediate interests of the individuals or institutions who were professionally involved; there was the fear that lawyers' client bases would diminish, there was the wish on the mayors' part not to get involved in family quarrels, and the judges' concern to keep control over the breakdown of family life.

The Expert's Freedom and the Limits of his/her Influence

As far as the role of the expert is concerned, it will suffice to refer to the thoughts of Irène Théry herself.[56] She emphasised both the freedom that was given to her and the limits of any influence that she could bring to bear. This liberty found expression as much through the choice of experts who took part in the preparation of the report as through the absence of any sort of political pressure. This freedom for the expert was equalled only by the lack of political interference in the proposals made, though these were not perceived as being in any way binding.

The editor who draws up an official report today is no more or less than a frail craft that offers a brief view over the sea of democratic opinion. Launched as a kind of pilot boat on the waves of public debate, it may serve essentially to test the water. From the safety of the port, one will be able to see the squalls that he has to face or, on the other hand, the soft winds of consensus that he will have been able to summon up. Then, if the weather is fair enough, the politicians will jump into the water. And because it is their responsibility to take decisions, they will choose what they have remembered of what the editor has said and of the proposals he has made. Perhaps this will be substantial, perhaps slight, but always different.

Law and Custom

We know the saying according to which, as far as family matters are concerned, "law follows custom". As a final reflection, one could ask oneself whether this might apply to the question of administrative divorce. For in the end, if public opinion is very much in favour of a peaceful manner of divorce, it is still very much the case that divorce is characterised, in practice, by a conflictual dimension. We are not just thinking here of the persistence of divorce with an element

---

[56] On this question see Malaurie (1998), pp. 815–22 and Théry's reply (1998b), pp. 823–32. See also the round table organised by Ined, 14 September 1998: "La place de l'expert en sciences sociales dans le débat public".

of guilt, but also of the cases of non-payment of maintenance that are still very numerous in France. We are also thinking of the breakdown of ties between children and the parent with whom they do not live, and even of the cases of alienated separations where, because they cannot speak to one another, the couple separate without settling anything between them. When one considers this state of affairs, one cannot help thinking that as far as divorce is concerned, as with other aspects of the ways in which families function, hopes are far in advance of the reality of the situation. We may be told that the introduction of administrative divorce could be part of the "pedagogic" aspect of the law, which can also be found when family mediators are called upon. This no doubt is true. But it is still the case that opposition from lawyers, judges and mayors refers us back to the idea that public opinion is not yet "mature" enough for justifying the step of putting non-judicial divorce in place.

REFERENCES

Bastard, B. and L. Cardia-Vonèche (1995) "Inter-professional tensions in the divorce process in France", *International Journal of Law and the Family*, no. 9, 275–85.
—— (1996) "Les professionnels du divorce", *Droit et Société*, no. 33.
Cardia-Vonèche, L., S. Liziard and B. Bastard, (1996) "A judge in charge, or a judge at a loss? Redefining the role of the judge in divorce cases", *Droit et Société*, no. 33, 277–98.
De Munck, Jean (1999) *France: Les Révolutions Invisibles* (France: Invisible Revolutions) (Paris: Calmann-Lévy and Magnum Photos Press).
Ganancia, D. (1997) "Towards a divorce for the XXI century", *Gazette du Palais*, no. 108–9, 18–9 April, 16 and 33–9.
Maclean, M. (1996) "Looking to the future: towards a new way of reducing professional involvement in the area of divorce in the United Kingdom", *Droit et Société*, no. 33, 299–316.
Malaurie, P. (1998) "Réformer le droit de famille. Sur le rapport d'Irène Théry", *Commentaire*, no.83, 815–22.
Théry, I. (1993) *Le Démariage* (Paris: Odile Jacob).
—— (1997) "Questioning the social union contract", *Notes de la Fondation Saint-Simon*, October.
—— (1998a) *Couple, Filiation et Parenté Aujourd'hui. Le Droit Face aux Mutations de la Famille et de la Vie Privée*. Report prepared for the Minister of Employment and Solidarity and for the Garde des Sceaux (the Minister of Justice) (Paris: Editions Odile Jacob—Documentation Française), 122.
—— (1998b) "Droit, famille et vie privée: le pari du débat", *Commentaire*, no. 83, 823–32.
Typhaon Commission (1998) "Should divorce be more run of the mill?", Papers delivered at Colloquium on 6-Parenting held on 12 June 1997, *Dialogue*, no. 1412.

SECTION 2

THE PARTY POLITICAL AGENDA

6

Regulation of Same-Sex Partnerships from a Spanish Perspective[1]

ENCARNA ROCA

THE REGULATION OF same-sex partnerships in Spain has not been the subject of major sociological inquiry, nor are there any relevant judicial decisions on the matter as cases have not been brought before the Supreme Court. But for political reasons some of the Autonomias, including the autonomous Communities of Aragon, Catalonia and the Pays Basque, have supported the creation of a legal context for same-sex cohabitation which will lead to legal consequences for this form of family life. As the reasons for the decisions taken must be considered as exclusively political, aiming to emphasise the ability of the local governments to act independently, they have left unanswered a number of the demands of the gay and lesbian community, particularly those related to eligibility for Social Security benefits, mainly pensions, which are only available to families based on marriage. The policy agenda which has driven these autonomous Communities in Spain to provide same-sex partnerships with legal effect was not a family policy, which, as expert commentators have noted, does not exist in Spain.[2] The political objectives are of a different nature and range, from short-term election strategies to the long-term goal of seeking to establish their place among the community of "progressive" countries.

Those who are not familiar with the legal framework in Spain may be surprised by the fact that it is the autonomous Communities, which have been taking the legal initiatives on this subject. It may therefore be helpful to set out as background how the legislative competencies of the autonomous Communities are defined.

Spanish civil law, of which family law is a part, is regulated by the Spanish Civil Code. In addition, some autonomous Communities can make their own Civil laws, which are ranked alongside the Civil Code. The Civil Code regulates marriage (capacity, formalities, registration), marital rights and duties, nullity, separation and divorce on a national basis. But several of the individual

---

[1] The original Spanish version of the text was translated by Asunción Esteve Pardo, *Licenciada en derecho*, and has been revised by Eugeni Bou.
[2] Flaquer (1998), p. 141.

Communities have autonomous status.[3] The constitutional problem lies in assessing whether these autonomous Communities with legislative powers, who may not legislate concerning marriage, may or may not pass legislation concerning unmarried couples. The underlying issue from a family policy perspective would be whether or not same-sex cohabitation is to be considered as a form of marriage or as something different (see the discussion of the PACS above p. 75). From a political perspective the issues are rather different, and focus on the extent of the legislative powers of the autonomous Communities.

Article 149, 1–8, of the Spanish Constitution gives the State the exclusive power to legislate on "private legal relationships related to the forms of marriage". This permits us to state, as a first conclusion, that autonomous Communities cannot pass an Act that establishes forms of marriage different from those provided by the State legislation. That is to say, no alternatives to marriage are to be created. But, this does not prevent the autonomous communities from regulating the *effects* of these kinds of partnerships, as these are private effects that *can* be regulated by autonomous Communities. They have nothing to do with forms of marriage, which are reserved to the national legislative bodies, under the said Article 149, 1–8 of the Spanish Constitution.[4] But even so, the autonomous Communities cannot make provisions on many of the issues which are of practical importance in giving effect to such partnerships, such as, Social Security pensions, taxes or issues connected with criminal law, because these are also exclusively within the jurisdiction of the State.

Where do the boundaries lie around the effects of same-sex marriage for which the autonomous Communities are empowered to legislate? They cannot establish a civil registry system similar to that for marriage, because this issue can only be regulated by the State; but they can fix the moment in time when these kinds of partnerships are able to produce legal effects, establishing objective factors which prove the existence of the partnership. Under this jurisdiction, the autonomous Communities of Aragon and Catalonia have passed legislation on this matter: the Catalan Parliament passed the Stable Unmarried Couples Act 10/98, on 15 July 1998 and the Aragonese Parliament enacted the law 6/1999, on 26 March 1999, related to non-married stable couples.

In 1997 the Spanish leading political party, Partido Popular, put forward a Proposal to regulate the effects of what were called "private Partnership Contracts".[5] This Proposal came in response to the disagreement created by the different Proposals put forward by the Socialist Party and the Canarian Party in

---

[3] This is the case for the following autonomous Communities: Pais Vasco, Cataluña, Galicia, Navarra, Aragón and Baleares.

[4] The scope of the power to give provisions on civil law is one of the most controversial issues of present-day jurisprudence in Spain regarding Private Law. The Constitutional Court has pronounced its view on this matter in the Decision 88/1993, 12 March. See Roca and Ferriol-Roca (1998), I, at p. 37 et seq.

[5] It is the Proposal of Private Partnership Contracts Act, submitted to the Congress by the Popular Parliament Group. BOCG-CD, IV Parliament Period, 29 September 1997, Serie B, number 117–1, at pp. 1–5.

the corresponding Congress Sub-commission. Both Bills are still in Parliament and they have not yet been passed at the time of writing (May 2000). The model submitted by the Partido Popular closely follows the structure of the French First Proposal on Private Partnership Contracts.

THE FRAMEWORK UNDERLYING THE SPANISH LEGAL SYSTEM: THE BILL OF RIGHTS

Spanish private legislation is determined by the Constitution of 1978. This Bill of Rights establishes the family law principles which must be respected by any later Act. Therefore, this chapter starts by defining the limitations that bind the legislator—either from the State or from any autonomous Community— regarding the regulation of same-sex partnerships. The additional problem of considering them as families will be discussed in the last part of the chapter. We need first to consider the legal framework and basis for regulation, and the solutions eventually provided.

It is a fact, confirmed by statistics, that marriage has undergone progressive decline in western societies. The number of so-called unmarried couples, that is, cohabitants who have children and whose social behaviour is almost the same as that of married couples, has increased especially in urban areas. The reasons for this increase are very diverse, and are part of the changes in social values that have taken place in the twentieth century, from the 1970s onwards.[6] Some of the reasons for this change lie in the fact that people are becoming more and more aware of their own freedom, and the growing recognition of affectionate relationships between people who could not, until quite recently, exercise the right to express their feelings and live as same-sex couples.

This social situation implies a new concept of the family, and obviously a decline in marriage. However, marriage is at the same time becoming thought of as more and more important a force for social stability, and for this reason it is included in the laws that recognise fundamental rights. One solution provided by a group of European countries consists of marking out a difference between marriage and other kinds of partnerships, which are given different status according to their circumstances. The different categories are: (i) couples who refuse to get married (heterosexual couples); (ii) couples who cannot get married (same-sex partnerships).

Article 12 of the European Convention of Human Rights establishes that "on reaching the age of puberty, men and women have the right to get married and establish a family". This provision has been interpreted many times by the European Court of Human Rights as referring to the right to get married, and not to other kind of partnerships. Member States can, however, provide such partnerships with rights according to their own criteria.[7]

---

[6] Flaquer (1998), at p. 85 and p. 148 et seq.
[7] See *The Rees Case* [1987] 2 FLR, 111; *Cosey* v *UK* [1991] 2 FLR, 492; *B* v *France* [1992]; and *X, Y and Z* v *UK* [1997] 2 FLR 892.

Article 32 of the Spanish Constitution states that "a man and a woman have the right to get married on equal legal terms".[8] This provision recognises the right to get married, which does not rank as a fundamental right. It is only considered as the consequence of the fundamental right to freedom. Therefore, according to the Spanish constitutional system, the right to get married is one of the manifestations of the basic right to freedom. The Spanish Constitutional Court stated that marriage is an institution directly protected by the Constitution, which implies that a legislator can establish, without infringing the Constitution, legal provisions for partnerships other than marriage (Constitutional Court Decision 184/1990).[9] However, Article 32 of the Spanish Constitution has consequences for stable unmarried couples. This provision implies that any issue connected with this matter must be regulated by an Act. Therefore, only an Act can determine how the right to get married is to be exercised, by establishing who can marry whom, provided they are of different sex. This statement has been confirmed by different decisions of the Constitutional Court (for example, the case mentioned above and the Constitutional Court Decision 222/1994, 11 July 1994).

But all this does not exclude the possibility of giving legal effects to another kind of partnership. Article 32 of the Spanish Constitution regulates the right to get married, and therefore public institutions, on facing the social evolution of marriage and the increasing number of unmarried couples, have to consider whether to introduce legal provisions for such partnerships. These provisions should take into account two different situations: (i) people who refuse to exercise the right to get married, and consequently live together without being married, although they could be married because they are single; and (ii) the situation of people who cannot get married because they are not entitled to do so, that is same-sex couples.

The solutions provided by comparative European Law are quite uniform in this respect.[10] Most European legislations respect the right to reject marriage. In fact, they do not provide cohabitation outside marriage with legal effects, which would provide the necessary protection for any particular and possibly unequal conditions of the cohabitants. This would be reflected, for instance, in the recognition of the cohabitants' right to claim a house tenancy or certain compensations in case of the breakdown of their relationship. However, in the case of

---

[8] For the scope of the right to get married see LaCruz (1997), at p. 29; Reina-Martinell (1995), at p. 289 and Gomez (1990), at p. 231 et seq.

[9] The Constitutional Court Decision 184/1990 introduces the crucial issue: marriage and unmarried couples are not equivalent. Marriage is a social institution granted by the Constitution, which is not the case of unmarried couples, and therefore, the right to cohabit outside marriage is not constitutionally granted. According to this Decision marriage involves rights and duties, whereas extramarital cohabitation does not. That is the reason why, for the Constitutional Court, legal provisions distinguishing married and unmarried couples are entirely constitutional, because they are not equivalent situations that allow people to opt for one of them. The legislator can therefore provide different effects for different situations, although the Constitution allows him to make the effects coincide.

[10] See Martin (1995), at p. 1722 et seq. and Bradley's well-known work (1996).

same-sex partnerships, the solutions provided in comparative law are different, because same-sex couples tend to be provided with legal effects similar to those of marriage, on condition that there has been a formal act establishing their relationship. But even though the legal provisions for both cases are equivalent, same-sex couples are not considered to be the same as married ones.

The Spanish Constitutional Court has recognised the existing difference between unmarried couples and same-sex partnerships. In relation to heterosexual unmarried couples, Constitutional Court Decision 184/1990 states that:

> "it is clear that according to the Spanish Constitution of 1978 marriage and cohabitation outside marriage are not equal realities. Marriage is a social institution granted by the Constitution, and the right of man and woman to get married is a constitutional right (art. 32.1). This is not at all the case of the cohabitation *more uxorio*, which is not a legally granted institution and there is no such constitutional right to establish it. If the right to get married is a constitutional right, it can be concluded that in principle the legislator can establish different treatment for marital and extramarital unions."[11]

The Constitutional Court has applied the same criteria to same-sex partnerships. The Court has only once expressed its views on this matter, when it did not grant an appeal brought by a same-sex partner against a court decision that did not give him the right to obtain a pension from his deceased partner's estate. The Constitutional Court Writ 222/1994, states:

> "the absolutely constitutional character of the principle defines matrimonial unions as heterosexual; so that, public institutions can give more privileged treatment to family groups formed by a man and a woman, than to same-sex partnerships. That does not exclude the establishment of equitable provisions to make same-sex cohabitants benefit from the all the rights and benefits of marriage, as the European Parliament advocates."[12]

The conclusion is that the Spanish Bill of Rights, that is, the Constitution, does not prevent the legislator from providing rights for either heterosexual or same-sex partnerships, although these are not equivalent to marriage as an institution, and in the case of a legal vacuum, marriage provisions cannot be applied to such partnerships, because they lack the resemblance demanded by Article 4.1 of the Spanish Civil Code in order to apply provisions by analogy.[13]

THE SOCIAL SITUATION

The Preamble of the Catalan Stable Unmarried Couples Act 1998 (Caplan Act), which also includes provisions for same-sex couples, justifies the legal option on

---

[11] See in this respect Constitutional Court Decision 66/1994, 28 February; see also Constitutional Court Decision 222/1992, 11 December, which is the first to give an unmarried couple the quality of a protected family according to constitutional principles, but not including same-sex couples. Ferreres (1994), at p. 172.

[12] European Parliament Resolution, 8 February 1994.

[13] Supreme Court Decisions, 18 February and 22 July 1993; 30 December 1994.

social grounds. After stating that Catalan society is mainly based on matrimonial families, it adds that:

"In recent years the increasing number of the so-called stable unmarried couples has been noticeable, in parallel and coincident with a growing recognition of them inside our society, a recognition that applies to all types of couples, including those of the same sex, and supports an increasing body of opinion in Catalan society, that supports the regulation of this kind of partnerships."

The same intentions are expressed in the preamble of the Aragonese Non-Married Stable Couples Act 1999 (Aragonese Act):

"Together with the stable heterosexual couple, another similar phenomenon, but with different features and effects, is the same-sex stable partnership, which is becoming less strange and marginal. The principle of individual freedom, based on the Constitution, which is traditionally essential and basic in Aragonese Civil Law, compels the Legislator to accept that each person has the right to build an effective relationship in accordance with his/her sexuality. This is a growing phenomenon, generally accepted and assumed by the social body, which in practice generates difficult problems and unfairness."

What is the factual basis underlying the statements made in the Preambles of both these laws? The answer to this question is difficult because there was no data about same-sex couples in Spain before the analysis of the 1996 census, which is still not complete. This data has not yet been studied by sociologists. This section of the chapter, therefore, relies on some preliminary data, which is of interest. This data refers only to Catalonia, where the census analysis has been completed more quickly.

Number of Same-Sex Couples

According to the 1991 census, there were 21,726 people living together as homosexual cohabitants in Catalonia. They were distributed as shown in Table 1 according to age.

From this data, Martin[14] considered that in 1991 there were 1.79 same-sex couples per thousand inhabitants in Catalonia. According to the Catalan

Table 1: Distribution of same-sex couples in Catalonia according to age.

	Men	Women	Total
Younger than 25 years	604	932	1,536
25–39 years	2,976	3,584	6,560
40–54 years	2,714	3,524	6,238
55 years +	3,206	4,186	7,392
Total	9,500	12, 226	21,726

Data collected by the *Institut d'Estadística de Catalunya* CP/91 (17).

Statistics Institute, the 1996 census contained 17,149 same-sex couples, which makes a total amount of 34,298 people living together as same-sex cohabitants. One might think that the number of same-sex cohabitants is increasing but this statement cannot be made with any exactitude because the 1991 census did not ask any direct question about this kind of cohabitation, whereas the 1996 census did ask for objective data on this issue. At any rate, the average proportion of the Catalan population who live together as same-sex couples is 0.55 percent. According to the census data from 1996, same-sex partnerships in Catalonia are distributed in accordance with the details specified in Tables 2 and 3.

An issue of a different kind is how widely such couples are recognised and accepted in Catalan society. A poll carried out by the Catalan Justice Department in 1997, on the occasion of the preliminary surveys for the 10/1998 Act, provided the following data in answer to this question, which indicates a widespread acceptance of the situation:

Acceptance of same-sex cohabitation:

Yes: 50.3%
No answer: 4%
It depends: 7.7%
No: 38%

Source: Catalan Department of Justice, 1997.

Registration of Unmarried Couples[15]

The European Parliament Resolution of 8 February 1994 introduced a special official system to record unmarried couples—the local registry. These registries have no significance for marital status, they are merely instruments to evidence the cohabitation and work as administrative registries.[16] The first was created in Vitoria-Gazteiz, in the Pays Basque, by a Major decree on 28 February 1984, and many others have followed it. Due to their very nature these registry offices are not highly efficient and very few couples have opted for this solution. However they can provide some interesting data in respect of same-sex couples,[17] and in Table 4 we consider the most relevant information.[18]

[14] Martin (1995), at p. 1721.

[15] In this section of the chapter, I have taken into account the data gathered in the thesis "Hacia una construcción jurídica de las uniones de hecho en el Derecho español," written by Dr Pedro A. Talavera Fernández, supervised by Dr Javier de Lucas and Dr Rosa Moliner, and submitted to the tribunal in Valencia on 5 March 1999. I was a member of the tribunal that evaluated the thesis and the information on unmarried couples' registries can be found at pp. 99–111 therein.

[16] On local registries, see Valpuesta Fernandez (1995), at p. 63 et seq. and Villagrasa Alcaide (1998), at p. 517. On local registries in Catalonia, see Martin (1995), at p. 1711.

[17] The Unmarried Couples Registry from Valencia does not give information on the sexual orientation of the recorded couples. Talavera Fernández (1999), at p. 108.

[18] Talavera Fernández (1999) states that there are hundreds of local Unmarried Couples Registries: there are 34 in the province of Madrid and more than 40 in that of Barcelona. Martin (1995) at p. 1711.2, holds a similar opinion regarding the situation in 1995.

Table 2: Male cohabitants in Catalonia according to age.

	Under 20	20–24	25–29	30–34	35–39	40–44	45–49	50–54	55–59	60–64	65–69	70–74	75–79	80–84	85+	Total
Under 20	0	0	0	0	0	3	0	1	0	0	0	0	0	0	0	4
20–24	1	9	7	12	3	2	15	2	12	0	2	1	1	1	3	71
25–29	1	11	65	26	14	17	1	6	4	3	3	9	5	0	2	167
30–34	0	5	64	188	50	15	2	7	3	3	1	7	2	1	2	350
35–39	0	5	15	159	239	56	20	8	11	4	0	0	3	2	2	524
40–44	2	1	7	26	181	173	48	13	3	3	1	6	1	4	1	470
45–49	0	6	4	5	40	180	186	39	5	10	5	1	1	1	0	483
50–54	1	11	14	7	20	35	161	172	30	7	1	1	2	1	3	466
55–59	0	8	12	10	7	7	34	140	119	31	6	1	1	1	3	380
60–64	0	12	16	16	13	4	10	40	128	141	35	6	8	1	4	434
65–69	1	9	22	24	11	7	7	9	25	111	124	33	8	6	1	398
70–74	0	1	8	18	6	10	12	7	14	34	102	120	29	3	3	367
75–79	0	2	5	5	10	7	14	5	5	10	22	99	57	9	4	254
80–84	0	1	4	0	4	5	6	12	13	1	8	39	51	50	7	201
85+	0	0	2	3	8	5	12	8	9	8	11	15	23	39	38	181
Total	6	81	245	499	606	526	528	469	381	366	321	338	192	119	73	4750

Table 3: Female cohabitants in Catalonia according to age.

	Under 20	20–24	25–29	30–34	35–39	40–44	45–49	50–54	55–59	60–64	65–69	70–74	75–79	80–84	85+	Total
Under 20	1	0	4	12	18	29	13	1	5	8	7	0	2	0	3	103
20–24	0	8	10	17	34	21	32	9	6	12	13	2	3	3	1	171
25–29	1	15	56	44	18	26	15	21	12	10	6	5	2	3	5	239
30–34	1	3	71	183	62	24	8	7	5	3	6	3	2	2	2	382
35–39	6	6	20	148	247	52	9	9	3	4	3	5	2	0	3	517
40–44	10	13	6	35	187	224	52	18	5	6	3	0	4	4	1	568
45–49	5	23	12	10	45	213	243	40	8	11	4	2	0	1	5	622
50–54	3	14	16	7	20	49	183	182	41	20	10	4	11	4	3	567
55–59	3	8	13	17	10	8	32	164	139	29	7	1	3	9	9	452
60–64	0	14	15	32	16	16	28	58	159	141	32	15	1	3	16	546
65–69	0	2	21	25	23	23	17	12	51	133	159	26	3	3	15	513
70–74	0	1	6	23	26	33	27	32	21	45	113	98	30	5	14	474
75–79	0	3	3	8	17	29	21	38	23	19	44	86	58	16	26	391
80–84	0	0	5	8	14	11	16	31	17	18	17	26	67	53	12	295
85+	0	0	3	14	13	14	15	19	21	33	31	13	20	29	48	273
Total	30	110	261	583	750	772	711	641	516	491	449	290	204	144	161	6113

Data collected by the *Institut d'Estadística de Catalunya*. Generalitat de Catalunya, 1999

Table 4: Number of cohabiting couples recorded in various local registries.

Registry	Total number	Couples	Average
Vitoria-Gazteiz (1994–8)	450	13	2.88%
Barcelona (1994–8)	531	99	18.64%
Asturias (1994–8)	82	8	9.75%
Madrid (1995–8)	1200	141	11.75%

The *total number* refers to unmarried couples officially recorded, either heterosexual or same-sex; *couples* refers to those couples officially recorded in the registry as same-sex, including both gays and lesbian couples.

In conclusion, the evidence we have on the social context of the legislation indicates that not very many people are involved in same-sex partnerships, and that there are no religious limitations on the admission of legal provisions on this matter, even though the Catalan poll showed that only one in three practising Catholics thought that same-sex partners should be regarded as forming a family with entitlement to social and legal protection, compared with one in two of the population as a whole. Moreover, the conservative governments of Catalonia and Aragon have carried out the task of providing a legal framework for same-sex couples.

THE CONTENT OF THE CURRENT SPANISH PROVISIONS: THE PRINCIPLES

There is no national uniform legal framework for same-sex couples in the areas that have not legislated for them directly. There are only scattered provisions in the State law, but two autonomous Communities, Catalonia and Aragon, have provided comprehensive legislation on the effects derived from same-sex cohabitation. These provisions, however, do not lay down a compulsory form for these partnerships. This could only be achieved by the State law, and the autonomous Communities with jurisdiction on civil matters do not wish to infringe this exclusive jurisdiction.

One can find some references to same-sex cohabitation in the State law which provides for legal effects. Perhaps the most important provision in this respect is the Urban Renting Act 29/1994 which entitles the surviving same-sex partner to succeed to a tenancy on the death of his/her partner, if he or she was sole tenant or the date of death. Article 16.1(b) of this Act establishes that this right should be recognised for

"the person that has been constantly living with the tenant for at least two years before his death, in a similar affection relationship to that of a spouse, regardless of his sexual orientation."[19]

[19] Perez Cánovas (1996), at p. 247.

The only other provision for the effects of same-sex cohabitation can be found in the Aid for Sexual Offences Victims Act 35/1995 (Article 3), and the Aid for AIDS Victims Act 34/1996, which recognise some rights for the cohabitants in a formulation quite similar to the one used in the Urban Renting Act.[20]

These provisions will not be the object of thorough analysis or criticism here,[21] but it is interesting to examine the principles they embody, and the solutions they propose. These principles embodied are legal security, free will and protection against unfair enrichment.

(i) *The legal security principle* requires the legislator to provide solutions for determining when a same-sex couple is formed. One has to bear in mind that marriage is excluded from these situations, and that the autonomous Communities have no jurisdiction to establish a specific form for these partnerships, so it is necessary to fix the moment when cohabitation starts producing effects between the cohabitants, and against third parties. The Catalan Stable Unmarried Couples Act uses a system of public deed (Article 21.1), that requires the statement of the cohabitants to accept the effects provided in the Act from that moment on. But if they want to obtain the effects, cohabitants must be of the same sex (Article 19), and the Catalan Act does not regulate the problem of transsexuals, who have the right to record in the registry their change of sex,[22] but not a clear entitlement to claim a right to get married.

The Aragonese Act, on the other hand, does not differentiate between a hetero(trans)sexual and same-sex couple in order to determine the requirements for considering that a stable couple has been constituted. Article 3 of the Aragonese Act admits two possibilities for the existence of a same-sex stable couple: (a) continuous cohabitation for at least two years, and (b) public deed, which must contain a clear declaration by the cohabitants. Article 2 of the Aragonese Act also foresees the creation of an Administrative Registry (not civil) in which cohabitants must record their union, if they want the "Administrative provisions" to be applied to it (Article 2).

(ii) *The principle of free will.* Article 22.1 of the Catalan Act declares cohabitants have the free will to establish the personal and material consequences of their partnership. Their free will extends to the possibility of dealing

[20] There is an allusion in the Children Protection Act 7/1994 passed by the Valencian Parliament, whose Article 24 contains a provision that was considered to authorise the adoption of children by same-sex couples. Actually it states that "the type of partnership that those who claim adoption have decided to establish can by no means be regarded as discriminatory". This provision must not be interpreted in relation to adoption claimed by a couple, but to individual adoption, so that it tries not to discriminate against individuals, regardless of their partnership: marital, extra-marital, heterosexual or same-sex. See Plaza Penades-Tamayo (1998), at p. 407.

[21] On the Catalan Act, Roca and Trias (1998), II, p. 445 et seq. and Martin (1998), p. 143 et seq.

[22] See Supreme Court Decisions 2 July 1987; 15 July 1988; 3 March 1989 and 19 April 1991. This last Decision states that the authorisation to record a change of sex in the registry does not imply "an absolute equivalence with female sex regarding the celebration of some act or contracts, especially that of contracting marriage as transsexual". On this topic, see Gordillo Canas (1989), at p. 324 and Lopez-Galiacho (1998), at p. 343.

with the effects of the breakdown of the relationship. But this principle is not absolute in the Catalan Act, because it imposes certain effects connected with financial support and succession, which cannot be overridden by the partners at the time their relation ceases. This is also the case in the duty to maintain the partner, guardianship of a mentally disordered partner, and the cohabitants' obligation regarding payment of their common expenses, which cannot be rejected by either of them. All this puts the free will principle in doubt, in spite of the Act's official declaration of this principle.

The consequences of the Aragonese Act seem quite different, because the effects of a same-sex partnership are regulated mainly by the will of the cohabitants. When a declaration is lacking, the Act will provide them with a status, established by Article 3.3.

(iii) *The protection against unjust enrichment.* One of the main principles declared in these Acts is to seek a balance between the cohabitants' property, which implies that once the relationship comes to an end (by unilateral or bilateral decision), financial compensation is compulsory for cohabitants only in cases where the cohabitation itself has produced an imbalance in their properties "that implies an unjust enrichment" (Article 31.1 Catalan Act and Article 7.1 Aragonese Act). Therefore, on providing these financial compensations, the Acts try to compensate one of the partners for the damages that might result from the partnership. This solution is given in the absence of specific regulation for cohabitants of property settlement in the way that former married partners have.

THE CONTENT OF SPANISH CURRENT PROVISIONS: THE EFFECTIVE RIGHTS

On the basis of these principles, we should examine the provisions that establish the constitution of a partnership, its permanent effects, the effects produced by the breakdown and the succession effects.

Legal Constitution of a Same-Sex Partnership

In order to constitute a partnership, members are required to be of age (Article 20.1.b Catalan Act), and not previously married (Article 20.1.b), or part of a stable unmarried couple (Article 20.1.c.). They should be neither full-nor half-blood relatives, nor should they be adopted.[23] The Aragonese Act establishes the same requirements in Articles 1 and 4.

[23] The previous statement could lead us to think that there has been an infringement of the exclusive State power to legislate on the form of marriage. This statement should not be accepted, because the Act does not establish a form of marriage for same-sex couples, but provides a kind of security for cohabitants and third parties. The public deed is not a new form of marriage, but a system to determine the existence of a partnership and an instrument for the partners to declare their intention.

The signing of a public deed provides the partnership with legal effect. The reason for that is that same-sex couples cannot marry, and therefore their partnerships must be regarded as a form of extra-marital cohabitation. Their signing of a public deed does not convert their cohabitation into marriage, but provides it with a basis that makes it possible to regulate some aspects of their partnership and its breakdown. The same effects are given by the Aragonese Act for the two-year cohabitation group.

The public deed must contain two statements; the first refers to the cohabitants' determination to accept the benefits provided by law; the second statement contains the cohabitants' declaration that they know of no impediment as to why they should not be part of a same-sex partnership. Without these statements, the cohabitation has no effect, either because cohabitants lack free will or because they do not satisfy the conditions imposed by law.

The laws also demand that the couple should be stable, and this is considered to be fulfilled when cohabiting (Article 19 Catalan Act and Article 3 Aragonese Act). Only the Catalan Act demands that at least one of the cohabitants should have "vecindad civil" in Catalonia.[24] The aim of this provision is to avoid "sexual tourists" in search of more advantageous legal provisions in order to obtain benefits.

The Effects of Same-Sex Partnership

The Catalan and Aragonese Acts establish different effects for a same-sex partnership. In addition to the effects established by the partners themselves, the Catalan Act provides the following effects:

(a) Maintenance (Article 26);
(b) Guardianship (Article 25);
(c) Obligation to pay the expenses of the partnership: the costs of maintenance, payments necessary for the upkeep of the house or its improvement and the charges for medical care. The obligation only exists if the costs are appropriate to the standard of living cohabitants agree to have (Article 23). Cohabitants are compelled either to pay or to do the housework themselves, although they can contribute in any form;
(d) Cohabitants are entirely free to deal with ownership of their separate property, but if one of them causes one of the above-mentioned expenses, both are obliged to pay it;

---

[24] The "vecindad civil" is a Spanish criterion to determine the applicable law in Spain. Spain is a pluri-legislative State, which demands a system of inter-regional law similar to that of private international law, in order to determine the applicable regional law. Articles 14 and 15 of the Spanish Civil Law provide regulation for the whole State on this matter.

(e) Finally, any act relating to the selling or renting of the dwellinghouse must be made with the non-tenant cohabitant's agreement. This requirement has been introduced according to the European decisions on this matter.[25]

The provisions of the Act do not contain specific regulation for cohabitants' rights on property as spouses have: therefore, no provisions are made by the Act in this respect, except for admission of the cohabitants' right to keep the ownership, tenancy and administration of their property (Article 22). Neither does the Act give same-sex couples the opportunity to adopt children in common.

By contrast, the Aragonese Act allows same-sex cohabitants to make an agreement about the specific effects of their relationship. If there is no agreement, the Act provides some requirements. These are: the obligation to pay the expenses, such as maintenance and expenses for housekeeping, according to their incomes (Article 5); guardianship (Article 12); and maintenance (Article 13).

Adoption

Both the Catalan and Aragonese Acts do not allow joint adoption, but no provision states this clearly; that is, both Acts foresee that only heterosexual couples can adopt jointly (Article 6 Catalan Act and Article 10 Aragonese Act), and nothing is laid down for same-sex couples.

Partnership Breakdown and its Legal Effects

The Acts provide the grounds on which these partnerships will be held to have broken down and the effects of the breakdown. These grounds can be the death or marriage of one of the cohabitants, and unilateral or bilateral breakdown. However, the main issue here is not the grounds for breakdown themselves, because these partnerships depend exclusively on the cohabitants' will, and therefore the breakdown will also depend on their decision. The problem is the effects of breakdown. Supreme Court decisions related to the breakdown of heterosexual unmarried couples have always refused to apply marriage or company provisions to these cases by analogy. Extra-marital cohabitation does not rank with marriage as an institution, so the latter provisions cannot be applied to the former on the basis of analogy.[26] On the other hand, company provisions cannot be applied because unmarried couples do not satisfy the condition imposed on any company, namely, *lucrum animus*.[27]

[25] It is Recommendation 15 of the Council of Ministers from the European Council of 16 October 1981.

[26] This is declared in the Supreme Court Decisions of 22 July 1993; 30 December 1994 and 10 March 1998.

[27] See Supreme Court Decision, 18 February 1993.

The Catalan Act provisions on this respect are based on a Supreme Court Decision (dated 11 December 1992) which held that the contribution made by the cohabitant's looking after her partner's welfare was not compulsory, because marriage did not exist, but it recognised that her contribution caused his enrichment and the correlative

> "impoverishment of the plaintiff because no remuneration was paid for her looking after the defendant's social relationships and her performing of domestic duties, in such a way that there is no doubt about the correspondence between the service provided by her and his financial benefit".

and this is assumed because

> "the legal framework does not specify that extra-marital cohabitation imposes on cohabitants an obligation to give each other support in their social life, professional career and domestic life".[28]

Following the Catalan Act, the Aragonese Act accepted the same solution.

One has to bear in mind that the Supreme Court has applied these solutions regarding the financial consequences of extra-marital cohabitation breakdown, just as in the case of heterosexual couples. The courts in Spain have not made any financial provision orders in respect of same-sex couples, yet the Acts base the regulation of this matter on the Supreme Court Decision.

Cohabitants are provided with two rights when the relationship comes to an end (only in cases where the end is not due to death). These rights are: to claim a lump sum of money as financial compensation (Article 31 Catalan Act and Article 7.1 Aragonese Act); and to claim income support (Article 31.2 Catalan Act and Article 7.2 Aragonese Act), in accordance with the following provisions:

(a) the cohabitant who looked after the house, or the other cohabitant with little or no remuneration, is entitled to claim financial provision. This contribution must have disrupted the balance between the cohabitants' properties by causing an unjust enrichment to one of them. In other words, there must be correspondence between the enrichment of one of the cohabitants and the other's impoverishment.

   The compensation will consist of money to be paid on the breakdown as a damages claim, unless the parties had previously agreed different terms. The cohabitant can decide the way to make the financial provision, but in case of disagreement, the courts can make orders.

(b) The entitlement of the cohabitant whose potential earning capacity has diminished during cohabitation, to claim income support from the partner, if the claimant cannot afford maintenance. Periodic payments should be terminated after three years. There is thus compensation for difficulties in re-entering the labour market that the claimant may experience as a

---

[28] See Supreme Court Decisions, 27 May 1994; 16 December 1996; 10 March 1998.

consequence of having lived with another person under these circumstances. Sometimes, returning to the job market poses serious problems for cohabitants after the breakdown, and it is impossible for them to recover their job or get a new one (Article 31.2 Catalan Act and Article 7.2 Aragonese Act).

Death of One of the Cohabitants

The Catalan Act recognises more rights for same-sex couples than heterosexual couples. On the other hand, the Aragonese Act recognises the same rights for both heterosexual and same-sex couples, but they are different from those recognised in the Catalan Act, because heterosexual partners in Catalonia have no rights in the succession of the deceased partner's estate. The succession rights are:

(a) the right to live in the family home for one year after the death of the tenant's unmarried partner. This right includes the tenancy of chattels, fixtures and fittings, regardless of the succession dispositions (Article 33 Catalan Act and Article 9 Aragonese Act);

(b) the right to be a successor to the cohabitant in cases where the partner dies without leaving a will. The surviving same-sex cohabitant can, therefore, apply for provision in the case of intestate succession: he shares this position with the deceased's brothers and sisters and can take one-half of the deceased's whole estate (Article 34.1.b Catalan Act). This right has not been recognised in the Aragonese Act;

(c) if the successors are the deceased's children, parents and grandparents, and he dies without leaving a will, the surviving same-sex cohabitant is entitled to claim a quarter of the intestate's whole estate, if the claimant cannot afford maintenance (Article 31.a Catalan Act);

(d) this same right is also provided to the surviving cohabitant if the deceased cohabitant made the will without making a bequest to the partner (Article 15 Catalan Act).

A FAMILY OUTSIDE MARRIAGE?

So far, this chapter has described the social situation and the state of law regarding same-sex couples in Spain. We know that there are two different approaches to the issue in Europe at the moment: one that follows the so-called *Nordic model*, which accepts registration for same-sex couples, and while not offering them the civil status of marriage does provide the couple with its effect; and the *Dutch model*, which is closer to the recognition of the matrimonial character of such couples. In addition, there is also the French PACS model, which a hypothetical Spanish Act could follow, if it were based on unions that are not identified by reason of the gender of the partners. However, it is difficult to predict at this time what kind of solution Spain will finally adopt, if any.

What are the main problems that follow the Constitutional Court Decisions on family and marriage in Spain?

1. The first issue discussed in our jurisprudence is the different treatment given to marriage and the family. Marriage is an institution with constitutional status and is therefore specially protected by Article 32 of the Constitution. As for the family, it is protected by Article 39 of the Constitution, but this Article does not specify whether the family should have its origin in marriage or not. This is the reason why the Constitutional Court has admitted that although unmarried couples are not equivalent to married, they are not absolutely excluded from constitutional protection.[29]

The Constitutional Court Decision 222/1992 introduces a new element to the discussion, which completes the comments already made on the difference between matrimonial families and non-matrimonial families. The decision states that:

> "Our Constitution has not identified the protected family with the matrimonial family; this conclusion must be respected . . . considering the protective dimension under which the Bill of Rights always deals with the family, specially in art. 39, as a response to the mandatory rules derived from the 'social' character of our State (art. 1.1 Spanish Constitution) and to the attention consequently provided to any sort of partnership in our society."[30]

and on this basis concludes that:

> "it is not possible to extract from art. 39 a necessary differentiation between matrimonial families and non matrimonial families."

But it is one thing to extend the constitutional protection for all types of families, regardless of their origin, and quite another to draw or to make necessary distinctions between them and to establish different provisions for situations that are absolutely different. One has to bear in mind that the Spanish constitutional framework contains a special protection for marriage, so that any provision that does not take it into account would be unconstitutional. In fact, the Constitutional Court Decision 222/1992 repeats what the 184/1990 Decision had previously stated:

> "mandatory protection of the family does not involve the duty of local authorities to provide care for all kinds of families without making differences or exceptions: it is

---

[29] The Supreme Court Decision 29 October 1997 declares that "the social situation shows that such unions [the heterosexual couples] follow the features of the legal family".

[30] The apparent contradiction between the Constitutional Court Decision 184/1990 and the Constitutional Court Decision 222/1992 is difficult to justify. Ferreres (1994) at p. 191 states that "there are no institutional reasons that can justify this diversity", although he finds reasons to justify the Constitutional Court Decision 222/1992. This Decision held that limiting the right to claim a tenancy of the house on the death of the tenant to married couples is unconstitutional and should be extended to heterosexual unmarried couples.

obvious that the legislator can differentiate between types of families based on, for example, criteria of relative necessity or similar criteria that can be rationally established."

2. The next question has much to do with an issue introduced at the very beginning of this chapter: does the right to marry, recognised in Article 32 of the Spanish Constitution, also include the right of people of the same sex to get married? If we take into account what the Constitutional Court Writ 222/1994 says, the answer should be negative, because these situations are different.

The usual interpretation of Article 32 of the Spanish Constitution coincides with the European Court of Human Rights, so that marriage, as a constitutionally protected institution, can only be contracted by two people of different sex. Even in the case of transsexuals—although the Supreme Court has admitted the validity of the official recording of their change of sex, after undergoing an operation—it has repeatedly denied the right to marry someone of the same previous sex.[31]

The General Register Office Resolution (on 21 January 1988) expressly rejected the possibility of allowing partners of the same sex to enter into legally recognised marriages:

"It is not necessary to point out that marriage has always been thought of as an institution where sexual differences are essential. This is the traditional concept that has been adopted by the legal provisions that are in force in Spain, correctly interpreted. Actually, when art. 32 of the Spanish Constitution declares that 'man and woman have the right to marry on equal legal terms', that does not allow us to conclude that by the absence of the expression 'each other', the Constitution allows marriage between people of the same sex."[32]

---

[31] The General Register Office Resolution, 2 October 1991, revoked the Court's authorisation (Court number 35 from Madrid) of a marriage between a transsexual and a man. It was considered that "the fundamental right of man and woman to get married . . . is limited to people of different biological sex", and added that "the spouses' agreement to get married . . . is not the simple agreement for a contract but a mutual agreement where both parties take into account sexual differences as a way to complement each other in an institution created by the legislator". Some Courts have authorised marriages of transsexuals. See the information in Lopez-Galiacho (1998), p. 329. See Perez Cánovas (1996), at p. 151 et seq.

[32] The resolution mentioned in the text agrees with the thesis that is sustained by the regulations and international treaties of which Spain is a part, On the contrary, it is very significant that Article 32 of Chapter II on Fundamental Rights and Liberties, in Section I of the Constitution, is the only provision that makes it clear that "man and woman" are entitled to the *ius nubendi*, whereas all the other provisions use impersonal forms such as "everybody", "every person", "it is granted", "it is recognised", without considering it relevant to correspond the right with the sex of the person. This very same criterion is followed by international treaties on this matter that have been ratified by Spain, which are to be taken into account by interpreting the provisions related to fundamental rights and liberties (cf. Article 10.2 Spanish Constitution): that is the case of Article 13 of the Rome Convention, 4 November 1950 on the protection of Human Rights and Fundamental Liberties ("on reaching the age of puberty, man and woman have the right to get married and establish a family") and Article 23.2 of the International Agreement on Civil and Political Rights of New York, 18 December 1966 ("the right of man and woman to get married and establish a family is recognised").

Therefore, there seems to be little discussion in Spain about the acceptance of the principle that requires parties to be respectively male and female for the validity of the contract of marriage.[33]

3. An entirely different issue is whether same-sex couples should be considered as a kind of family or not. It has already been pointed out that according to the Constitution marriage is not the only way to build a family and thus obtain the protection provided by Article 39 of the Spanish Constitution, which is not denied by the Constitutional Court: what the Court demands is that such legal recognition must be explicit and according to specific circumstances.

Legislation on same-sex couples has followed this opinion, but has been criticised for not adopting a method that allows this statement to be made clearly. Both the Catalan and Aragonese Acts are indeed autonomous laws that have not been absorbed within the legal body containing the Family Law provisions. In Catalonia objections have been raised showing disapproval of this method, because it is thought that by excluding the Act from the Family Law provisions, one is in fact excluding these couples from a family context. Reasons for this thesis could be found in the Preamble of the Catalan Act 10/1998, on the grounds of the differences made by the Constitutional Court Decisions mentioned earlier.

However, the autonomy proclaimed for these couples, when compared with married couples, is not very accurate. If we interpret freely in accordance with our whim rather than the legal methodology, we can reach the conclusion that the solutions provided for marriage are the same as those given to solve the problems that arise with same-sex couples.

As a matter of fact, if one compares the effects of marriage in the private sphere with those provided for same-sex couples, one arrives at the conclusion that they are the same, except for the obligation of marriage settlements and the different formalities. Why sustain the argument that marriage constitutes a family and same-sex couples do not? If the law does not distinguish between their effects it may be because it considers the social function of the family as established by Article 39 of the Spanish Constitution to be present in both marital and extra-marital relationships. Therefore, my conclusion is that the regulation of the effects between parties made by the autonomous Acts provides same-sex couples with a familial status. Although there are no formal declarations about their consideration as families, the effects of the cohabitation are familial.

However, the State's, and the autonomous Communities' different legislative power present a legal vacuum: the autonomous Communities are not endowed with the power to make provisions relating to taxes and Social Security, so that some of the relevant effects linked to family relationships such as the widow's pension, or the effects connected with income or inheritance taxes, are not regulated. With respect to these issues, cohabitants are treated like strangers.

---

[33] Surprisingly, the Spanish lawyers dealing with Matrimonial Law do not mention the gender condition for the validity of the contract of marriage.

CONCLUSION

The present-day legal provisions for same-sex couples focus on regulating the parties' private sphere. That is to say, cohabitants must make financial provisions for maintenance during cohabitation, and for compensation after a breakdown, in case of dissolution by mutual agreement or during the union by unilateral decision. It is true that the Family Law system works like a *mixed system* in Spain, where financial provisions for family members come both from public institutions and family resources. But this opportunity is not given to same-sex couples. If one has to evaluate the solution from this perspective, one must finally agree with those who criticise either State or autonomous Communities public institutions for their lack of family policy, whatever the term is intended to convey. This allows us to state that the use of a family model does not solve any of the problems that remain in the relationship between public institutions and same-sex couples. Imposing a system of rights and duties limited to the private sphere can even be held to infringe their right of freedom, because since they have contractual capacity, they already have the right to regulate them privately.

Perhaps if the impetus for legal change had come from family policy rather than from the political agenda of the autonomous Communities seeking to flex their legislative muscles, these complex issues might have benefited from more consideration. Future development along these lines might benefit from serious attention from analysts of both family law and family policy.

REFERENCES

Bradley, A. (1996) *Family Law and Political Culture* (London: Sweet and Maxwell).
Ferreres, (1994) "El principio de igualdad y el 'derecho a no casarse' (A propósito de la STC 222/1992)", *Revista Española de Derecho constitucional*, Madrid, no. 42, 163–96.
Flaquer, (1998) *El destino de la familia* (Barcelona: Ariel).
Gomez, (1990) *Familia y matrimonio en la Constitución española de 1978* (Madrid: Centro de estudios constitucionales).
Gordillo, (1989) "Comentario a la sentencia del Tribunal Supremo de 3 marzo 1989", *Cuadernos Civitas de Jurisprudencia civil*, Madrid, Civitas, no. 19, 314–25.
LaCruz, B. (1997) *Elementos de Derecho civil IV. Derecho de familia* (Barcelona: José M. Bosch).
Lopez-Galiacho, P. (1998) *La problemática jurídica de la transexualidad* (Madrid: McGraw Hill).
Martin, (1995) "Informe de Derecho comparado sobre la regulación de la pareja de hecho", *Anuario de Derecho civil*, Madrid, 1709–808.
—— (1998) "Aproximación a la Ley catalana 10/1998, de 15 de julio, de Uniones estables de pareja", *Derecho privado y Constitución*, no.12, 143–87.

Perez Cánovas, (1996) *Homosexualidad, homosexuales y uniones homosexuales en el Derecho español* (Granada: Editorial Comares).

Plaza Penades-Tamayo, C. (1998) "Artículo 28 de la ley autonómica valenciana 7/1994, de la Infancia, y sus repercusiones en materia de adopción por los posibles integrantes de una unión de hecho", in Martinell-Areces (ed.) *Uniones de hecho (*Lleida: Edicions de la Universitat), 401–13.

Reina-Martinell, (1995) *Curso de derecho matrimonial* (Madrid: Editorial Marcial Pons).

Roca, E. and P. Ferriol-Roca (1998) *Institucions del Dret Civil de Catalunya*, 5th edn (Valencia: Tirant lo Blanch).

Roca, E. and Trias (1999) Full relevance to be supplied at proof.

Talavera Fernández, P.A. (1999) "Hacia una construcción jurídica de las uniones de hecho en el Derecho español" (Tesis doctoral inédita, Valencia).

Valpuesta Fernandez, (1995) "La institucionalización jurídica de la pareja de hecho. Registro de parejas de hecho", in M. Paz Sanchez Gonzalez (ed.) *Las uniones de hecho* (Jerez de la Frontera), 47–66.

Villagrasa Alcalde, (19??) "Los registros municipales de uniones civiles", in   Martinell-Areces (ed.) *Uniones de hecho* (Lleida: Edicions de la Universitat), 513–26.

7

"Pro-Family Policy" in Poland in the Nineties

MALGORZATA FUSZARA and BEATA LACIAK

W HEN THE POLISH transformation began in 1989, no one would have predicted that the family—particularly its shape and the extent of state interference in family matters—would so soon become the subject of heated political debate. At that time, the political language, when discussing the economy and political institutions, referred most frequently to a liberal model, which sought the minimum of activity from the state. It might therefore be expected that, following this same principle, the state would refrain from interfering in family matters. However, this was not to be the case at all. Analysis of actual Polish practice in this area during the ten years since June 1989—that is since the first post-Communist parliamentary elections in Poland—tells a different story.

One of the first draft bills to be submitted at an early stage in the reform process in 1989 dealt with abortion. The original version provided for an absolute ban on abortion, and a subsequent modified version proposed a considerable reduction in the number of situations where abortion would be permitted. The draft was highly controversial, giving rise to public demonstrations and heated discussions, and these recur from time to time whenever a new draft amendment of the relevant regulations appears.

Similarly heated discussions about the extent of state interference in family life also accompanied the publication of the series of drafts for the new post-1989 Constitution. There was debate about whether the Constitution should contain any provisions concerning the family at all, as this area of life belongs to the private sphere. Other heated discussions concerned the question of how to define the family: if the family is to be regulated at the constitutional level, the question of its definition must be addressed. Ultimately, the following provision was included in the Constitution: "Marriage is a union of man and woman, the family, maternity and parentage receive care and protection from the Republic of Poland". The final decision was to state explicitly that only the union of a man and a woman is treated as a marriage in Poland; and that a rather vague form of care and protection was to be rendered by the state to the family.

Relations between the state and the family were also discussed when religious instruction was introduced into schools, following the long period of exclusion under the former regime. The discussion concerned the extent of parents' influence in deciding what should be taught to children, and the degree of freedom for the state to shape the content of religious education. Who should decide whether religious instruction should be given in school or in church? Should this be decided by parents? If classes are to be held in school, should attendance be obligatory or voluntary? And—an issue that closely concerns the family, parental authority and the autonomy of family members—who is to decide about attendance or non-attendance, the child or his/her parents? To what extent, and from what age, should the child rather than the parents be permitted to take such decisions?

Such discussions accompanied the introduction of a great variety of different legal regulations, some of which were only indirectly related to family matters (e.g. the religious instruction issue). Parallel to these, however, there were also discussions about regulations which directly affect the family, particularly concerning divorce and separation. A wide variety of conceptions about the shape of the family, the autonomy of individual members and individual freedom to establish and dissolve a family were revealed.

A number of trends can be identified at an early stage in the policy debates, beginning with the aim of supporting marriage. A vision of the evil involved in a broken home appeared during political debates and especially in the electoral campaign, and was reflected in the legal sphere in drafts to reform the law by making the divorce procedure more difficult and introducing separation as an option. Among other things, the reform was intended to achieve a reduction in the number of divorces granted.[1] We turn now to consider the way in which

---

[1] The Provisions regulating the institution of divorce in force today were originally introduced in 1964. Under those regulations, a spouse may move for dissolution of marriage if there has been a permanent and complete disintegration of the matrimonial life. Thus "permanence" and "completeness" of disintegration are so-called "positive prerequisites" that have to occur for divorce to be granted. Provisions do not oblige the court to appraise the weight of the causes of disintegration; yet the Supreme Court's guidelines state that this does not relieve the judge from the duty comprehensively to clarify the factors that led to such disintegration. This directive determines the course of judicial proceedings, defining the judges' interpretation of their duties in a divorce case. Polish law also provides for the so-called negative prerequisites of divorce, that is, circumstances that make dissolution of marriage inadmissible despite ascertainment of a permanent and complete disintegration of the matrimonial life. Thus, under the relevant provisions divorce is inadmissible if it would infringe the interest of the spouses' minor children; if a grant of divorce would be against the principles of social coexistence; and also if the divorce claim has been lodged by the spouse who bears exclusive guilt for the disintegration, unless the other spouse who does not bear any guilt consents to be divorced, or that latter spouse's lack of consent would be against the principles of social coexistence in the concrete case. The Polish family and guardianship code provides that on granting a divorce, the court should also decide about guilt, stating which of the spouses (if any) bears the guilt for disintegration of the matrimonial life. However, if both spouses unanimously move for a no-guilt divorce, the decision about guilt is left of the proceedings. In this case, the judicial proceedings may be simplified and shortened, especially if there are no minor children from the marriage at the moment of divorce. In the decision granting divorce, the court is obliged to settle a number of additional questions. These are: parental authority over minor children from the marriage; maintenance for such children; and the manner of using the ex-spouses' jointly owned

these changes were introduced, the arguments used, and the effects of these kinds of reforms.

1. LAW AND THE PERMANENCE OF MARRIAGE: CHANGES IN THE DIVORCE LAW

Reforms aiming to reduce the number of divorces were introduced in the 1990s by changing the competency of courts. Until 1991, divorce cases had been examined by the family courts attached to district courts, that is, the courts of first instance. There were two hundred and eighty-two such courts. In 1991, divorces were handed over to provincial courts, of which there were at that time forty four. The official justification for this change was the need for high quality decision-making in divorce cases, which were seen as difficult and requiring extensive judicial experience—both legal and personal. Yet the hope of achieving higher quality decisions was not likely to succeed if we look at the way in which the changes were introduced. Following discussions several years later in connection with suggestions about reinstating the district courts' competency in divorce cases, many of the district court judges who had originally dealt with divorce cases were appointed provincial judges in 1991, and were thus "transferred" to the courts of higher instance together with their speciality. Although this could not be avoided in view of the shortage of judges in the provincial courts, such mass promotion called into question from the very start the possibility of achieving the declared purpose of the reform, that is higher quality decision-making in divorce cases.

The official ground for the change in the competency of the courts was probably only one of a number of reasons why the reform was actually launched. Other reasons, which were left out of official statements, can only be the subject of speculation. At that time, a draft amendment of the family and guardianship code was submitted to Parliament, which provided for reintroduction in Poland of the institution of separation. That first attempt at reintroducing separation failed, as Parliament turned down the bill. The handing over of divorce cases to higher instance courts was made through an Act at a lower level, and was therefore much easier to introduce. According to widely held suspicions (also voiced during subsequent parliamentary debates about reintroducing separation), the reform was actually designed to limit the right to divorce. The transfer of divorce cases to provincial courts was among the steps aimed at making it more difficult to get a divorce in Poland.

All of these changes were introduced or drafted in a country with a very low divorce rate. Interestingly, the rate had been decreasing even before the reform, in the late 1980s. From 1985 to 1987, there were 1.31 divorces per 1,000 of the

apartment (if any) until they can find separate lodgings. The court may also divide the ex-spouses' joint property if this does not lead to excessive delays in the whole of proceedings.

population, falling to 1.27 in 1988, 1.24 in 1989, 1.11 in 1990, 0.88 in 1991, 0.84 in 1992 and 0.73 in 1993. The drop in the late 1980s is said to have been the result of mainly demographic factors; yet whatever the interpretation, the fact remains that access to divorce was made more difficult at a time when the number of divorces in Poland was decreasing—remaining perhaps too low compared to many other European countries, indicating a restricted capacity to leave an unacceptable situation.

From 1994, there has been a slow but systematic increase in the number of divorces in Poland. In 1994, the rate was 0.81 per 1,000 of the population, rising to 1.0 in 1995 and 1996 and 1.1 in 1997. This means that in 1997, the divorce rate returned to the level where it stood before the transfer of divorce cases to the higher instance courts.

The effect of that transfer can be clearly seen in the considerable differentiation in access to court once divorce cases were handed over to provincial courts. Compared to the inhabitants of the big cities, people from small towns and villages were particularly affected. For the former, the transfer of divorce cases was practically insignificant: the district and provincial courts in a big town are seated not only in one and the same locality, but often in the same building. The situation is different in small towns and villages, where the reform made the distance from the court much greater. This difference was reflected in the statistics: in the 1980s, the growth of divorce cases was faster in rural as compared to urban areas, though the number of divorces in rural areas has always been much smaller than in urban ones. In the 1990s, however, the divorce rates in rural areas fell more rapidly. On analysing the court statistics on divorce cases, the impact of the "distance to court" on the number of cases filed can be clearly seen. In some provinces, the divorce rates dropped rapidly after the change: the number of divorce suits filed in 1993 amounted to a mere 49 percent of the 1991 figures. A drop as rapid as that was found mainly in the provinces where no provincial courts had been set up, and the inhabitants' distance from the divorce court was particularly great.

Thus the steps taken in the 1990s hindered divorce, and reduced the number of divorces. However, in that same period (1995) another legislative initiative was submitted, which also aimed at simplification of the divorce procedure. The initiative was launched by the Parliamentary Women's Group, which submitted a draft amendment of the family and guardianship code. The draft proposed handing over the initiative for resolving most divorce-related issues to the persons concerned, and thus made it easier to get a divorce. The duty to state the so-called positive prerequisites of divorce was removed: thus the court would not ascertain whether permanent and complete breakdown of the marriage had taken place. One of the spouses would simply have to file the divorce suit, and divorce would duly be granted. Another radical change contained in the draft was the departure from the conception of fault: the court would not decide whether matrimonial life had broken down, and therefore would not inquire which of the spouses (if any) bore the guilt for such disintegration. The draft provided for one negative requirement only: divorce would not be granted in violation of the interest of minor children. In this case, the draft went somewhat further than the current legal regulation, as it did not contain the requirement that the children involved should be those from the marriage. It has to be stressed here, though, that the negative requirement relating to the interest of children, which has been part of Polish law for a long time, provides the grounds for refusing divorce in only a very small proportion of cases. In Poland, where few divorce suits are filed, divorce is seldom refused, the proportion traditionally ranging from 1 to 2 percent of cases. It happens much more often that parties themselves withdraw the proceedings they originally instituted. Yet the vast majority of people genuinely seeking a divorce do get it, and it hardly ever happens that the interest of minor children is considered to prevail.

As the authors of the draft stressed, the present divorce procedure in Poland often forces people who want a divorce to reveal intimate matters, which are of no interest to anybody but those directly involved. Many parties to divorce proceedings not only feel that they are treated as immature persons incapable of deciding about their lives, but also consider themselves to be the victims of the morbid curiosity of judges who decide which intimate confessions to demand from divorcing spouses. The judges for their part—and this is not always clear to the parties—have to proceed this way because of their duty to state in each and every case whether permanent and complete disintegration of matrimonial life has taken place, and to learn about the causes of that disintegration. Thus the authors of the draft assumed that mature people should have the right to dissolve their relationship, parallel to their right to establish it. The State should act merely as the institution stating a specific legal position or "translating" a private decision into a legal one, rather than making its own decision. All matters settled by the parties by agreement would merely be confirmed by the court. Points of issue concerning, for example, parental authority or division of property, would be settled in separate proceedings; in this way, the divorce itself would not be delayed. Another proposal contained in the draft was to return divorce cases to the district courts. These would be geographically closer, and thus more accessible, to the parties, and would thus lower the costs of the procedure, especially for people from areas other than big cities, who usually file for divorce only in very serious cases of marital problems, such as violence in the home.

The draft was referred to the competent parliamentary committee and discussed there. The discussion was rather brief, as the forthcoming parliamentary elections minimised the chances of completing the legislative procedure before the end of that term. The committee was, however, highly critical of the draft, and hostile to the main idea behind it, that is, the simplification of procedure and greater availability of divorce.

Quite obviously, both advocates and opponents of the draft were guided by different conceptions of the freedom of the individual to contract and dissolve a marriage. The authors of the draft assumed that the decision, taken by adults, to dissolve their relationship was as much their private affair as was the decision to establish the relationship in the first place, and thus State interference should be kept to a minimum. Such interference might be justified in the rare cases where preservation of the marriage would be in the interests of the children. The opponents of the proposed changes stressed that if "the legal system treats marriage as a legal institution, it ceases to be a private matter for spouses. It acquires the nature of a social institution in itself, and not only because of the interests of the children. . ." (opinion of First President of the Supreme Court, 3 November 1995). It was also argued that "Polish family law is based on the principle of permanency of marriage", and that marriage "is also protected constitutionally"; thus reducing the so-called negative prerequisites (that is, factors making divorce inadmissible) to the child's interest only "would be groundless" (opinion of Professor Tadeusz Smyczyski, Polish Committee of the International Year of the Family). Thus—if we understand the opponents' reasoning correctly—what should be protected is not only the children's interest (which sometimes is against the divorce), but also the institution of marriage as such, even if the parties to it are not convinced as to the value of its preservation in their specific case. The justification for this approach lies in the constitutional provision on state protection of marriage.

Another type of reasoning, expressed quite often in opinions on the draft, included—as can be surmised—opposition to departure from the concept of fault, and especially from the situation where a spouse who is actually to blame for the disintegration of the marriage would be in a position effectively to demand divorce, and the innocent spouse would be unable to counteract it. It was argued that such provisions would establish "rewards for the irresponsible and dishonest, and particularly for the immature 'youngsters' who contribute to the disintegration of their marriage through alcoholism and unfaithfulness". In a letter from two family judges from the Lublin Provincial Court, it was argued that the proposed changes could result in a greater number of hasty marriages, and thus also of divorces, followed again by new marriages and further divorces. From these arguments it can be concluded that the authors of such opinions treat the divorce procedure not only as the means of dissolving a marriage but also as quasi-penal proceedings (though of course not in the legal sense), where at the demand of the innocent person, the guilty person is not only labelled as such but also forced to remain in a formal relationship with the person from whom he/she wants to separate legally.

In some cases, the reasoning is surprising: the argument is reiterated in many letters that the proposed amendment would "reward" irresponsible persons, such as alcoholics or those who make light of the other spouse, making it possible for such people to get a divorce despite the guilt they carry for the disintegration of the marriage. This reasoning completely neglects the reality, whereby the wives of excessive drinkers file for divorce and have to demonstrate before the court that a permanent and complete disintegration of the marriage has indeed taken place. The party who does not agree to divorce in such cases is usually the alcoholic husband who derives numerous benefits from the marriage. These husbands are frequently dependent on their wives, drink away the entire family budget, and treat the wife and children with cruelty. It is unlikely that the alcoholic husband would file a divorce suit, with the wife protesting and exercising her right as the innocent spouse to refuse the divorce. Thus if family law awards any "bonuses" in this area, it is the alcoholic husband who gets such rewards in the present system: he can stay married to a person who sees to all of his needs and finds it difficult to get a divorce.

Another recurring argument against simpler divorce that has already been quoted is that concerning the possibility of ill-considered entry into marriage. It can be summarised as follows: if divorce can be obtained easily, it will also be easy to decide to get married; yet the decision may well be ill-considered and lacking the necessary sense of responsibility for the relationship. This reasoning, however, neglects the fact—obvious in both Polish and West-European marriage statistics—that the choice is not between irresponsible marriages and responsible marriages being contracted in large numbers, but rather between such hasty relationships and cohabitation, that is living together without getting married—which is most certainly not ideal in the minds of the rightist advocates of the traditional family who are the opponents of easy access to divorce.

A number of opinions were also expressed against the return of divorce cases to the lower courts, although some participants in the discussion supported this solution. Those against it argued that the judges in district courts are mostly very young, often the same age as the children of the divorcing spouses. As a result, they lack the necessary experience and their involvement in the case would be embarrassing to the parties. It remains a matter of conjecture as to why those holding this view are willing to grant to these young judges the right to decide in cases that often dramatically affect the life of others (e.g. to sentence defendants in criminal proceedings to prison terms), but refuse them the right to decide about divorce. Another argument referred to what its advocates considered the higher quality of decision-making in provincial courts. There were, however, also some who argued that the transfer of divorce cases to provincial courts had failed to produce this result in practice.[2]

[2] In my survey of 1999, persons whose cases had been decided both by provincial and by district courts were examined. Generally speaking, the respondents' appraisals of provincial courts tended to be polarised. The provincial court was praised by a somewhat higher proportion of respondents (63%) than the district family court (59%). Yet on the other hand, the provincial court was also much more often decidedly criticised (37% compared to 28% decidedly critical appraisals of the district family court). Yet it is not only the general opinions of the court's work that matter, but also the type of objections raised. Thus the courts and judicial proceedings were criticised for slowness, incompetence, excessive costs, dryness, formalism, failure to let parties speak up, neglecting motions, indifference, bias in favour of men, bias in favour of women, undue inquisitiveness leading to the "washing of dirty laundry" in public, permitting abuses, tolerating fictitious divorces, indifference to the child's interest, manipulating the child, injustice, bribery, ineffectiveness manifested in the impossibility of executing the decision. Characteristic are the serious accusations against judges, formulated by persons whose cases were examined by the Provincial Court in Warsaw—one of the courts that were to guarantee a higher quality of decisions. The accusations were mostly made by men involved in divorce cases; they concerned the judges' complete disinterest in the case

The many politicians who did not take part in the debate on the divorce law, suspecting that it would never go to the vote, proved right. The 1997 parliamentary elections put a stop to work on the draft bill, and this was not resumed by the next Parliament. The discussion on this draft demonstrates the different approaches to the family by different communities and political parties. A further opportunity to investigate such differences is provided by the electoral campaigns. Let us now take a look at one such campaign and analyse what the programmes of the Polish parties offered to the family.

2. THE ELECTORAL CAMPAIGN: THE FAMILY IN THE PROGRAMMES OF POLITICAL PARTIES

Electoral campaigns provide extremely interesting materials demonstrating the intentions of individual political parties in the area of state policy with respect to families. In the 1997 campaign the parties tended to include detailed offers in their programmes, and to make numerous promises concerning protection of, and support for, the family.

Promises to families were most prominent in the campaign of Solidarity Electoral Action (Akcja Wyborcza Solidarno, AWS).[3] The family appeared in its main slogan, "Always Poland, freedom, and the family". In its electoral programme, AWS declared: "The nation is a family of families. . . The family is the foundation of society; it is within the family that an individual grows and develops".[4] The following elements of social policy, aimed at protecting the family, were listed:

(i) the tax policy was defined as "pro-family policy", though without providing any details on the actual nature of that "pro-family" quality;
(ii) assistance to mothers of small children;
(iii) assistance to large families;
(iv) development by the state of the social and economic conditions for harmonious functioning of families; and
(v) parents' right to bring up their children.[5]

Individual candidates provided some of the details of this programme during their pronouncements in electoral TV broadcasts produced by AWS. Promises

("the judge was reading a newspaper") and partiality (including a statement "the court was partial to my advantage"). There were also some extremely critical opinions: "that was absolutely idiotic", or "the court was hopeless", etc. Thus, although a considerable majority (64%) of parties to divorce proceedings praised the work of courts, those who criticised that work formulated most serious accusations. Such accusations are even more often addressed at provincial as compared to district family courts, which means that both the hopes for a better quality of decision and the arguments that the quality has actually been raised must be seen as pointless.

[3] A right-wing party formed immediately before the elections, combining the "Solidarity" trade union and a number of anti-Communist, rightist and Catholic parties.

[4] Electoral programme of Solidarity Electoral Action, p.1.

[5] TV electoral spots of Solidarity Electoral Action, Channels 1 and 2 of Public Television.

were made relating to the economic and social foundations of family functioning, as well as general promises such as "Pro-family activity is our inevitable focus",[6] including slogans such "Housing for each and every Polish family",[7] referring to the housing shortage in Poland and promising to solve this problem (at least this is what might be concluded from the declaration). Another promise concerned the introduction of allowances for every child ("Your vote cast for AWS means a pro-family policy and a monthly family allowance of PLN 50 per child"[8]). With reference to the promise of a "pro-family tax policy", it was suggested that the child allowances should be deducted from the tax base ("The basic child allowances should be deducted from the tax assessment base; this should of course apply to each and every child"[9]; "It is indispensable that a pro-family tax system be introduced; at present, neither parenthood nor the number of children is taken into account"[10]).

The principle of "the parents' right to bring up their children" was referred to by AWS candidates who said, "I declare support for . . . the grant to families of control over schools";[11] they did not, however, provide any details of the proposed manifestations of such "control".

AWS was not the only rightist party to promise what was called "pro-family policy" before the elections. Another rightist party whose programme devoted a lot of attention to this issue was the Poland Reconstruction Movement (Ruch Odbudowy Polski, ROP). It promised mainly changes in the tax system towards giving due consideration for three factors: the number of children per family, children's education, and the fact that one of the parents provides for the other one. We quote here an example of this kind of electoral promises:

"We shall introduce a pro-family tax system. Parents who care for a larger number of children will pay lower taxes. . . . We propose the introduction of a social minimum wage per family member, which would be tax-free. The amount would be duly raised (by 50%) in the case of families where one of the parents is providing for the other one, and also raised during the period of the children's education (e.g. by 25% per child)."[12]

A third rightist party that devoted a lot of attention to the family in its programme was the National Christian-Democratic "Bloc for Poland". Beside declarations concerning changes in the tax system, the party also promised assistance to the mother and child, and openly declared for "protection of the unborn", which in practice amounts to tightening up the abortion regulations. The following are quotations from the Bloc's electoral leaflets:

[6] Ibid.
[7] Ibid.
[8] Pronouncement of Ms E. Lewicka in a TV electoral spot of AWS, Channel 1 of Public Television.
[9] Ibid.
[10] Pronouncement of Ms E. Tomaszewska in a TV electoral spot of AWS, Channel 1 of Public Television.
[11] Ibid.
[12] "Programme Assumptions for Socio-Economic Reconstruction of Poland", Programme of the Poland Reconstruction Movement, p. 4.

"The foundation on which the Christian-Democratic party must necessarily base its political activity, is the family. . . For this reason, the Bloc for Poland declares for a family-friendly policy of the 3rd Republic. Specific legal solutions are proposed, e.g. reduction in the income tax due from parents, or joint taxation of parents and children, which would be to the advantage of Polish families."[13]

"We say 'yes' to the big and many generation family. The 'yes' includes both protection of the unborn and assistance to mother and child."[14]

The pronouncements of the representatives of this party clearly encompass a specific vision of the "perfect family": large, composed of several generations and also—as follows from other pronouncements—what is called "complete" ("The entire State and tax system should serve the family . . . a normal family is one composed of the mother, the father, and children; this family is the foundation of society. . . It is wrong to make the large family carry the entire burden of transformation"[15]).

It was not only the rightist parties in Poland who decided to include promises relating to the family in their programmes. Such promises were also made by the leftist parties (Labour Union, Democratic Left Alliance). The Labour Union proposed tax reductions for parents and reminded the voters of the fact that during its previous parliamentary activity, "it had been the first party to move for assistance to large families".[16]

The post-Communist Democratic Left Alliance mentioned the family in its programme among their fifteen paramount principles and values, stating as follows:

"We declare for a pro-family social policy, for the creation of conditions for the preservation of the family's health and stability and of its performance of educational functions. . . What we see as the basic instrument of that policy . . . are family allowances and other forms of assistance to indigent, and particularly large families."[17]

Thus before the recent parliamentary elections in Poland, both the rightist and the leftist parties included promises of "pro-family policy" in their programmes; that policy, however, resisted definition. It was made up of the following main elements: declarations concerning tax reductions related to parenting, to children's education etc.; declarations concerning the parents' right to bring up their children in accordance with their own convictions; material support to parents through taxes and a system of allowances, bonuses and reductions; support to large families; and support to the mother and child. The

[13] "From Non-Party Bloc for Co-operation with the Government to the National Christian-Democratic Bloc for Poland", electoral leaflet of the Bloc for Poland.

[14] "Programme Declaration of the National Christian-Democratic Bloc for Poland", p. 4.

[15] Pronouncement of Mr M. Giertych in a TV broadcast "Candidates on Channel 2", Channel 2 of Public Television, 16 September 1997.

[16] TV electoral spot of the Labour Union, Channel 1 of Public Television.

[17] "A good today—a better tomorrow", electoral programme of the Democratic Left Alliance, p. 4.

programmes contain formulations indicative of the specific vision of the family for which its authors declare their support: in the case of the rightist parties, it is the so-called complete, large and multi-generation family. The Freedom Union—a centrist party with an anti-Communist opposition background—did not make such promises. In its campaign, the Union focused on presenting its economic programme as "securing material improvement for all Polish families"[18].

In the new Parliament, a majority coalition was formed by the Solidarity Electoral Action (43% of seats) and the Freedom Union (13%). The opposition included the Democratic Left Alliance (36%) and some other parties (e.g. Polish Peasant Party and Poland Reconstruction Movement), which together won about 8 percent of the seats. The Parties making up the ruling coalition differed quite considerably on many issues. A coalition agreement was signed, therefore, which contained elements pertaining, among other matters, to the family. One of the "crucial objectives in the interest of the Republic" was described as the "improvement of the people's living standards and the enhancement of economic self-dependence for families; including pro-family financial, tax and relief policies". But the agreement went beyond such general statements, and provided specific commitments:

"1.1 Within 6 months, the Government shall analyse the impact of current provisions on the situation of Polish families and draft a proposal of amendment to the families' advantage of the tax system, family allowance, and family relief systems, including social welfare.

1.2 The target principle of a five-day working week shall be specified so as not to hamper the growth in employment.

1.3 Enhanced assistance to families and to all mothers caring for small children.

1.4 Through appropriate pro-family policy, special care shall be secured for large families.

1.5 Gradually, in co-operation with local governments, relief to children from indigent families should be enhanced in schools, through meals and purchase of school books among other forms."[19]

Yet in this area—as in many other spheres—most of the electoral promises and coalition agreements remained as nothing more than declarations. Let us therefore answer the question, what elements of family policy were actually introduced by the Government, and what related pronouncements of politicians accompany that introduction? Another question concerns the differences between parties. From a comparison of electoral programmes it follows that the right and left wing do not differ significantly on this matter. An attempt should therefore be made to discover a specific "hidden programme", which may differ greatly from what was declared before the elections, and may also tell us more

---

[18] "Electoral Programme of the Freedom Union", 1997, p. 14.

[19] Coalition agreement between Solidarity Electoral Action and Freedom Union. After E. Olczyk, "Zebysmy zdrowi, bogaci i madrzy byli" ("May we all be healthy, rich and wise"), in *Rzeczpospolita* of 2 November 1998.

about differences between parties with respect to the vision of the family, the autonomy of its members and views on its permanence and insolubility.

In 1991 the office of Plenipotentiary of the Government for Women and the Family was established; the Plenipotentiary's responsibilities included the co-ordination and implementation of family policy. After the formation of a new Cabinet in November 1997 the office was transformed into that of Plenipotentiary of the Government for Family-Related Matters, whose responsibility was to "initiate and co-ordinate activities for the shaping and implementation of State policies with respect to the family".[20] The office's main activity was the preparation of two documents, "Assumptions of Pro-Family Policy" and "Report on the Situation of Polish Families". The former planned joint taxation of parents and children, which would be tantamount in practice to lower taxes for parents. It also proposed simplification of the adoption procedure, promotion of the traditional Polish family model in the media, payment of regular salaries to women who leave work to become housewives and retirement pensions for women who had never been employed but cared for their children and ran the house. The ideas were criticised in many press articles; their authors stressed, quite rightly for that matter, that "the grant of retirement rights to persons who had never been employed is inconsistent with the essence and meaning of that allowance". They asked who would pay the salaries and retirement premiums, and stressed rather that for the women, "a career would therefore be a crime, punished with the double burden: retirement premiums paid for themselves and for others. This is the more unjust as most female employees do the chores of wives and mothers anyway, on coming home from work".[21]

Just as controversial was the other document submitted to the Parliament in September 1998, the "Report on the Situation of Polish Families". The Plenipotentiary stressed what he considered to be particularly alarming phenomena, that is a growing number of divorces, a drop in the number of marriages, more and more children born out of wedlock and a drop in the birth rate. Characteristic of the document itself and of the Plenipotentiary's parliamentary pronouncement is the vision of a traditional family and the phenomena seen by the Plenipotentiary as a threat, i.e. divorces, late marriages, a growing number of informal relationships and a drop in the birth rate.

The blame for these phenomena was placed on harmful educational influences. According to the Plenipotentiary,

[20] Ordinance of the Council of Ministers of 7 November 1997, appointing the Plenipotentiary of the Government for Family-Related Matters, Journal of Laws No. 138, item 927.

[21] J.A. Majcherek, "Polityka prorodzinna—pole do naduzyc" ("The pro-family policy—opportunities for abuse"), *Rzeczpospolita*, 16 March 1998.

"the pro-family policy programme should aim at securing the exercise ... of the parents' right to educate their children in accordance with their moral and religious beliefs, including the right to control the sexual aspect of their children's education".[22]

The list of dangers encountered by children and the young included parental indifference, propagation of life-styles based on consumption, the breakdown of the school's authority, sects, pathological families, drugs and the harmful impact of films, journals and computer games.

The recapitulation contained recommendations as to the desired state policies with respect to the family. Some of the proposals are rather controversial, and it is surprising that while some issues receive an extremely broad treatment others are completely ignored. The recapitulation lacks any suggestions whatever as to the prevention of family pathologies (alcoholism, violence) or the equalisation of educational opportunities for children from different backgrounds. Instead, the authors state that

"the State and social institutions should follow the principle of helpfulness, supporting the younger generation of Poles so that they may live in a social order they accept, and not just respect or tolerate".[23]

The recapitulation also states:

"The important responsibilities of the state should include a policy of support for the permanence of marriage, at the same time making it possible for women to become mothers".

Both this statement and the Plenipotentiary's activities indicate that preservation of the stability of the family has become a priority within the "pro-family policy". In addition it may be surmised that the Plenipotentiary is guided in his decision to negate the need for action against family violence by the aim of preserving families at any cost. One of his first decisions in office was to stop a programme of emergency assistance to victims of family violence. The "Report" criticises the campaign against family violence, launched at that time by the media. It argues that the campaign

"may be perceived as a warning against marriage and against trusting a fellow man ... In some periodicals, the Polish man is shown as an alcoholic who ill-treats his wife, a primitive degenerate who rapes her and sexually abuses his children. The man's caring attitude is shown as his *domination*, and what he expects from his wife—as *oppression*."[24]

The media were also accused of propagating models of independent women, pornography, and "stress on sexually arousing contents".[25]

---

[22] Parliamentary pronouncement of Plenipotentiary of the Government for Family-Related Matters, K. Kapera, 3rd term of the Sejm, 29th session, 22 September 1998.

[23] Ibid., p. 221.

[24] "Raport o sytuacji polskich rodzin" ("Report on the Situation of Polish Families"), Office of Plenipotentiary of the Government for Family-Related Matters, Warsaw 1998, p. 174.

[25] Ibid., p. 176.

4. PROTECTING THE PERMANENCE OF MARRIAGE RE-EXAMINED: THE QUESTION OF SEPARATION

While it has not been possible so far to realise the aims mentioned in electoral declarations such as changes to the tax system or easier access to housing, reforms aimed at supporting the permanence of marriage proved easy to introduce. This was probably one of the purposes of a new draft amendment of the family and guardianship code of 1999, which provides for the reintroduction in Poland of the institution of separation. This reintroduction had been discussed repeatedly: participants in the debate mention a total of six such drafts submitted during the 1990s. Two draft bills were recently submitted, prepared by the Government and a group of deputies respectively. The Sejm (Parliament) examined both. On the one hand, the two drafts were similar to each other; on the other, the opinions prepared for the Chamber chiefly referred to the faults in the deputies' draft. Numerous participants in the parliamentary debate stressed the fact that the deputies' draft had been submitted once again in the exact shape in which it had been originally rejected, with no corrections whatever, despite extensive criticism of its provisions. This was said to indicate the authors' unwillingness to discuss the institution of separation, and to amount to their attempt at forcing a specific approach upon the Parliament.

The deputies' draft on separation repeated practically the whole of the regulation for divorce, the basic difference being the separated spouses' incapacity to contract a new marriage. Many of its solutions were criticised, including the fact that, with the requirements for divorce being absolutely the same as those of separation, it would be illogical to expect the court to state the existence of the former and not of the latter. As a result, the entire justification—based on the reasoning that it is easier for separated but not divorced spouses to resume matrimonial life and thus to annul the separation—was found to be pointless: either the court would have to be mistaken in stating the permanent and complete breakdown of married life, or it would not be possible to resume such life. But this was not the only objection to the deputies' draft.

Probably as a result of the criticism with which previous drafts had been met, the authors of the Government draft tried to avoid this kind of trap. Their draft provided for the possibility of separation in cases of complete breakdown, but there was no requirement for the court to recognise the permanency of such disintegration. The court would refuse separation in cases where it would be against the interest of minor children or the principles of social coexistence. A separated person would not be permitted to contract a new marriage. In all remaining areas, the effects of separation would be the same as those of divorce.

A lot of attention was devoted in the discussion to the competency of the court. It was proposed that unanimous motions for both separation and cancellation of separation should be examined by lower instance (district) courts, and disputed cases by the provincial courts, as is the case with divorce. In cases of one spouse's divorce suit accompanied by the other spouse's separation suit, the court would first examine the former as the farther-reaching one.

In a justification quoted by the authors, and also delivered in the Parliament, it was stressed that separation is an institution much-desired by many people, especially those who do not want a divorce bearing in mind the children's interest, religious reasons, or the opinions of their local community, but who would like a legal settlement of their relations with the spouse from the broken marriage. On this occasion, extremely paternalistic pronouncements were made. For example, on presenting the Government draft in Parliament, the Under-Secretary of State in the Ministry of Justice (Janusz Niemcewicz) said, "rural women in particular—often ill-treated and intimidated—will ask for separation where they would never ask for divorce". None of the participants in the discussion pointed out that nobody has to ask anybody else for anything in judicial proceedings (with the exception of defendants in criminal cases who ask for leniency). Instead, the question was posed: where had the Government and deputies been when these solutions to women's disadvantage were introduced into Polish law, if they now wish to say that they care?

The authors argued that separation offered a better chance for spouses to reconcile. People who do not establish a relationship with another person (or who at least cannot legalise such a relationship) might be more willing to be reconciled with their spouse. During separation, with all legal issues settled, there are no conflicts; therefore, the whole relationship can be reconsidered and a decision reached that would not be tinged with violent emotions. The advocates of separation stressed that it would prevent ill-considered dissolution of marriage and offer the possibility of a relatively easy reunion. Many of the arguments were also of a fundamental nature: the draft was said to meet society's expectations based on respect for the "fundamental values such as the family and marriage". One of the advocates, however, pointed out the inconsistency of this assumption in that the institution of separation cannot be shown as evidencing respect for marriage and the family if it in fact legalises the breakdown of matrimonial and family ties. Others referred to the consistency of the draft with canon law and the Concordat to justify the advisability of introducing separation into the Polish legal system. According to those who put forward these arguments, the decided prevalence of Catholicism is a justification for the conviction as to the need for and desirability of separation.

This latter argument was at the same time, however, the basis of the main objection raised by opponents of the draft. They argued that the draft was in fact a specific step—and not the first one at that—towards introduction of canon law into the constitutional law of Poland, and expressed their fears that the next step would involve limitation of divorce. Data was quoted on the grounds for divorces—family violence and alcoholism in particular—and the question was posed: why and in whose interest should such families be protected, and how could the spouses be expected to become reunited in this situation? The proposed change which was being presented as offering a greater choice (divorce or separation) could in fact lead to loss of the right to divorce. Doubts were also raised on a number of detailed points. For example, concerning tax regulations, would it be possible for separated spouses to be taxed jointly, or for one separated spouse to be taxed together with his/her child, etc.? Pertaining to a child born during the separation, what would be the position concerning the use of the family name, inheritance, joint property and so on?

The debate was highly emotional. Besides the deputies who took the floor on behalf of their parliamentary clubs (they all spoke for referral of the draft to parliamentary committees), and other deputies who asked questions but failed to declare clearly for or against the drafts, long speeches were also made by twelve deputies, seven of them representing the right wing, and five the leftist Democratic Left Alliance. Of these twelve speakers seven were women and five were men. All the members of the rightist parties supported the draft, and all those from the left wing spoke against it. (Five of the women—all of them members of the leftist party—were decidedly against both drafts; the remaining two (members of the rightist Solidarity Electoral Action) as well as all of the men (also representing the right wing) were for the draft.) The draft was duly examined by the competent parliamentary committee and sent back to the Sejm, which eventually adopted the bill. It has yet to be examined by the Senate.

Finally, the findings of relevant opinion surveys should be discussed, the more so as advocates of the draft bill referred to its consistency with social expectations. Public opinion seems divided on the introduction of separation. The proportions of respondents who declared for and against it were almost identical (41% and 36% respectively). Thirty three percent had never heard of the plans to introduce separation. Respondents were also asked to consider the desired negative prerequisites for separation: should the children's interest constitute an obstacle to separation, and should the spouse who bears the guilt for disintegration of the marriage be permitted to file a separation suit? The public proved highly restrictive or perhaps simply accustomed to the regulations pertaining to divorce: in both cases, the largest proportion said that separation should not be granted in such cases.

After over sixty years of absence from the Polish legal system, separation can be expected to reappear quite soon. An external observer might be surprised at the heat of the discussions involved and the highly emotional atmosphere accompanying the debates. Only experience will show whether this highly emotional treatment of the issue was indeed justified. Perhaps the authors of the solution were right, and separation will provide the possibility of legal regulation for those who no longer want to stay together but cannot divorce for important reasons. Yet it may also be the case that in a country where divorce was only denied in a few exceptional cases, the incidence of such refusals may increase. We may also see considerable social pressure towards separation rather than divorce. In itself, this would not be alarming, were it not to be interpreted as a stage in the gradual introduction of Catholic principles into the legal system.

5. PRO-FAMILY POLICY, LARGE FAMILIES AND THE TAX SYSTEM:
PROPOSALS FOR CHANGE

The concept of "pro-family" policy proved extremely broad, and differences in
its interpretation could be seen not only within the coalition, but also within the
Solidarity Electoral Action party itself. The Federation of Life Defenders'
Movements, within its pro-family activities, demanded restoration of the legal
ban on abortion on social grounds. The Christian-National Union brought a
legislative initiative aimed at extending paid maternity leave from sixteen weeks
to six months. The Association of Catholic Families sees pro-family policy
mainly as a struggle against pornography and protests against the introduction
of sex education into school curricula.

Changes in the tax system were often mentioned in the electoral declarations
as mechanisms for implementing a pro-family policy. The issue recurred during
the discussion of taxes in 1999. Individual members of the coalition made radically different suggestions on this issue. One of the members—the Freedom
Union—suggested a linear tax and cancellation of all allowances, in order to aid
economic growth and thus to improve the situation of families. Parties in the
AWS proposed the opposite: joint taxation of all parents and children, joint taxation of all relatives within one household, and tax reductions for each child,
which means that the actual amount of tax reduction would depend on the number of children.

Some politicians of the Solidarity Electoral Action suggested introducing a so-
called family quotient in the income-tax return, that is division of common earnings between spouses and their children. Deputies of the Christian-National
Union, a party included in the AWS, submitted an even more radical draft,
which permitted the taxpayer to be taxed jointly with all relatives living in the
same household provided that such persons were dependent on him. The
Government Centre for Strategic Studies suggested the conception of a base
amount: the parents would deduct a defined amount from their tax depending
on the number of children. Thus 25 percent of the basic amount would be
deducted for the first child, 50 percent for the second child, 100 percent for the
third child, 50 percent for the fourth child and 25 percent for the fifth, sixth, etc.
The leader of the other party in power with AWS submitted an entirely different conception. He suggested a single tax rate (lower than in 1998) for all, independent of earnings, and the abolition of all reductions, joint taxation of
spouses and single parents included.

Suggestions for radical changes to the tax system were criticised chiefly
because their introduction would involve extremely high expenditure. The family quotient concept was additionally criticised for bringing greater benefits to
richer families. When commenting on the suggestion of reductions dependent
on the number of children in the family, economists from the Adam Smith
Centre stressed that

"this tax system would hardly stimulate greater thrift and diligence, but would rather help large families to enhance their levels of current consumption. . . . Yet truly pro-family assistance would in fact be entirely different, mostly education coupons and a system of scholarships and credits for students".[26]

In the press comments it was suggested that income per person should matter more in the tax return than the number of children. The suggestions submitted by AWS and other rightist parties very clearly stressed the need for a tax system that would help large families. This aim of support to such families can also be found in other drafts prepared by rightist politicians, including the report submitted by the Plenipotentiary of the Government for Family-Related Matters, and in various joint initiatives of the rightist parties, the Catholic Church and Catholic social organisations. Ways of supporting large families and stimulating procreation were discussed, for example, in March 1999 in Czestochowa within a national debate on "Social Welfare During State Reform". The debate was organised by the Independent Trade Union "Solidarity" and the Polish Federation of Associations of Catholic Families. AWS politicians submitted a draft law on pro-family allowances that would be paid automatically to all families with at least three children. A conference on a similar topic was organised in the Parliament in April 1999 by the Christian-National Union. During that event, the party's leader addressed the Prime Minister, demanding that pro-family policy be made the Government's priority as:

"the Crisis of the family and the demographic crisis are today the two greatest threats in Poland. . . The crisis of the family and the ageing of society may in future lead to economic crisis. Only young nations can be resourceful, enterprising, and innovative; only such nations develop. . . The decreasing birth rate is a threat to Poland internationally also. The proportion of Poles in the population of Europe and the world is radically reduced . . .".[27]

Laying the stress chiefly on procreation does not help to develop thinking about family policies, for as well as the low birth-rate, a number of other social problems appeared in the 1990s which are probably much more important, such as unemployment, poverty, homelessness. An increase in the birth rate, the favourite slogan of rightist politicians, will not contribute to solving those problems but rather to their expansion, the material situation of large families being the worst of all. This is described in the "Report on the Situation of Polish Families", which states that 63 percent of families with three children and 80 percent of those with four children live below the social minimum. Added to this is the fact that large families often accumulate a variety of problems (e.g. poverty, pathology, low educational levels, and thus also a greater threat of unemployment). It is therefore only natural that both the Plenipotentiary of the Government for Family-Related Matters and AWS politicians are criticised for

[26] *Wprost* of 20 September 1998 (825), p. 21.
[27] Pronouncement of President of the Christian-National Union Mr Marian Pika, in *Gazeta Wyborcza*, 19 April 1999, p. 14.

abusing the term "pro-family policy" and for supporting growing birth rates only. Polemical statements are appearing in contradiction, such as:

> "Being bigger does not mean that families will live a better life. The State should intervene in family matters as little as possible, if at all, and such interventions should be limited to situations of violation of human and individual rights within the family. The State should counteract pathologies and violence against women and children. This would be a genuine policy in support of the families that are not doing well."[28]

6. PRO-FAMILY POLICY AT THE LOCAL LEVEL

Pro-family policy may also be important at the local level. It appears that there, too, implementation proves difficult, and the idea itself is subject to various interpretations. From the findings of a questionnaire survey organised in May 1998 by the Polish Towns Union among its member towns,[29] it appeared that in almost all the towns in the sample (128 of the 130 that answered the questionnaire), the commune authorities felt that they were actually helping families, and interpreted pro-family policy as performance of the commune's obligatory tasks in the area of social welfare or education. Local authorities in one-third of the towns had formed Family Commissions or other commissions with the word "family" in their name next to education or social policy; and the municipal authorities of 15 percent of the sample had also adopted specific resolutions concerning pro-family policy. Initiatives to support the family mentioned by the local authorities included: organisation of family assistance centres; free meals for school children; implementation of an anti-alcoholism programme; therapy clubs for children; and controlling crime and family violence. Most local authorities support families in exceptional situations: pathological (assistance declared by 93% of towns); the poorest (91%); large families (90%); the unemployed (87%); incomplete families (83%). In a majority of the towns the local authorities co-operate with nongovernmental organisations in assisting families. The greatest problem limiting the implementation of pro-family policy, as seen by local authorities, was lack of resources.

OBSERVATIONS

From the data provided by the sociological surveys to which we have access it appears that in 1996[30]—that is before the recent parliamentary elections—

---

[28] Pronouncement of Director of the Federation for Women and Family Planning Ms W. Nowicka, in *Gazeta Wyborcza*, 30–31 May 1998, p. 3.

[29] Findings based on a summary prepared by A. Krec and A. Porawski, "Polityka prorodzinna" (Pro-family policy) on the Polish Towns' Union's website.

[30] Centre for Opinion Surveys Newsletter: "Polityka panstwa wobec rodziny—ocena, spoleczne postulaty" ("State policies towards the family: appraisal and social postulates"), December 1996.

Polish society was critical of State family policy, and the activities of the new Cabinet have led to little change in this respect. This can be seen, for example, by a demonstration, organised in May 1998 by the Silesian branch of "Solidarity" trade union. Its participants demanded that the AWS should start implementing the pro-family policy promised during the electoral campaign. The question might thus be worth asking as to exactly what kind of State family policy society expects. From an opinion survey[31] it appears that the majority would like the State to create appropriate conditions for families to meet their own needs independently. Forty-four per cent of respondents said that the State should support all families irrespective of their life situation. A majority approved of help to families with a handicapped child (98%), incomplete families (92%), large families (92%) and families with children in difficult conditions due to poverty, unemployment or illness (97%). The forms of State relief to the family most expected by society include: available and cheap housing credits (96%), cheap and available infant day care centres, kindergartens, school clubs (93%), available and cheap credits for children's education (91%), higher family allowances (87%), tax reductions for parents (87%) and benefits in kind (85%).

It appears that the "pro-family policy" advertised during the electoral campaign by the parties now forming the ruling coalition is not only conceptually unclear, but also unclear in directing official actions with respect to the family. The parties' electoral declarations differ radically from what was actually introduced during the rule of the rightist coalition. The only measures introduced are simple legal regulations with the hidden aim of increasing the permanence of marriage. Various methods are employed in this aim: the physical distance to courts in divorce cases is increased; separation is reintroduced as an alternative to divorce; the programmes that offered the chance of escape to victims of family violence have been stopped; and campaigns to reveal family violence are criticised. The sole reference to such actions in the electoral programmes is the promise that the State would develop social and economic conditions conducive to harmonious functioning of the family. It seems unlikely, however, that the voters interpreted that promise this way. There has been no introduction of any of the mechanisms originally promised to increase protection to mothers or large families; nor has the pro-family policy been defined with any amount of precision. Surveys of local authorities and public opinion surveys show that what is seen as pro-family actions are traditional elements of social welfare. There are reasons to doubt whether these actions contain any new element which could justify the grandiloquent name of "pro-family policy".

---

[31] Centre for Opinion Surveys Newsletter: "Polityka panstwa wobec rodziny—ocena, spoleczne postulaty" ("State policies towards the family: appraisal and social postulates"), December 1996.

8

The Bulgarian Children Act: A Battlefield for Adult Policies or a Genuine Commitment to Children?

VELINA TODOROVA

INTRODUCTION

WIDE-REACHING REFORM in the field of family law and child protection is under discussion in Bulgaria. The initiative for change got underway formally at the end of 1997 when four legislative Drafts for Child Protection were brought to the Parliament. Although the intention was to bring about reform in the public protection of children, the impact was far wider, and these proposals have helped to accelerate the entire reworking of legal regulations in the area of family relations. In 1998, drafting began for a new Family Code. The aim of this chapter is to outline the nature of the debate on the development of the Bulgarian Children Act (BCA). On the one hand, there was growing recognition of the need for such a law; on the other hand, however, it became clear, that there are serious obstacles to the social and parliamentary discussion. The passing of the law has already been postponed for a second year.

The chapter will describe the continuing conflict in Parliament and its causes. It will also reveal some of the general characteristics of the legislative process in Bulgaria during the ten-year period of political instability and transition from one social system to another. In this macro-environment little political attention is paid to the family, to children or to private problems. The conceptual vagueness, the uncertain alternatives in social practice and the lack of serious pressure on behalf of interested groups are the actual reasons for postponing the debate on the Draft in question. But shortcomings in the legislative procedure itself should also not be overlooked. As a result, the debate on this Draft exemplifies a crisis in the legislative response to social and political transition.

This analysis is being made from the standpoint of a participant in the process, which, I must admit, is hard to combine with the standpoint of an unbiased commentator. It is from the perspective of two years of complicated and exhausting work towards overcoming suspicions, traditional expectations and personal ambition that I will review the reasons for the delay in the debate and the possible fate of the BCA.

In 1991 Bulgaria ratified the 1989 United Nations Convention on the Rights of the Child (UNCRC) with enthusiasm. This provided a serious external stimulus for reconsideration of child policy and legislation in the country. The ratification, however, remained only a political token. Regardless of the automatic incorporation of the Convention into Bulgarian domestic law, pursuant to the 1991 Constitution, the Convention still remains no more than a moral document.[1] Any direct effect or even the priority over domestic law provided by the Convention to the Bulgarian Constitution cannot be realised due to the lack of institutional infrastructure and proper mechanisms for implementation.

In 1993 drafting began for the Initial Report of the Republic of Bulgaria under Article 44 of the Convention. It became the reason for the articulation of the commitments of the state arising from the Convention. The same period witnessed a more serious campaign and pressure from nongovernmental organisations (NGOs) and experts for legislative change. A decision was made by the Government to begin working on a Draft Children Act (1994). Although the decision was affected a great deal by pressure and personal contacts between experts and state officials, this pressure was not based on clearly formulated theses and requests. It was nourished more by enthusiasm for the ratification of the Convention and dissatisfaction with the inactivity of the state. This was the early period of emerging civil society.

After political change during which two cabinets came and went—first a coalition and then a socialist one—work on the Draft was abandoned. Serious economic problems meant that political priority was given to economic reform and back-up legislation. For the same reason, work on the Initial Report was delayed. It was presented before the UN Committee on the Rights of the Child after a two-year delay, and was reviewed in January 1997.

At the end of 1997, four legislative Drafts on Child Protection were brought into Parliament by women parliamentarians from various political persuasions.[2] A fifth Draft was presented some time later. In addition to creating a precedent in parliamentary procedure, this fact also raised a number of questions about the motivation of the MPs and the reasons for their unexpected

---

[1] According to Article 5, para. 4 of the Constitution, international instruments, ratified and duly promulgated, become integrated in domestic law and have supremacy over norms which contradict with them.

[2] According to the Constitution, the legislative initiative is vested in the Government or a Member of the Parliament. They have equal authority to bring drafts in for consideration by Parliament. The governing party, UDF, Socialist Party, Agrarians and Eurolefts lodged drafts on Child Protection.

activity on a subject that had been disregarded for years. The presentation of all five of the drafts became even more paradoxical, after it became apparent that they were all based on different concepts. Furthermore, there was no parliamentary mechanism to enable the presenters to unite and to avoid introducing different texts simultaneously for a first reading.

In May 1998, the first four drafts were incorporated into a single one, which was presented to Parliament for a second reading. According to the existing procedure, all interested Ministries were approached for comments. In essence, the comments were critical, and this led to a procedural trap for the Draft, so that when lodged for a second reading it was rejected by the Government. The reason announced publicly for postponing the reading of the Draft in Parliament was the necessity for its harmonisation with the Draft Family Law Code being drawn up by the Government.

Paradoxically, bringing the drafts before Parliament could not bring about the desired political prioritisation for the Act. A rule had been established in Bulgarian political life, after the changes in 1989, that the legislative agenda was to be defined by the executive power. There is almost no precedent for a law to be passed outside of the political programmes of the Government, and this was to be the case for the Draft Children Act. The Government refused to participate in the considerations, and this seemed to predetermine the failure to move ahead.

What the parliamentary debate did lead to, however, was the use of the child problem for political purposes. The first draft, for example, brought to the foreground a formerly peripheral partner in the coalition. Other drafts were used to demonstrate the political energy and the unprecedented unity of the major political forces represented in Parliament, which was to be attained later. The child issue suddenly became useful for demonstrating political consensus in a situation of constant political confrontation and the lack of parliamentary dialogue. Paradoxically, this resulted in the public and categorical rejection of the least politically biased project, i.e. the fifth Draft, which was the only one drawn up by well-known experts in the area, who publicly put their names to it.[3]

This was how the BCA provoked two sets of conflicts. The first emerged between MPs themselves, with conceptual incongruity at the heart of it. The second conflict appeared between the two powers, the legislative and the executive. When the drafts were presented, the Government did not have its own view on the matter and was not even ready to accept the need for such a law. For this reason the independent initiative of the parliamentarians posed a challenge to the Cabinet. Its first public reaction came in January 1999 after almost two years of

---

[3] This Draft was drawn in the framework of the project of the Bulgarian–British Children Initiative, financed by the PHARE Programme and the British Know-How Fund. The project is being developed with the co-operation of the Bulgarian Association of Women Lawyers and British Bulgarian Law Association. The Fifth Draft received very positive comments from experts and NGOs. It was recognised both by the general public and the lawyers as a successfully made and professionally designed piece of legislation as well as a good basis for further discussions.

silence. The Prime Minister declared that the Cabinet was not satisfied with the Draft but would give its support to a law that could ensure the effect of the UNCRC in compliance with existing Bulgarian legislation.[4] This meant that the need for passing a law for child protection had finally attracted the Government's attention. From this point onwards, the Draft was turned into a political issue. However there was still no solution.

WHY IS THE LAW NECESSARY? WHAT TYPE OF LAW IS NEEDED?

The discussion of the BCA was useful in two ways. Firstly, the necessity for the Act was problematised in public, without it being categorised as a political priority. The legislator must respond to existing public expectations. Subsequently, as a result of public pressure and the efforts of the experts, the politicians admitted that the condition of children and their rights, together with the international commitments assumed by Bulgaria, required legislative measures for the implementation of the rights recognised in the UNCRC. However, this fell short of recognition of the need for state policy towards families and children to be reconstructed in harmony with the new values and social tendencies.

Secondly, in spite of the delay on the Draft, the ideas brought out by the discussion of it had set in motion an overall move towards legislative reform of the public protection of children. As a result a Draft on Family and Child Allowances was drawn up and some of the BCA concepts were borrowed by the Draft Family Law Code. A number of problems were calling for the development and improvement of the legislation for children in Bulgaria.

(i) Social Necessity

The liberalisation of social relations after 1989 had provided a new social and economic environment for families and children to which not only they, but also the social mechanisms applicable at that time, responded inadequately. The reduction of social expenditure by the state[5] and the impoverishment of families had led to serious deterioration in the welfare of children. Access to even basic services such as health care[6] and education was reduced.[7] According to the

---

[4] Shorthand records of the Prime Minister's answer to a parliamentary interpolation, 29 January 1999.

[5] The GNP portion allotted to social support is constantly dropping: from 1% in 1993 and 1994 to 0.9% in 1995 and 0.76% in 1996, which covers not more than 20% of the population with extremely low transfers in the situation where 90% of the families could be characterised as poor (see Stoyanova et al. (1997), pp. 59–60).

[6] The low salaries in the health care system and the low social expenditure on it (2.8% of GNP in 1996, 3.05% of GNP in 1998) have corrupted the system, which resulted in the doubling of the payments: social contributions and cash payment during treatment.

[7] Education is also turning into an expensive service. In addition to the school aid (a set of textbooks costs $1/3$ of the average monthly salary), the fees for additional training courses (without which it is impossible to pass examinations) make even secondary education hard to afford.

Ministry of Education more than 3 percent, or 50,000 children, were dropping out of school annually. The reasons were mainly economic. This figure includes a drastic increase as far as Roma children are concerned: 52 percent of Roma children aged 7 to 16 do not attend school at all. The number of children who begin work (usually in an unhealthy environment) before they turn sixteen, is rising progressively. The growing tendency of children to use drugs is especially troubling. Child prostitution has developed. Nearly one thousand children live on the streets, where they become victims of brutal violence. The child-care establishments have accommodated about 30,000 children, which is equal to one fifth of all Bulgarian children. Only 4 percent of them are orphans. About 40 percent are put up for adoption, and each year 20 percent of them are adopted by Bulgarian parents, and about 300 to 350 are adopted by foreign families (most of them from France, Italy and the USA).

(ii) Public Care for Children, and Its Agents

Five ministries and two central committees have responsibilities for children.[8] To a large extent their policies are inconsistent and often controversial, which presupposes their low efficiency. Departmental interests can often be seen to prevail over special care for children. Local departments of the Ministries of Education and Health deal with administrative issues rather than serving the interests of children. There are no authorities at the local level to implement public care for children. The various departments carry out statistical research, based on different criteria. This results in a lack of reliable statistics and opportunities for monitoring the indicators for the welfare of children. Only the processes in the demographic area are being monitored.

The police have no special obligations or authorisation for the protection of children. The only provision particularly targeted at children in the Ministry for Home Affairs Act (1997) authorises the police to take into custody for delinquent behaviour, children who have run away from their homes or other places where they have been placed for reasons of safety (Article 70, s.4). Policemen are sometimes accused of violence towards street children.

At present, special authorities are dealing only with juveniles suffering the effects of asocial behaviour. According to the Juvenile Delinquency Act (1958), there is a Central Commission, and local commissions which take administrative measures against parents neglecting the upbringing of their children and educational measures for juvenile offenders. The Child Pedagogical Departments are also at municipal level. They have a special duty to "search and identify children subjected to criminal offence, abuse or left without supervision".

The large network of day-care establishments and institutions for children with special needs is the only mechanism to provide public care for children.

[8] Ministries for Health, Education, Labour and Social Policy, Justice and the Central Commission for Children with Delinquent Behaviour, and Youth and Sport Committee.

The system helped to support both the full-time economic occupation of both parents as well as public control over the education of children.[9] Regardless of its good aspects—including easy access for families, due to the token fees and widespread availability, good living conditions and care—it nevertheless produced many negative results. I do not want to repeat the critique of institutional care, but I feel tempted just to mention some shortcomings of the system that are typical in Bulgaria. They resulted from the monopoly status given to institutions in the framework of care measures. That is why we witnessed a shift in their policies away from serving children and their needs, to the staff and the existence of the institution itself.

Regardless of the practices established with Bulgarian families in the fairly recent past, no family-based alternatives were developed in Bulgaria for children with specific needs: children without parents, handicapped children, or those suffering from chronic diseases, violence, etc. The only possibility for bringing up these so-called "problematic" children remained the residential establishments, with their isolation from social monitoring and control. There are various reasons for this, ranging from political to ideological. In general, the state monopolisation of public life imposed the exclusive position of the state, and would not allow admission of children to the private care of foster families and voluntary organisations.

The upbringing and education of children was left mainly to the care of the public and the functions of the family in this area were suppressed. The assumption by the state of almost the entire responsibility for the children and freeing of the mother from it brought about changes in values and family behaviour. Parents expected far too much from the state, which to some extent resulted in irresponsible parenthood. For example, an almost unrestricted opportunity arose for the parents to leave their children to the care of the state. Statistical

[9] The upbringing of children was entrusted to a network of nurseries (for infants from 6 months to 2 years) and kindergartens (for children aged from 2 to 6). They received large subsidies from the state budget and therefore, were affordable for most of the families willing to use their services. The social policy on children after 1944 was related to the equalising of the rights of the sexes (1945) and the gradual and almost full occupation of women in labour, necessitated by the policy of accelerated economic growth after World War II. As shown in the following table, the labour occupation of Bulgarian women is characterised by the highest values as compared to the occupation of women in other parts of the world.

Women in the workforce as a percentage of the total

Year	Rest of the world	Developed countries	Europe	North America	Eastern Europe	Bulgaria
1950	31.2	31.8	33.0	28.3	40.9	40.0
1975	35.0	36.6	36.2	37.4	43.7	46.1
1980	34.8	37.1	36.6	38.1	43.7	48.5
1985	36.6	36.1	36.9	38.4	43.8	49.5
1990	–	–	–	–	–	48.6
1996	–	–	–	–	–	41.5

data reveal that most of the children entrusted to residential establishments today come from known and living parents. It is also known that most of the children are being left there for social reasons. Another major reason (together with poverty) may be physical or psychological handicap of the child, or a severe disease. As poverty in Bulgaria is directly related to ethnic origin, most of the children in the homes are Roma. Their admission is usually the result of the parents' volition, since the establishments provide free support for the children.

The same situation applies in the specialised homes for mentally handicapped children. The parents are motivated by medical personnel to leave their children there. The homes can hospitalise even healthy children. Obviously, the entire system of entrusting children to institutions began, at some stage, in order to justify their own existence. It serves the needs of the staff and the respective departmental authority, and not the needs of the children.[10]

On the other hand, the patriarchal culture and traditions did not allow for the child to be considered as an independent consumer of individual services. Also, it was denied that socially significant conflicts (except for divorce) could exist within the family. The absence of individually targeted social services did not allow for child protection against possible domestic violence. In Bulgaria we do not have any known or accessible authorities where cases of violence or other risk for the child can be reported. No mechanism is provided to respond to a call for help and provide the child with immediate assistance. Currently, the only protection available is through the police and prosecution authorities. This is cumbersome, hard to initiate, and does not provide a fast or adequate reaction to the needs of the child.

(iii) Legislative Situation

It is a constitutional principle that both society and the state should provide care for children. According to Article 14 of the Constitution "The family and children . . . are placed under the protection of the state and society", whereas Article 47, para.4 reads: "Children left without the care of their relatives shall be placed under the special protection of the state and society." In practice, however, the mechanisms for implementing these principles are outdated and ineffective.

It is already ten years since the 1989 changes, and Bulgaria has not seen significant reform in its *social legislation*. The current law cannot respond adequately to the social needs arising in the process of transition, especially those related to children and family. The public care of children is being implemented mainly on the level of financial support for families and children. The second level of public services for children and parents remains undeveloped. Institutions for child upbringing constitute the only available public service.

[10] See Todorova (1994).

These offer day care or permanent residence in establishments meant for orphans or children exposed to risk.

The system for social support is defective, in spite of being based on a new Social Support Act (1998). The experts state that

"regardless of the constituted priority orientation to monthly support provisions for children and families through average coefficients, the low level of the basic minimum income as well as the rigid, extremely low standards for support eligibility, have led to a situation where the objects of support are only the single-member households, the lonely old people and the families of the unemployed".

Single parents, large families, parents of handicapped children and families exposed to multiple risk remain unsupported or are provided with inadequate support. In parallel with the normative restrictions, there are other factors for this, such as payments overdue, ignorance of one's rights, lack of activities for targeting the clients, etc.[11]

To a great extent, *family law* is also outdated in terms of philosophy and regulation. Together with procedural legislation, it preserves an emphasis on the rights of the parents, and therefore the tendency to preserve and reproduce patriarchal relations in the family. The philosophy of the law is that the children are a part of the family, they belong to their parents and what they need is only protection and prevention from harm. In spite of the provision of a broad range of opportunities for consulting children over a number of family conflicts, there are no procedural means for hearing the voice of the child. The lowest level of change in legislation lies in the area of regulating parent–child relations, and establishing mechanisms and institutions for the protection of children and their rights. In general the legal norms date from 1968. The next Family Code (1985) introduced some changes but the judicial supremacy of the Supreme Court, whose decisions are binding on the courts of inferior status, dates back to the 1970s.

The experts also assess as ineffective the regulations for the protection of children from domestic violence. Although violence against children is already publicly spoken of, there are no mechanisms for the identification of violence, and no suitable measures for the protection of children. The Family Code still supports the myth of parents being the best protectors of the child's rights and interests and the only conscientious representatives of the child, who needs to be protected and kept away from court proceedings affecting his/her interests. The legislators hold back from introducing the figure of the child's special representative (GAL).

The system for fighting juvenile crime is also exposed to severe attacks. Its character is extensively repressive and does not involve preventive intervention, nor can its re-socialisation mechanisms serve the interests of the child.

---

[11] See Stoyanova et al. (1997).

(iv) Changes in the Family, Children and Childhood

The need for revision of the law relating to children is generated by the changes in social behaviour. Changes can be seen not only in family patterns but also in the relations between the family members. In the context of the Bulgarian cultural milieu, the child is seen as one of the supreme family values, but not as a value in itself. The economic dependence of the child and the historical tradition were the cornerstone of unquestioned parental (mainly paternal) authority in the Bulgarian family. Until the very recent past, it was normal for parental and economic support for children in Bulgaria to last a lifetime. On the one hand, this was due to the poverty of society in general; on the other hand, the seclusion of the society and the lack of significant individual prospects for most Bulgarians turned the child into the main reason for the existence of the family. The conscious choice not to have children, which is popular in Western societies, is uncommon. This is why family legislation has always preserved the paternalistic relations between the child and the parents.

Recent years have seen a change in this respect, too. Sociologists claim that the young have a more emancipated economic position and values.[12] Their economic dependence on the older generation is decreasing in favour of the reverse tendency. While, before the transition, an economically independent life was impossible for a young family until the spouses were middle-aged, now it is impossible for older people to survive without the support of the young.[13] According to sociologists, this destroys paternalistic relations and questions the established pattern of "possessive" parentage. The loss of power over the young generation is being taken very dramatically by the older generation. The value orientation of child-rearing patterns is also changing. Sociological surveys indicate the answers young parents give to the question of "What qualities do you want to see in your child?" are almost entirely oriented to "modern" qualities as "independence and active position", "flexibility and adaptability".[14]

The forms of cohabitation are also changing. Demographic research shows the drop in the marriage coefficient in Bulgaria after 1980, and especially after 1990.[15] One-quarter of Bulgarian children are born outside marriage, which does not necessarily mean that they are reared by a single parent as, in fact, most of them are brought up by parents who live together out of wedlock. There are no sufficient guarantees, however, regarding support for children by parents who live apart.

---

[12] See *The Human Development: Bulgaria* (1998), publication of the UNDP, pp. 61–2.

[13] Unfortunately, this is due both to the broadened prospects of the young to increase their earnings and the miserable incomes of the retired.

[14] See *Demokratsia* (Daily), issue no. 54, 1996.

[15] In 1990 the number of marriages was 59,900, and the coefficient of marriage was 6.9 per 1000. In 1997 the numbers were respectively: 34,700 and 4.2 per 1000. Statistical Annals of the Republic of Bulgaria 1998.

The cases of domestic violence are the subject of wider discussion. In addition to media attention, practices are being established to help the victims of violence, and lobbying has begun for legislative changes.

In the light of the situation outlined, we must conclude that new legislation is expected not only to set up mechanisms for more efficient protection of the children's welfare, but also to support the emerging social relations and status changes. The different Drafts, however, provided different answers to the questions posed here.

THE CONCEPTS BEHIND THE VARIOUS DRAFTS

It was not surprising that the four Drafts introduced different ideas about the Act. It appeared that the experts for each MP had different ideas and their own emphasis and philosophy on the subject of the law, for instance:

- family support and allowances;
- list of rights and the establishment of the office of ombudsman;
- reform in adoption procedures;
- an infrastructure to guarantee the wellbeing of children.

Common ground had to be found in this conceptual diversity on which to build agreement on standpoints for the protection of children. This did not appear to be an easy task, but not because of the lack of legal arguments. The problem was that in Bulgaria there is still no sociological, philosophical and political discourse on child protection and rights. In this respect the legal experts were left on their own to elaborate the concepts.

In the course of the search for a harmonising philosophy, the following problematic areas were identified:

- Two of the Drafts proposed outdated legal techniques for normative enforcing of desired behaviour: restriction, prohibition, sanction.[16]
- Three of the Drafts were affected by social expectations and offered catalogues of rights without guarantees and implementation mechanisms. The listing of the rights was redundant not only because they are provided for in the current legislation, but also because it duplicated the Convention that already has the status of a domestic legislative Act. For example, the Draft presented by the European Left Party is a kind of code or a constitution of the child containing regulations of a moral rather than a legal character.[17]

[16] For example, it is provided that "The freedom and privacy of correspondence shall not apply in the relations between children and their parents, trustees and guardians" (Article 3, para. 3 of the Draft of the Agrarian Party). The same Draft prohibits the establishing of organisations by juniors and gives special authority to parents to select the information that can be used or known by their children.
[17] For example, Article 5, para. 2 reads that the child "shall participate in an appropriate manner in the taking of the decisions on issues concerning him/her". This is a wonderful provision, but it adds nothing to the actual provisions of the Convention.

- In two of the Drafts, subject matter was overlapping and mixed social support, rights in private and public relations and adoption regulation procedures.[18]
- Four of the Drafts demonstrated uncertainty about the grounds for the public protection of the child. In general they did not go beyond child protection without offering guarantees for respecting the autonomy of the child.

It was the setting up of a system of authorities (municipal and central) to provide the public care for children that emerged as a common concept envisaged by four of the Drafts. The suggestion was generated in an initial text, drawn up by experts at the Ministry of Justice. This was new and unfamiliar to Bulgarian practices, and naturally became the focus of the main discussion. These Drafts also suggested commitment of NGOs in the activities of child protection, and an ombudsman in relation to children.

Unfortunately, the consolidated version of the Draft, which is lodged for the second reading, demonstrates the drawbacks of the initial versions. They could be summarised as follows: lack of a basic concept of the interest of the child and the authorised bodies meant to protect him/her, a complicated and bureaucratised system of bodies dealing with children at risk; no concept of family-based alternatives for bringing up homeless children; cumbersome administrative procedures without serious guarantees for the rights of the parties; no concept about the grounds for public care; no child participation and representation; and as a result of that, non-compliance with international standards. Therefore, the Draft received serious criticism and was set aside for further elaboration.

On the other hand, the Fifth Draft has been recognised as a promising basis for discussion. It introduced concepts compatible with the international standards incorporated in the UNCRC and the European Convention on the Exercise of Children's Rights. Its key points, influenced mainly by the UNCRC and the English Children Act 1989, are as follows: the child is a holder of certain rights and can exercise them; the right to independent representation in legal and administrative proceedings is ensured for the child as long as her/his interests are implicated; and larger guarantees for informing the child are presumed. Formation of local authorities as well as a central body to co-ordinate the policy of public care for children is assumed. Social workers can intervene in the family to protect the child. The grounds for intervention are harm, or serious risk for the child of being harmed (serious neglect and abuse). Creation of family alternatives to institutions is envisaged.

---

[18] There were also some genuinely funny and paradoxical formulations such as the provision of special protection for "outstanding, gifted and talented children" and also a provision prohibiting "all forms of sexual exploitation and sexual violence against children".

148   *Velina Todorova*

THE REASONS FOR THE FAILURE OF THE DEBATE

Despite the serious efforts of the various organisations and experts, the Draft was not passed. The discourse of legal experts and children advocates appeared to be insufficient to attract the attention of the Government. Various reasons can be identified which lie behind that. Some failings in the legislative process are visible. For example, there are no parliamentary practices for research on the legislative situation and the use of expertise. A more important reason, however, is the delay in the reform of social policy. Because of that some fundamental structures and interrelations between them in Bulgarian society are still at an embryonic stage. Additional difficulties resulted from restrictions on state expenditure imposed by the International Monetary Fund. The Government did not want to get involved in the establishment of a new administrative structure.

The Law-Making Process in Bulgaria? Mechanisms and Driving Forces

The debate on the Draft, indicated earlier, brought into the open the conflict in the legislative process between the Parliament and the Cabinet. Although Bulgaria is a parliamentary republic and legislative power is vested in the Parliament, the Government's legislative programme in practice determines the legislators' agenda. This advantage is pressed to the limit, with a confrontational atmosphere in Parliament and without mechanisms for the minority to enforce their ideas. Behind the conflict in question, however, more profound reasons can be identified which worked against smooth and successful adoption of the BCA.

An active and accelerated legislative programme was a dominant feature of public life in the years after the political changes. Legislative activities were concentrated mainly in the area of the economy and the objective was to establish the legal basis for the transition from a regulated to a market economy. In this respect, a German scientist stated that: "What the other countries have been building for years and decades in terms of legal regulation, has emerged in Bulgaria in an extremely short period",[19] in effect in seven to eight years. What would evoke the astonishment of a foreign observer is merely the norm for Bulgarians.

Periodically, Bulgaria faces the need for forcible modernisation of its economic relations and legal regulations.[20] This is why mistakes and imperfections

[19] See Paschke (1997).
[20] This happened for the first time at the end of the 19th century, when the liberation of Bulgaria from the Turkish Empire played the role of a bourgeois revolution and the country needed to catch up with the historical time. The second time Bulgaria faced this need was after the end of the Second World War, when it transformed its economic and social life under the directions of the Communist ideology. At present, the third "revolution" within a period of 120 years is in progress in Bulgaria.

in the legislative process recur. This time, however, the goal was not only to establish a legal basis for economic change, but also to satisfy international criteria for the admission of Bulgaria into European structures. This objective was announced as the main political goal of the current rightist Bulgarian government.[21] The development of normative regulations today are determined, therefore, not only by political priorities, but also by external pressure coming from various sources.

In the first place, pressure arises from the European agreement on integration, according to which Bulgaria is required to harmonise its economic legislation with the law of the EU. This does not include policy in relation to children. In the second place, serious requirements are posed for the harmonisation of domestic legislation with international law on human rights. In this area, however, the efforts are much more modest and the changes are made sluggishly. As a rule, we enthusiastically join in international agreements, after which we delay fulfilling the obligations arising from them. In most cases, the ratification is meant as a political token aimed at international recognition. It is not preceded or accompanied by analysis of domestic law or of the economic and social consequences for the country. This is how the UNCRC was ratified.

So, Bulgarian law at present is once again in a position to help to construct change. The pressure of time for the regulation of interrelations is yet again leading to the dominance of law over economic relations. There are also few opportunities for translation into the domestic law of the criteria valid for highly industrialised and rich countries. Bulgaria is a country that is only just beginning to transform its centralised planned economy into a free market. Subsequently, the new legislation has serious drawbacks.[22] For example, laws are adopted which are not applicable due to the lack of certain objective conditions.[23] The repeated introduction of revisions and amendments in the law generates instability and unpredictability in legislative regulations.[24] The rapid legislative changes aimed mainly at constructing economic behaviour affected the ethical image of law. In many cases basic principles of law were suppressed, including the principle of justice and equality before the law.

[21] At the end of 1997 the country went through a very severe financial and economic crisis which brought about a political crisis. The socialist government resigned. The pre-term parliamentary elections gave power to a right-oriented government, who identified themselves as Christian Democrats and had the Agrarian Party as their coalition partner. The Cabinet started a liberal policy in the economic and social security areas.

[22] See Bulgarian Laws and *The Ability to Hurry Slowly, Capital* (weekly), issue no. 12, 18 September 1998.

[23] For instance, Protection of the Competition Act (1992); The Law on Securities (1993).

[24] One of the popular examples is the Privatisation Law (1992) which was revised 20 times, and the Trade Law (1991) which was revised 15 times. There are also other examples of laws which have been revised prior to being enacted.

Political Priorities or Social Needs

The speed of legislative activity in the area of economic relations was in sharp contrast with the precaution, the delay, and even the fear of change in the social sphere. This holds true for all the governments that have come into power since 1989. Attention in that field was focused on relieving the situation of the two vulnerable groups affected by the change: retired people and the unemployed. As far as the creation of new policies for families was concerned, no significant steps have been taken in the last two years. The measures were limited to partial changes in the financial support for families and children in harsh circumstances.[25]

The usual explanation for this is lack of resources and because of that, lack of political will. The real reasons, however, should be sought in the lack of strong public pressure by interested groups and professional communities. Tradition also hinders change, especially in the field of family law and child protection. Moreover, for historical reasons, Bulgaria has never experienced a special policy aimed at families and children in terms of housing, taxes, services, etc. Therefore, regardless of their having inherited a Draft Children Act (drawn up by the previous Cabinet), the present Government was in a rush to pass it, like a hot potato, to the parliamentarians for whenever an opportunity manifests itself. The Government was conceptually unprepared to start a debate on the subject.

The Government has initiated changes in the fields where Bulgaria already had experience; that is financial support and family relations. As a result of the debate on the BCA, a Draft on Family and Children Allowances was drawn up within a short period and with comparative ease. It responds to the changes in social behaviour and attempts to stimulate the birth of a second child. The monthly benefit for a child remains universal, but the amount is related to the needs of the child. The amount depends on age and receipt is related to meeting the needs of the child on behalf of parents (for example, the child has to attend school). Another effect of the debate on the BCA was the rapid (within six months) drafting of a new Draft Family Law Code. The Draft incorporated some of the basic ideas of the BCA: the setting up of municipal services for child protection, the possibility of entrusting the child to a foster family, orientation of adoption in the child's best interests. The incompleteness and one-sidedness of the regulations in the Draft Family Law Code, however, reveal that the concept of a modern child protection policy has not been grasped. The unwillingness to base a modern regulatory system on the rights of the child is clear.

[25] See Social Assistance Act (1997).

The Draft on Child Protection and the Public Expectations[26]

Parents and specialists working for children inspired by the concern about social hardship focused their views on criticism of the existing relevant legislation. The legislative activity of the last ten years had led Bulgarians to hope that problems could be solved by law reform. That is why the BCA began to be regularly discussed in the media. Public concepts and expectations, however, did not agree as to the contents of the BCA. Subsequently the legislator received many and various messages. Unfortunately, until very recently, similar uncertainty was the case among the experts and is currently the case with most of the politicians.

The uncertainty is mostly due to the fact that the child and its specific legal protection have never been the focus of social debate or legislation. Bulgaria has never had a special law on child protection, such as modern European countries have, only a special Juvenile Delinquency Act, in effect since 1958, which protects society from children rather than children from conflicts in the family and society.

Therefore, at the opening of the debate, the initial public expectation was that this law would *codify* legislative matters referring to children. Society expressed its hope that the law would become a panacea for all the serious current problems of children, which had become evident since the political change, the liberalisation of economy and the gradual withdrawal of the state from the social sphere. Reaction by the state was demanded concerning the new and unfamiliar phenomena of the sexual and economic exploitation of children and the use of drugs. Actually, it was expected that in terms of child protection the state would be restored to its traditional position and provide ready-made solutions to the problems. Three of the Drafts made an attempt to respond to this expectation. They offered a list of rights but with no legal guarantees or back-up mechanisms for realisation.

Gradually it became clear that it was impossible and unnecessary for the entire complex of issues concerning children to be covered by a single law. The many risks to which children are exposed must be at the heart of how effective the protection is, and whether the means to implement protection would need an additional mechanism to provide for the uniform action of the legislative package. This concept was the basis of the Fifth Draft, which proposed the setting up of an infrastructure of local authorities to implement protection for children.

Some time later public expectations began to differ and messages became more specific. The most serious concerned the change in social support for parents and children. The withdrawal of the state from the social sector and the policy of restrictions in social support provoked the first protests among parents

---

[26] This part is not based on data collected through a socio-legal survey, which has never been done. The analysis uses materials from media and interviews with specialists working for children.

and generated ideas about changes in child legislation.[27] That is why the prevailing expectation in 1996–7 was for the new law to regulate financial support for families with children. The "monthly allowances" had been the only concrete link between state and parents. Due to high inflation since 1990 that link almost disappeared, and parents' reacted with a strong demand for changes in the law. This subject matter was tackled in one of the Drafts. A change in family allowances was envisaged and supported with alarming data about the demographic processes in the country.

In recent years, media attention to the problems of children and the relevant legislation has been developing, together with social expectations. In the beginning the media responded to the obvious without trying to form and direct public opinion. They provided coverage of the social and economic problems of families and children and the demographic problems in the country, without attempting a more serious analysis and proposals for change of child-related policies.

The most significant progress was registered in raising awareness of domestic violence, which had been invisible in the public domain in recent years, as well as other subjects hidden from the general public until very recently, e.g. the high rate of institutionalisation of children and the lack of policies towards children in the streets. Disclosure of information about children in institutions led to strong criticism. Another very relevant message that was made public was the need for setting up the infrastructure to provide public care for children.

It also became clear from the media that the public still maintains an aggressive attitude towards irresponsible parents, formed by the previous policy. The majority, even among the specialists, suggest repressive measures be undertaken against such parents, for example to initiate penal proceedings under Article 182 of the Penal Code, the parental rights to be terminated and the child placed in an orphanage, etc.

It is difficult at this stage to assess what the public reaction will be to the newly emerging alternatives to public care, such as providing for the child to be brought up in family foster care, rehabilitation centres, etc. It was a pity that the authorities did not make any effort either to research the dynamics of the social opinion in this area or to identify the newly emerging social norms and to legitimise them. No official attempt is being made to identify and support the new tendencies in families, as well as the practices set up by civil organisations such as adoptive families, social centres servicing the victims of domestic violence, family mediation, etc. Therefore, it was not a matter of lacking political will; to some extent development has already started.

---

[27] The monthly child allowances were in fact the only form of state support addressed to every child and family. Therefore, the first reaction was against the inflation-ridden monthly support payments. The law which provides for the support was adopted in 1958. It played a role in solving the demographic problems of the nation. The amounts were proportional to the number of children and there were special incentives for the birth of a third child in the family.

The Emerging Civil Society and its Role in the Legislative Process

It must be stated that a major contribution to raising the issue of the necessity of adopting the BCA and for most of the lobbying for a good law was made by civil associations and local and foreign experts. Some international organisations and institutions have also played a role in this respect—UNICEF, the Council of Europe, the World Bank, etc. The pressure for adopting the law was organised in two directions. The first was to identify the main problematic issues in policies for children and to pave the way for the legislative changes; the second was to set up an alternative to the existing policy in practice.

The major civil organisations in Bulgaria emerged in 1989–91. The experts working for them were the vehicle for the penetration and the influence of Western philosophy and experience in the area of protection of children and their rights. Some research was carried out at that time which had no targeted recipients and did not bring forth significant consequences.[28] During the period, however, no serious discussion has been conducted on the need for changes in the policy and the legislation on children.

Bulgaria also enjoyed a boom period for charity and merciful treatment of children. In 1992–3 and 1996–7 many international and local campaigns were initiated to rescue children. These were the hardest years in terms of economic survival when the state faced immense difficulties in providing for the elementary needs of children, such as food, medicines and clothing. The children residing in institutions suffered most. For example, ten children placed in a home for severely handicapped children died in the winter of 1997. The reason reported was heart failure caused by physical exhaustion. During this period, some of the NGOs financed by western donors[29] began working on the establishment of new models of social care for children and assistance for parents. For example, regardless of the lack of a legislative framework, and by the use of some of the existing ones (that concerning guardianship, for instance) the gradual selection and preparation of adoptive families was started. Now there are fortyone educated and functional families where fortyseven children have been fostered. Family consultation centres[30] were set up, where child psychologists provide assistance to child victims of domestic violence.

There is growing activity by other organisations which hold educational seminars, discussions among professional societies, exchange of specialists between countries famous for their modern legislation and practices in child protection

[28] By the initiative of UNICEF a survey of domestic legislation was carried out in order to assess its compliance with the Convention on the Rights of the Child. Scientists from the Institute for Research on Youth (which was closed down shortly after 1989) published collected research on the situation of children (*Children in Crisis and the Crisis in Children* (1991) and *Children in the Conditions of a Social Crisis* (1991)).

[29] For instance, the Bulgarian "Orphan Foundation", financed by and working in co-operation with the Christian Children Fund of Great Britain; the Association of Social Workers, financed by Dutch foundations; the British Council, etc.

[30] Such centres are functioning in Sofia, Burgas and Plovdiv.

and media expression.[31] Also, the attention of the political forces was drawn to the problems of children due to the role of some foreign organisations (the Council of Europe, for example, within the process of monitoring Bulgaria's respect for its obligations and commitments to the organisation[32]). The policy on children was seriously criticised in a report written by a group of representatives of the World Bank, UNICEF and UNDP. The three organisations carried out a monitoring mission on the situation of children in Bulgaria at the end of December 1998 and came out with specific suggestions for changes in the policy and the adoption of new legislation on the protection of children and their rights.

In general, both missions confirmed the conclusions made by local organisations and experts. These conclusions and suggestions can be found in the Recommendations of the UNCRC on Bulgaria's Initial Report. Unfortunately, the efforts of the international community could not trigger dialogue on the subject at home. No attention was paid to the Recommendations of the UNCRC and the two other missions will probably be confined to promises only.

Traditions Versus Claims for Modernisation

One of the main reasons for the failure of the parliamentary debate was that it employed only moral and not economic arguments. The international commitment of Bulgaria arising from the UNCRC was the argument most frequently referred to. No economic reasons were provided, however, (such as the cost of bringing up a child in an institution as compared to the cost for a foster family). Bulgaria still does not have strong economic pressure for curtailing costs in this respect. The financing of institutions is still centralised and comes from the state budget. This is why the municipalities formally responsible for managing the establishments are not considering the lowering of costs and finding better alternatives. There is no economic demand for staff cutbacks and for searching for more effective economic solutions for child upbringing. This is why no pragmatic decisions in this area can be expected at the present stage. The lack of economic discourse was one of the consequences of the high level of centralisation of state care for children. Another, already mentioned above, was the lack of uniform public statistics on the situation of children. Centralised policy also prevented the local units from having flexible policies connected with the specific needs of the children. For example, there is no conception of how to realise

[31] For example, the project of the Bulgarian Association of Women Lawyers in co-operation with the British Bulgaria Law Association financed by the PHARE Programme and the British Know-How Fund.

[32] See the Information Report of the Commission on Observing the Obligations and Commitments by the CE Member States, drawn by David Atkinson and Heningh Gelerod, which emphasises the following problems: the practice of sending children who have committed crimes to isolated establishments without procedural guarantees for the protection of their rights, as well as the violence committed against children in the streets, doc. 8180/2 September 1998, *Human Rights Journal*, 3/1998.

the actual transition from institutions to foster families and smaller units for children. There is also a serious resistance by the staff to any changes aimed at the reorganisation or the closing down of the childrens' homes. For instance, there is also resistance against the measures of the Ministry of Education for the non-admission to institutions of children with parents, for the integration of children into mainstream schools, for the integrated training of handicapped children, etc. From the perspective of the personnel this is equivalent to job cut-backs and modification of teaching methods. The clash with conservatism and tradition is serious. Therefore, a clear political commitment is needed for the association of the change with measures for restructuring job positions, additional training of employees and a transfer of financing.

Probably the most significant reason for the failure of the debate was that owing to the previous policy, there are no professional communities in Bulgaria (such as social workers and child psychiatrists) to serve children. The newly emerging professional community of social workers is still incapable of serious contributions to the development of universal criteria and objectives in child policy. Social work training was started only in the 1990s in several Bulgarian universities. The group itself is still amorphous, without common interests and cannot exercise any serious pressure for the reform of the law. The only professions related to work with children are teachers and medical workers. They are traditionally occupied with children, but still within the framework of the old concepts and paradigms.

Contacts and communication between professionals—physicians, social workers and lawyers—attending to children are just beginning to emerge. In fact there are no lawyers qualified specifically to work with children. The curriculum for legal training is underdeveloped and there is no development of sub-specialities within the main branches of law. This was also a reason why the legal community, unlike the social workers who did not take great pains to grasp this concept of a new law, were unable to fully comprehend the idea. As potential specialists servicing children social workers are not yet strong enough as a professional group, nor do they have any broader representation in society. The need for their profession is still unacknowledged and they do not enjoy wide recognition and popularity among people.

For various reasons, no tradition has been established in Bulgaria and no services were set up to address the individual needs of children and their parents. Public policy for family and children was oriented to the specific objectives of society, which lay in its economic, demographic, social and even political development. Therefore, the services oriented to the collective needs of children as a special group of the population languished. Public upbringing and education of children by child institutions and organisations constituted the total care of the state and society for them. Their specific interests and needs were not addressed.[33]

---

[33] It should be admitted that such conclusions could be easily made in the current environment when the comparisons both with the international standards set up by the UNCRC and successful modern policies are widely debatable.

The patriarchal family tradition was the main factor barring the development of demand for professional support and consultations for family members. In the cases of personal failure, a family conflict, or for the upbringing of their children, Bulgarians prefer to rely on relatives from the extended family. With the emerging individualisation of personal life, however, and the gradual loss of the strong bonds between the extended family members (such as proximity of residence, common business, etc) it can be stated that there is a growing demand for the helping professions.

CONCLUSION

The experience derived from drafting child protection legislation in Bulgaria in the last three or four years has revealed the discrepancy between the political priorities determining the legislative agenda and the concepts of experts. It appeared to be very difficult for the two groups to hear each other due to the lack of interactive communication in that particular field. The two parties in this "battlefield" have not yet put their arms aside, and the chance of reaching a reconciliation is slight. Government seems to take the initiative from the parliamentarians, but is not eager to go ahead. The experts are convinced Bulgaria must have a Children Act that is expected to deal with the deficiencies of current policy. It should regulate the relations for public support for children and families by the development of a system of social services and agents to provide them to the parents and the children who need them. It is not easy to foresee, however, how long the children of Bulgaria will have to wait for it. And a doubt still remains: is this an experiment and if so, are we ready to pay the social cost of it?

REFERENCES

Atkinson, D. and Gelerod H. (1998) Information Report of the Commission on Observing the Obligations and Commitments by the CE Member States *Human Rights Journal*, 3.

Demokassia (1996) issue no. 44.

Institute for Research on Youth (1991a) *Children in Crisis and the Crisis in Children.*

—— (1991b) *Children in the Conditions of a Social Crisis.*

Paschke, M. (1997) "The legal basis of Bulgarian economy from a German point of view", *Targovsko Pravo* 2 (a report presented at a seminar held at Bischofsgruen, Germany, May 1996).

Stoyanova, K. (1997) *Family Social Policy: Problems, Priorities, Implementation*, Gorex Press 59–60.

—— *Hurry The Ability to Slowly, Capital* (1998) (weekly) issue no. 12.

Todorova, V. (1994) "Adoption and the legal defence of children residing in social establishments" *Modern Law*, 4.

UNCRC (00) *Recommendations on Bulgaria's Initial Report.*
United Nations Development Programme (1998) *The Human Development: Bulgaria —*
    pp. 61–2.

SECTION 3

THE RIGHTS AGENDA:
RHETORIC AND REALITY

9

Legislating for the Child's Voice: Perspectives from Comparative Ethnography of Proceedings Involving Children

ANNE GRIFFITHS and RANDY FRANCIS KANDEL

I. LEGISLATING FOR THE CHILD'S "VOICE": THE THEORETICAL QUESTIONS

THIS CHAPTER EXPLORES how legislation and legal ethnography can shape the process of developing and implementing legislation under Article 12 of the UN Convention on the Rights of the Child (hereafter UNCRC). It raises a seriess of questions that are both explicit and implicit in terms of direct or indirect representation, welfare and rights perspectives, and taking into account the developmental capacity of the child. These issues are explored in the context of a comparative ethnographic research project on local practices in proceedings involving children in Glasgow, Scotland, and Canal County (pseudonym) in New York State, which began in 1997.[1]

A. The Convention's Questions

Article 12(2) of the UNCRC provides, in pertinent part, that "the child shall in particular be provided the opportunity to be heard in judicial and administrative proceedings affecting the child." The provision opens up an international legal "sound space" for the child's "voice"—to be implemented through domestic legislation in the signatory states (for general discussion of children's rights under the UNCRC see Cohen, 1997; Cohen and Kilbourne, 1998; Detrick,

[1] This comparative research project, funded by the Anneberg Foundation in the USA, examines (through observations and interview data) the ways children's views and needs are expressed and determined, how children participate directly and indirectly through representatives, and the role of children's representatives in child care proceedings with special emphasis on the role of safeguarders in Sotlands and law guardians in New York State.

1992).[2] But, the "right to be heard"—like any basic legal right or standard (e.g., equal protection, due process, reasonableness)—has no single, self-evident meaning and, therefore, its meaningful incorporation into domestic legislation requires that the standard be glossed with some grounded set of requirements.

What these requirements should be, in any given country, for any particular type of proceeding, for children of any particular age or in any particular provision or predicament, can only be decided by choosing policies responsive to the numerous sub-questions implicit in the amorphous standard of "being heard". What are these sub-questions? The UNCRC itself explicitly addresses three of these sub-questions, allowing for a range of national options. The sub-questions are:

(1) Whether the child should be heard "directly" (actually speak at the hearing) or be "heard indirectly" through a "representative"? This choice of options is squarely presented in the language of Article 12(2) (stating that the child may be heard "either directly, or through a representative or appropriate body").

(2) How the law's determination of the child's developmental maturity should map onto the issues of whether the child should "express those views freely" (Article 12(1)) and how the legal system should be guided or obliged to respond to this expression. (See also Article 5 the UNCRC, providing that children have the right to gradually express the liberty rights guaranteed under the Convention in accordance with their "developing capacities").

(3) How the legal system's shaping, authorising and responding to the child's voice should balance (a) the dual and often conflicting categories of children's rights: welfare rights (those affirmative rights which responsible others perceive as being in the "child's best interests" and therefore the child is entitled to as beneficiary) and (b) autonomy rights—the right to independent decision-making choice, and the behaviour by the child.

Obviously, these three sub-questions are not independent of one another. For example, the determination of the child's maturity or developmental capacity (that is, sub-question (1), above)[3] impacts upon whether the child should speak directly or through a representative and who that representative should be (lawyer, parent, specially appointed lay person, guardian *ad litem*, or other) (sub-question (2), above) and whether that representative should take guidance from the child (an autonomy-based conception of rights) or advocate for the child's best interests (a welfare model of rights) (sub-question (3), above).

---

[2] The USA has not yet ratified the Convention but is family law courts and legislation reflect its ethos (see Part II A in the text).

[3] Anthropologists and other child researchers have critiqued the UNCRC as being "developmentalist".

B. Agency, Narrative and the Cultural Vision of Children

On a deeper still level still, culturally and theoretically, the very structure of these categories and questions resonates with a western jurisprudential vision of children as special and different (see Boyden, 1990; Dolgin, 1997(a) and 1997(b); Stevens, 1995): at once legally disabled (children historically do not have a right to sue and be sued in their own names) and deserving of extra protection and solicitude. Also, children are viewed as subject to a psycho-biological imperative (their specially protected status gradually giving way as they are socialised into adulthood acquiring adult legal responsibility).

Children are most often seen as sites of socialisation—a perspective deeply ingrained in the "soft" law of children's proceedings based upon helping the child to get out of or overcome bad environments and to be taught right from wrong (Caputo, 1995). Their role as creators and interpreters of culture and social norms is disregarded or disvalued (Caputo, 1995).

Consequently, developmental capacity becomes the threshold for ascertaining the respect to be accorded to the child's voiced expression of views on a deep societal standard. In determining implementing legislation, it is necessary to go beyond the Convention's categories and ask to what extent the requirement of providing a "sound space" for the child's voice should directly recognise the child's agency: that is the child's independent will to be a causal actor in society (not unrelated to the child's identity as a legal person); and to what extent the child's voice should be used as evidence of the child's condition—and hence, shattered and refracted through the analysis and interpretations of "expert" spokespersons such as psychologists, group workers social workers and teachers. Do we look at the child "as person" or the child "as patient"?

Yet more simply put—do we recognise children as equivalent to adults, as being full-fledged parties in legal proceedings whose stated positions, interests and accounts of facts are to be expected at face value (subject only more-or-less to whatever examination and cross-examination may take place in a legal forum) or do we view children as objects of study—whose statements must be analysed for their real meaning by professionals whose job is to study and interpret children? Whether we recognise children's agency or not has a profound effect on the kinds of legal narratives we expect to emerge when the child's voice speaks directly or indirectly and is heard in a legal proceeding.

C. The Structure of Forum and Role

Yet another vital component to consider in developing implementing legislation for the child's voice is the structure of the forum, and the role and position the child plays within it. For example, there may be great differences, in both fairness and solicitude towards children, for the way the child's voice should be heard—as to the narratives told, the nature of the expression (direct or via representative) and, if by representative, who that person should be—as between formal decision-making forums and informal consensus-building forums.

Further, and at least equally important, although often ignored, is the position (role) the child plays in the proceeding. In essence, there are four (non-exclusive) positions or roles in a legal proceeding: plaintiff, defendant, witness and victim. The role of "object of concern" may possibly be a fifth role in children's proceedings, although it is not clearly separable from that of defendant or victim. (A child who is the sibling of an abused child, might be a mere "object of concern" but is equally well-described as a "potential victim"). Even in informal children proceedings, where deliberate effort is made to avoid this labelling, these various roles exist de facto. The proceeding takes place either because the child has done something unlawful—placing the child in the position of de facto defendant—or something unlawful (neglect, abuse, etc.) has been done to the child—placing the child in the position of de facto victim and/or witness.

What position the child occupies may have profound importance for implementing legislation regarding the child's voice. For example, law and society research has consistently shown that plaintiffs have an edge of advantage in constructing the narrative, issues, and "facts" of a case in both formal and informal forums (Cohen, 1997; Cohen and Kilbourne, 1998; Cobb and Rifkin, 1991; Cobb, 1993; 1994). A plaintiff is a legal actor who intentionally uses the law to seek a desired result, based upon the plaintiff's version of the facts. Basically the same body of research has shown that the socially disadvantaged (by gender, race, education, etc.) have a more difficult time in getting their narratives and issues accepted in legal forms (White, 1991; Bellow and Minow, 1996). If the goal of the implementing of legislation for the UNCRC is truly to empower children, at least one legislative position to consider is to structure legal proceedings in a way that provides space for children's voices as plaintiffs or de facto plaintiffs. At present, such a space is virtually unavailable.

For example, while Scots law makes provision for children to participate in family actions (Act of Sederunt (Family Proceedings in the Sheriff Court) 1996 SI 1996 No. 2167) a child in Scotland cannot independently bring an action to be removed from parental custody because of abuse and/or neglect. While it may be possible for a child to apply for a specific issue order relating to residence or removal from the home (under s. 11 of the Children (Scotland) Act 1995), assertions of abuse or neglect would necessitate referring the matter to a children's hearing for disposal (under Part II of that Act). In this situation children can only exercise agency in such matter indirectly through the medium of state action promoted by the Reporter to the Children's Panel in Scotland. In New York State such children can only exercise agency in such matters indirectly (e.g., by notifying a social worker who might initiate state action against the parents).

Rather than being in the position of de facto plaintiffs in parental abuse and neglect cases, children are in the position of de facto witnesses and victims.

Their voices, in such roles, can be expected to be read for truth and value and expression of need, to be helped, healed, etc. In this situation, it is not the facilitation of agency, but the explication of damage that is paramount. Such a role, perhaps, leads most naturally to the refraction and interpretation of the child's voice by social workers, psychologists, and others—the vision of the child as "patient".

On the other hand, where children are offenders they may find themselves being treated differently and thus in the position of a de facto defendant.[4] In this position parties tend to resist the narrative that others lay claim to, rather than constructing an alternative account—which may be turned around and used against them. In such a position, which is so analogous to the criminal trial of an adult, the child may, logically, be best protected not by speech, but by silence—and not by direct expression but by indirect expression—and possibly by a spokesperson with legal training (as distinct from, for example, psychological background).[5] Implementing legislation must, at least, consider whether children in de facto defendants' roles are more like adult defendants or more like children in witness and/or victims' roles.[6]

The above synopsis of roles that children may occupy in legal proceedings relates primarily to the fact-finding stages of the proceedings, but both the Scottish hearings system and the New York State family courts recognise that there may be two stages in the process involving a fact-finding hearing and a dispositional hearing. In Scotland, the two are separated and dealt with in different forums. Where fact-finding involves adjudication on whether or not the grounds for referral apply, it must be referred to the local sheriff court for a decision (1995 Act, s. 65(7)). A hearing can only proceed where grounds for referral are accepted by both parents and the child on the basis that the hearing's function is to focus on a "consideration of the measures to be applied" (Kilbrandon, 1964: para. 72). In New York State, proceedings are divided into a fact-finding hearing and a dispositional hearing. The dispositional hearing raises novel issues regarding the child's voice and representation and the three sub-questions of the Article 12 requirement. Most particularly it raises issues regarding the

[4] While Scotland makes no distinction between the treatment of children as victims or offenders (in theory), interviews with Children's Panel members reveal that the Panel's approach to dealing with such children may well vary in practice according to the type and severity of the offence. In New York State, and the United States jurisdictions generally, these offences are divided into two categories: juvenile delinquencies (acts that would be crimes if committed by adults) and status offences (truancy and acts of disobedience at home, school, or community that would not be unlawful if committed by adults).

[5] It is based upon this understanding of the defendant's predicament, for example, that the United States Constitution gives criminal defendants the right to remain silent (not the right to talk) and the right to counsel (not the right to talk for oneself). This was also the case in the UK until recently when legislation provided that in certain circumstances the prosecution is able to comment adversely on the failure of an accused to give evidence (Criminal Justice (Scotland) Act 1995, s.32 and Criminal Justice and Public Order Act 1994, ss. 34–5 for England).

[6] The United States Supreme Court in a series of cases provided defendants' rights to juveniles, recognising that such proceedings were, in fact, quasi-criminal. *In re Gault*, 387 US 1428 (1967); *In re Winship* 397 US 358 (1971).

balance between children's "best interests" and children's wishes or "interests", as follows.

In dispositional hearings where parents have been found to be abusive or neglectful (and hence children are in the position of victims or "objects of concern") the overriding standard is the "best interests of the child". However, the best interests of the child, as perceived by third-party representatives—who may advocate the child's removal from the home—may often run counter to the stated preference of the child, who may want to stay with mummy or daddy. These wishes, although recognised to some extent, are typically rationalised by social workers, etc., as inappropriate psychological reactions (wanting to protect a parent, etc.)—pointing out the law's need to make choices between the child's "direct" voice and the child's voice as "interpreted" by mental health professionals.

In the offences category, children's wishes are viewed in the context of the child's best interests or welfare, which must be balanced against the interests of society in protection (ss. 16(5) and 17(5) of the Children (Scotland) ACT 1995). In New York, this has not only led juvenile delinquency proceedings to assume a quasi-criminal aspect which is not evident in Scotland, but also to operate in terms of a mindset that, conversely, engages in psycho-diagnosis and treatment. What is clear is that there is a need, whether dealing with fact-finding or dispositional proceedings, for legislation to address the issues of who speaks for the child (self, lawyer, child specialist), development maturity, and autonomy versus needs-based rights inherent in the Article 12 UNCRC provisions about voice.

II. THE INSIGHTS FROM ETHNOGRAPHY

In the formation of implementing legislation, answers to the questions posed above are best informed by incorporating understandings derived from local practices. This part of the chapter looks at different types of forums that have been established for dealing with children and legislative attempts to provide them with a voice. The UK ratified the UNCRC in 1991 subject to certain reservations, and in Scotland efforts have been made to implement the spirit of the Convention through the Children (Scotland) Act 1995. Although the United States has not yet completed the ratification process for the UNCRC and the American juvenile and family court system (first introduced in 1899) antedates the Convention, the spirit of the American family court system is in keeping with the Convention's ethos.

A. The New York Ethnography

Despite the fact that the American juvenile and family court system antedates the UNCRC, the spirit of the American family court reflects the Convention's ethos. Combining social welfare and judicial intervention (hence rights-based and welfare-based models) and taking into account the child's developmental needs and capacities, the American family court provides significant insight into the "sound space" of children's voices in a child-centred judicial system. The following discussion is based on analysis of New York State family law and an ongoing ethnography study (funded by the Anneberg Foundation) of the family court, in rural west central New York State county, (pseudonymously, Canal County).

1. *Description of the New York State Family Court System and the Child's Voice*

New York State Family Court jurisdiction includes the civil aspects of parental abuse and neglect actions (New York Family Court Act, Article 10), status offences (PIN—persons in need of supervision) (New York Family Court Act, Article 7), and juvenile delinquency (New York Family Court Act, Article 3). Cases are resolved in a two-step proceeding: an adjudicatory hearing and a dispositional ("sentencing") hearing. In addition, various feedback loops are possible, allowing for the "adjustment" of cases through the probation department rather then a full hearing process. In practice, fact-finding hearings are relatively rare. Rather, the social services attorney, and the small pool of attorneys from which the judges appoint counsel for the parents or law guardians (children's lawyers) know and trust each other well. Most attorneys sometimes represent parent(s) and sometimes represent children, the pool includes the former social services attorney, and the present social services attorney has been in the pool in the past. Within this work-group, cases are negotiated resulting in "bargained pleas" followed by rigorous discussion of dispositional alternatives.

2. *The Child's Voice and Admission of Evidence*

When there is an adjudicatory hearing, how does the child's voice enter? In abuse and neglect cases, the child's voice is virtually never heard "directly" or "audibly"—for their "protection" the children are often kept far from the courthouse door. Although the law does not prohibit the child from testifying in the open courtroom, the child's role as "witness" is usually effectuated through special evidentiary rules.

Broad exceptions to the hearsay rule allow for admission of the child's statements as reported speech. Section 1046 of the New York State Family Court Act provides in pertinent part that:

"(vi) previous statements made by the child relating to any allegations of abuse or neglect shall be admissible in evidence, but if uncorroborated, such statements shall not be sufficient to make a fact-finding of abuse or neglect. Any other evidence tending to support the reliability of the previous statements, including, but not limited to the types of evidence defined in this subdivision shall be sufficient corroboration. The testimony of the child shall not be necessary to make a fact-finding of abuse or neglect."

Another provision of Section 1046 (the evidentiary statute) provides for the routine admission (without foundational testimony by an in-court witness) of, among other things, routine records of public and private agencies (including hospitals where children's injuries are treated or the logs of social services caseworkers investigating or monitoring possible abuse/neglect cases). Through reporting and recording, the "indirect" voices of children give powerful, even dispositive, testimony.

The following example is based on the field data. The (unmarried) father testified that his son told him "Mommy left us alone all night without food in the house. I had to go to the pond and catch a fish for dinner." The case worker's logbook (opened after the father called the children's protective services) stated that the caseworker had visited the children's home in the evening. The mother was not there. The children said they had not yet eaten supper and the refrigerator was virtually empty. Under Section 1046, this testimony is sufficient for neglect finding.

This is not to imply that the testimony was fabricated. In all likelihood, the children were being neglected by the mother who apparently had a fairly serious drug problem. She did not appear at the hearing. However, excluding the child while allowing the child's hearsay in the name of protection, is fraught with difficulties of authorship and authenticity. As socio-linguistic research has revealed, reported speech is a present memory of past perception that is unlikely to be a verbatim repetition of the original statement (Tannen, 1989). Further, as speech within speech, it takes on the collaboration of the testifier's intent and not that of the original speaker (Bakthin, 1981). What the in-court witness repeats is not necessarily what the child said, or what the child as an in-court witness would actually say or would want understood.

Another method of taking a child's testimony outside of the courtroom is the "Lincoln hearing"—named after the eponymous case (*Lincoln v. Lincoln*, 24 NY 2d 270; 247 NE 2d 659; 299 NYS 2d 842 (1969)) in which New York's highest court (the Court of Appeals) upheld the use of private interviews with children by the judge in chambers, where custody was at issue. The court reasoned:.

". . . [T]he first concern of the court is and must be the welfare and the interests of the children. . . The rights of their parents must, in the case of conflict, yield to that superior demand. . . There can be no question that an interview in private will limit the psychological danger to the child and will also be far more informative and worthwhile than . . . an examination of the child under oath in open court. . . The test is whether the deviation will on the whole benefit the child by obtaining . . . significant pieces of information . . . to make the soundest possible decision. . . [W]e do not gainsay that there are risks involved. . . A child . . . [may be] subjected to emotional stresses . . . that may produce completely distorted images of its parents and its situation . . . its feelings may be transient indeed, and the reasons . . . indicate that no weight should be given to the child's choice. . . The dangers, however, can be minimised."

As employed in Canal County Family Court, the Lincoln hearing may provide testimony for both fact-finding and dispositional purposes. The judge, the child, a court stenographer and the child's law guardian are present in the judge's chambers. Sometimes the other lawyers are present, sometimes they submit questions. The judge and the law guardian ask questions (which may be indirect, such as asking the child what he or she would want if they had three wishes). A stenographic record is made, but it is non-public. The law guardian may review it for accuracy (in Canal County this is done in the judge's chambers in the courtroom). The transcript is sent to the archives of the state's highest court and sealed. If the parent(s)' lawyer(s) are present they, of course, may use what they know in negotiating for a particular disposition. But the requirement to seal the transcript is serious. Trial judges are reprimanded in writing, even in published opinions, for non-compliance.

In combination, the broad hearsay requirement and the closed Lincoln hearing make a curious mixture. The child's "indirect" voice has an enormous evidentiary "power" because the processes invoked to protect the child substantially shield the child's statements from cross-examination. However, these same processes which deprive the child of a direct in-court voice through which the child may strategically tell his or her case, may, curiously, disempower the child as an active agent in the legal process.

3. The Child's Voice and Legal Representation

New York law requires that all children in abuse/neglect, PINS and juvenile delinquency proceedings be represented by *law guardians*—a New York neologism that reflects the inherent role tension between being an attorney, advocating for the child's wishes and a guardian *ad litem*, taking an independent position based on the child's best interests. The law guardian is the child's primary spokesperson in court, examining and cross-examining witnesses if there is a hearing and stating the legal position the child wishes to take.[7]

The role of the law guardian in particular, and legal representation for children generally, has been the focus of much study and discussion (Appell, 1996; Buss, 1996; Duquette and Ramsay, 1987; Federele, 1996; Guggenheim, 1996; Haralambie, 1995; Kelly and Ramsay 1982–3; Kelly and Ramsay, 1985; Knitzer and Sobie, 1984; Mandelbaum, 1996; Margulies, 1996; Moore, 1996; New York State Bar Association, 1991; Peters, 1996; Shepherd and England, 1996; Wu, 1996).

The various (and sometimes conflicting) rules and recommendations (binding and non-binding) promulgated by the state courts and bar association generally advise law guardians that they are to function primarily as the child's

---

[7] Although the law guardian is the child's official legal representative, when a child placed in foster care has been working with a particular social worker with whom rapport has developed, and this social worker appears as a witness at the hearing for extension or termination of placement, the social worker may be a more personal knowledgeable spokesperson than the law guardian.

"lawyer"—a rights based stance (see particularly, New York State Bar Association, Committee on Children and the Law, 1996). However, in recognition of the child developmental issues, they allow a welfare/best interests-based approach where the guardian perceives the child's understanding to be immature and the child's wishes are contrary to the child's good (sometimes phrased as contrary to the child's best interests, sometimes a stricter standard such as detriment or harm).

In interviews, almost all the law guardians reported experiencing ambivalence between the advocate and guardian roles. The majority said that they primarily took a best-interests welfare view, but one informed by what the children said they wanted, even while explicitly acknowledging that the current thrust of the Third Judicial Department (where Canal County is located) is on advocacy. Almost invariably, law guardians reported using the welfare best-interests approach with younger children and acting more like advocates with older children. They also stated that they acted more in a welfare role when dealing with abuse and neglect cases and more in an advocacy role when dealing with PINS and still more with the quasi-criminal juvenile delinquency cases. These two continua are obviously interconnected. Dysfunctional family cases present as abuse/neglect charges with younger children, but as PINS/delinquency cases with older children and teens. Seemingly paradoxically, the law guardian's adoption of a stronger rights-based position does not imply a stronger "direct" voice for the child. Rather, the lawyer's advice in juvenile delinquency proceedings and sometimes PINS cases is what one would expect from a defence attorney—keep quiet and let the lawyer do the talking.

Further, in Canal County the Family Law judges know each lawyer's style and personally choose the law guardian for each case. Based upon the judge's preliminary assessment of the case's needs at the "initial appearance" when counsel is appointed, the judge may appoint a more rights-based or more welfare-based guardian. Several interviewees said that they could infer the judge's view of the case by who had been appointed as law guardian and who had been assigned to the parent(s).

Each law guardian's negotiation of the role conflict is more nuanced than the binary welfare-rights model would suggest because the law guardian must balance these roles at every step along the way. For example, a law guardian has a right/obligation to examine and cross-examine witnesses at a fact-finding hearing. But whether the questions the law guardian chooses to ask weigh in on the side of the guardian's view that the child's interest is in removal from the home or the child's statement that "I want to stay with Mommy," is only the law guardian's decision (the child is not even present at the fact-finding hearing).

Most of the law guardians in Canal County tend to trust the child welfare department's assessment that abuse/neglect exists. Even in the rare adjudicatory hearing, they shoulder little of the burden of examination. As one law guardian expressed it "My role in an abuse/neglect proceeding doesn't really begin until the dispositional hearing. And once the parent is found to be neglectful or abusive, the child's staying with the parent is not a legal option that the court will consider." At the dispositional stage, it is easier to reconcile the child's wishes and best interests. If the child expresses a preference—for example, placement with a favourite aunt as kinship foster parent, the law guardian can easily advocate or negotiate for this placement and, because of the adult-child affective bonds, also be advocating for the child's best interests, unless there is some secondary problem—such as a history of abusiveness by the preferred aunt.

Similarly, law guardians' best interests parentalism sometimes permeates rights-based advocacy in delinquency proceedings. For example, in one juvenile delinquency case (theft of a CD player), the law guardian said that he thought that technically, he could have got the case dismissed because of the technical failures in the juvenile delinquency petition brought by the county; but he was going to seek only Adjournment in Contemplation of Dismissal (a situation where the court holds jurisdiction for one year and dismisses if there are no problems) because he thought the boy needed that little "help" from the court to stay on the right path. In formal court, he told the judge that he thought the petition could be dismissed, but he was not going to put the county to the trouble of possibly drafting a new one, if they consented to "ACD" (Adjournment in Contemplation of Dismissal) it. The boy's view, when interviewed afterwards was that his lawyer and the county attorney had agreed on the idea of an ACD with some community service and that his lawyer was a good one because he wasn't going to get sent away to do time; but the dismissal with no ACD would be even better. The actual role of the law guardian seems to evolve situationally into a kind of hybrid parentalistic advocacy.

In addition, one of the most important roles of the law guardian is investigator. Law guardians said that judges preferably appoint as law guardians lawyers who are competent, thorough and skilful investigators. The law guardians interviewed all reported doing reasonably extensive "investigatory" work. Many visited children at their homes—talking to them privately in their bedrooms or taking walks with them. Others preferred that children come to their offices to see "that the law guardian is their lawyer." They conferred privately while the parent or other person who had brought them waited in the waiting room.

Law guardians sometimes met the child at school, and/or spoke to teachers, neighbours and others. The law guardians report that they are virtually never thwarted in these investigations once they identify themselves because people co-operate when children are at stake. In Canal County (although not everywhere in New York) the social services department and parent(s)' attorneys readily provide discovery materials (including many department of social services records) to the law guardians.

In combination, independent investigations and easy access to discovery materials renders a good law guardian very case knowledgeable and family court judges in Canal County and elsewhere in west central New York State rely to a greater and lesser degree on the law guardian's understanding of the case as an aid in decision-making. Knowledge enables the law guardian to play an informed and trusted role when dispositions are negotiated.

Ironically, but unsurprisingly, child interviewees do not view the law guardians as having the thoroughness and client-connection the law guardians attribute to themselves. Several PINS children summarised their interaction with their law guardians as having first met at the courthouse, the lawyer's using big words, telling them what to do and not really explaining things. Some saw the law guardians as relating more to the other lawyers and the judges who appoint them than to their child clients. Several pointed out that the law guardians were members of the community elite, and hence more connected outside the courtroom to judges and lawyers than to the working-class families who are typically the parties in family court.

4. Agency and the Child's Direct Voice

There being no space for fuller discussion, this section relates one episode, based on the field data, illustrating the social and emotional constraints that make it hard for children to directly tell their stories to the Family Court or to abusive or estranged parents. It also shows how children strategically exercise agency, and draw on the judicial and social services system, in round-about ways, to achieve their ends.

MaryAnne (a pseudonym[8]), a twelve-year-old girl, was PINSed by her father, because of acting out and hostilities with her stepmother. MaryAnne had been in foster placement for several years and came home for weekend visits. The father, who found her to be better behaved ("I don't expect to have a perfect child" were his words) wanted placement to be terminated. The child welfare department was recommending continuation of the placement for a year, based on the results of certain psychological tests and a psychiatric assessment of MaryAnne. MaryAnne wanted to continue weekend visits with her family, whom she loved, and where she got to spend time with her older sister and friends and babysit for her younger half-siblings, but she wanted to stay in placement during the week. She wanted her own personal space—to form friendships, see her boyfriend, write poetry and read books—away from her somewhat thinner, prettier and smarter competitive older sister, and her rather coarse and male chauvinist father, and her stepmother who still regarded her as the family troublemaker. MaryAnne told the researcher, and her caseworker, (with whom she did have a genuine rapport) that this was what she wanted, but that she was afraid to tell her father because he would be really angry. She also really didn't trust her law guardian (whom she thought of as a snob) to get her message across to the judge. The caseworker told the girl that the child welfare department attorney was going to recommend an extension of placement, but that if the girl wanted termination of placement she would try to testify in court.

[8] Pseudonyms are used for all children who are referred to in the text.

If the girl did not want termination, the caseworker would not say anything to the social services attorney and the judge would probably follow the attorney's recommendation. The caseworker would not have to testify (or even be present) at the brief continuation hearing.

The girl determined what she would do. At the continuation hearing, one of the rare times when the judge often asks a child in open court what their preference is, she would say that she wanted to go home. She knew that the child welfare department would recommend continuation, and that her father would get fuming angry—as he had for some time been angry that the child welfare department was holding his child against what he understood to be the wishes of both father and daughter. This anger would irritate the child welfare department, leading to greater in-court disruption, and would lead the judge to conclude that the family was not yet ready for the return of the child—continuing the existing placement but with lots of weekend visitation. Although the actual process of the hearing became a little bit more complicated because the social services attorney was off sick for several weeks, the gist and result of the hearing went exactly as planned!

B. The Scottish Ethnography

1. *Description of Glasgow's Children's Hearings*

In contrast with the New York setting, children in Scotland (whether abused or offending) are dealt with primarily through the Children's Hearing system which represents an alternative forum to formal court proceedings. Children's hearings were first introduced into Scotland under Part III of the Social Work (Scotland) Act 1968. Currently regulated under Part II of the Children (Scotland) Act 1995 (hereafter all references to section numbers refer to this Act) these hearings deal with children under 16 who are in need of compulsory measures of supervision. Such children include those who have committed offences as well as those who have had offences committed against them and who may be in need of care and protection due to others' behaviour, e.g., neglect or abuse.

The children and their families are referred by the Reporter to a lay panel of three members, known as the Children's Panel, who do not require a legal training, who are unpaid and who are drawn from all walks of life. The aim is to promote discussion of the child's particular problems (e.g., truancy or abuse) and to reach agreement with the family on how to deal with them in a setting that is non-adversarial and which focuses on the children's "needs" rather than "deeds".[9] Created as an alternative forum to a court-based system for handling juvenile justice, hearings aim to foster co-operation and consensus in the

[9] This philosophy which was embodied in the Kilbrandon Report (1964) and legislated for in the 1968 Act has been modified by ss. 16(5) and 17(5) of the 1995 Act which permit the "best interests principle" to be set aside "for the purpose of protecting members of the public from serious harm".

decision-making process as it affects children rather than relying on coercion and sanctions.

For this reason proceedings during a hearing are relatively informal compared with court proceedings to encourage maximum participation by children and their parents or other relevant persons. The aim is to assess what is going on in the child's life through direct contact with the family in a setting which is freed from the kind of constraints that formal legal proceedings entail. At the end of a hearing the panel has power to discharge a referral or to make a non-residential or residential supervision requirement. It may also terminate or continue an existing supervision requirement. The rationale behind the system has been to protect vulnerable children and their families from confrontation with, or intimidation by, the kind of legal process that operates in ordinary courts of law. To this end, although a legal forum, a hearing is not subject to the same rules of evidence or burden of proof as a court of law and while lawyers may be present (unusual) they do not speak for their clients. The dialogue is one that is managed by panel members who speak directly to the families concerned and to other professionals, such as IT (intermediate treatment) workers or social workers, who may be involved with the child or family.

In this process three overriding principles apply. These are that:

(i) the welfare of the child is paramount (s. 16(1));
(ii) children must be able to express their views and have them taken into account where sufficiently mature (s. 16(2));[10] and
(iii) that there should be minimum intervention, that is, that a hearing should only make an order if it is better for the child to make such an order than to make no order at all (s. 16(3)).

These principles represent an attempt to integrate welfare and rights perspectives with respect to children, but there are tensions in the ways in which they intersect which are discussed below.

2. *The Child's Voice and Admission of Evidence*

Children's hearings in Glasgow, unlike the family court in Canal County, do not engage in adjudicatory legal proceedings. As noted earlier, where the grounds of referral are disputed they must be remitted to a sheriff for proof and it is only after they have been established in that forum that the case will be referred back to the hearing for a disposal. Given that fact-finding with respect to abuse and neglect takes place elsewhere, that hearings draw no distinction (in theory) between children as "victims" and children as "offenders" and the emphasis that is placed on direct personal communication, it is not surprising to find that children generally appear in person during these proceedings. Indeed they are under a duty to attend (s. 45(1)(b)) unless the hearing dispenses with this requirement

[10] Note, however, that there is a presumption in favour of children aged 12 or over having such maturity.

on the basis that attendance is not necessary "for the just hearing of the case" or where "it would be detrimental to the best interests of the child" (s. 45(2)). Although these provisions allowing for non-attendance exist they are not routinely employed when dealing with children who have been the subject of abuse or neglect.

Not only does a child have the right to attend a hearing but, in line with Article 12 of the UNCRC, he or she must be given an opportunity to express his or her views and to have these views taken into account insofar as is practicable, taking account of the age and maturity of the child concerned (s. 16(2) and 1996 rules (hereafter r. 15(1)). Making space for the child's voice is reinforced by the requirement that a hearing may not reach a decision unless an opportunity has been given for the views of the child to be obtained or heard (r. 15(3)).

However, the requirement to take account of the views of children contained in s.16 is not a new development. Prior to the 1995 Act the Children's Hearings rules had required the views of children to be sought and taken into account and to be given "due weight" in all the circumstances of the case. Lockyer and Stone (1998:106) observe that the introduction of the age and maturity requirement into the new rules (15.(5)), while in line with Article 5, "could be regarded as a retrograde step for hearings in terms of the principle of listening to children". Geared to a developmental model of child development they do, however, point out that there is "nothing to prevent children's hearings continuing to elicit and take appropriate account of the views of the children of all ages"—without first considering whether they are mature enough to "'form a view".

But even where children are present during proceedings that affect them this does not guarantee their participation in terms of direct speech. While panel members who were interviewed all agreed that it is essential to hear the child's story about the circumstances giving rise to a referral directly from the child, most admitted that this is an uphill struggle. Observational data confirmed this view which has also been borne out by other studies (Hallett and Murray, 1998: 62,125; Gallagher, 1998: 89). There are a number of reasons for this. Many panel members observed that while some young children were happy to talk adolescents were much more reluctant to speak. This was often put down to the child's stage in the life cycle. Adolescents' relationships with adults are generally viewed as being more problematic and panel members were not therefore surprised if they were non-communicative and sat throughout a hearing with a baseball cap drawn firmly over their face.

In these circumstances, as in the family court, reliance is placed on indirect speech, that is, on what another person relays as being the child's views or wishes. In children's hearings these persons are nearly always social workers or other professionals or safeguarders (see below) who present written and verbal reports to the panel based on their contact with the child and his or her family and which make recommendations about what they consider to be in the child's best interests. Given that these experts, reports have been circulated prior to the hearing to all parties (including parents, but not children) and that their authors generally present their findings at the beginning of a hearing, children often find it hard to overcome the narratives that have preceded them by the time that they are called on to speak and which may characterise them as truants, trouble-makers or victims. In a setting where the ethos is one geared towards co-opera-tion it is easier for children to go along with what the experts report rather than to dispute what is said about them as persons, which makes them appear con-frontational.

The 1995 Act does recognise that children may be inhibited in their speech where family members are present, especially where decisions involve questions about contact or where the child is to live. To assist children in these circum-stances the Act now contains powers to enable the hearing to exclude a parent or "relevant person" from part or parts of the hearing to allow a child to express views or because their presence is causing, or is likely to cause, significant dis-tress (s. 46(1)). This is seen to be an improvement on the previous position where a Chair could only ask a person to leave but had no power to compel them to do so. However, where this is done the Chair has a duty to inform the child that the substance of anything that he or she says to the hearing must be relayed to those who have been excluded.

While the 1990 *Review of Child Care Law in Scotland* recommended that this should be the case (rec. 82) on the basis of allowing for open and frank discus-sion, the recommendation was subject to the caveat "unless that would be detri-mental to the child's interest". There is no such reservation in the 1995 Act, with the result that what is said by the child cannot be treated as confidential during the hearing (this may be contrasted with the power of sheriffs who can treat chil-dren's views as confidential in legal proceedings that come before them under the Child Care and Maintenance Rules 1997, r. 3.5(4)). Although what is said by parties to the process cannot be treated as confidential during the hearing, the hearing itself is conducted in private (s. 43 (1)) and treated as a confidential pro-ceeding so far as the outside world is concerned (ss. 44(1) and (2)).

3. *The Child's Voice and Legal Representation*

Direct speech is only one of the ways in which the child's wishes may be known to a hearing. Scots law, in keeping with UNCRC recognises that children's views need not only be relayed in person but may be presented indirectly through a child's representative. The question is what kind of person should ful-fil this kind of role given the format of the hearing system. Should this person be a friend or relative, or a professional of some kind, including a person with legal expertise? As things currently stand both parents and children are allowed to bring along one person to a hearing (1996 rules, r. 11). Nothing is said about who this person should be, so it may be any one of the above. Adults who knew about and took advantage of the provision called on a range of persons includ-ing, parents, grandparents, siblings and lawyers. Some adults stated that they did not feel the need to bring along a representative as they relied on their social worker to support them. Among the minority of children who were aware of this provision and elected to use it, there were a range of adults including a representative from the children's organisation Who Cares?, a school guidance teacher, a priest and an older sibling. In a few cases children were advised to have legal representation and instructed lawyers. In Scotland children under 16 can instruct solicitors in civil matters so long a they have a general understanding of what it means to do so and competence is presumed at age 12 (ss. 2(4A) and (4B) of the Age of Legal Capacity (Scotland) Act 1991). There is a practical problem here , however, in that most children and their families cannot afford to pay lawyers' fees. They rely on legal aid which is which is not available for legal representation at a children's hearing but only for legal advice and assistance given to parties prior to a hearing (in some cases), or in respect of hearings before a sheriff.

In addition to these persons, children's views may be presented to a panel by any safeguarder appointed by a hearing (s. 16(2), 1996 Rules r. 15(5)). Rarely used when introduced to the system in 1985, the number of appointments are increasing as a result of changes made by the 1995 Act which now require a hearing to consider whether or not to appoint a safeguarder in every case that comes before it (s. 41(2)) that involves a preliminary or intermediate stage in the process (Norrie, 1997: 14). The role of the safeguarder, however, is to act as an independent person appointed by the hearing to investigate and report on what he or she considers to be in the best interests of the child. All safeguarders interviewed to date expressed this view which is in line with the provisions of the 1995 Act (s. 41), although Lord Clyde in the Orkney Report suggested that safeguarders could play more of the role of a child advocate. Many safeguarders are lawyers, but they do not view their role as one of child advocacy in promoting the child's wishes, but rather, as one which involves making recommendations to the hearing based on their assessment of the child's welfare. Good practice requires safeguarders to establish whether or not the child wishes to express a view and, if so, to make sure that they are clear about what the child's views are. This is especially important where the child's views and those of the safeguarder conflict (Sutherland, 1996: 33). In this position the safeguarder's role is very similar to that of a *curator ad litem* in ordinary court proceedings (Clelland, 1996: 53–67).

There have been heated debates about the extent to which adults should speak to children's interests or rather on their behalf, and what role, if any, lawyers should play in this process (Hallett and Murray, 1998 vol. 1: 98–107, 1998 vol. 2: 5–12; Gallagher, 1998: 51–77) given the fact that lawyers are associated with an adversarial process and the spirit of the children's hearings is supposed to be non-adversarial (Edwards and Griffiths, 1997: 231). What is interesting is that some surveys conducted among lawyers in the UK who work with children reveal that, like the law guardians in Canal County, they operate on the basis of a welfare and rights perspective so that in practice the child's views are accommodated within a best-interests framework (Gallagher, 1998: 69; Masson and Oakley, 1999: 97–117).

4. *Agency and the Child's Direct Voice*

Although hearings are child-centred and every effort is made to engage the child in discussion, when it comes to the question of "voice", children's participation in the hearings system is constrained by a number of factors. These include:

Conflicting loyalties: Whatever the difficulties in the family a child may be reluctant to lay these open to strangers for discussion, especially where either or both parents may be presented in a negative light, e.g., as failing to take proper care of the child by ensuring his or her attendance at school, or through neglect or addiction. In the face of outside intervention children will often keep quiet about the difficulties they face, e.g., as in one case where a boy was reluctant to admit that he was a truant because his mother, who was disabled, wanted to keep him at home as a companion to provide her with emotional as well as physical support. Our preliminary research suggests that the majority of children who come before the panel come from economically and socially deprived families with a high rate of unemployment and/or alcohol or drug addiction.

Fear: Children, especially those who come before the panel for the first time, may be reluctant to talk because they are unfamiliar with the panel system and fear what the panel may do. There is a common misconception that panels exist to take children into care by removing them from their homes. In addition, the presence of family members may inhibit children from speaking freely because of the repercussions that this might have for family relationships outside of the hearing.

Disaffection: This is brought about by

(a) technicalities/procedures of the particular forum: the proceedings may be less formal than those in court but they still adhere to certain formalities, e.g., reading out the grounds for referral which must be accepted by the child and family before the hearing can take place. These are often quite technical and while the panel chair often attempts to put them in "user-friendly" language this does set a certain tone at the start of proceedings, which it is hard to displace.

(b) lack of communication: communication for children is a problem especially when they are asked to talk after all the experts have had their say. Over half the panel members interviewed to date (who also sit as chairs) noted that it was their practice to turn to the social worker after the grounds of referral are established to initiate discussion. There are a number of reasons for this—to bring the reports up to date—and to give the child/family time to get their bearings and relax. However, by the time the child gets to speak he or she may be intimidated by the various presentations of "self" that others such as social and IT workers and even parents have constructed. While it is generally stressed throughout the hearing that it exists for the benefit of the child, children do not necessarily perceive this. Attempts to put children at their ease, e.g., by asking them their names are viewed by some children as being "silly cos they've got that information written down in front of them". Others find the language that is used difficult to understand or to relate to. In some cases panel members come across as "snobby" and children resent them because "they try to speak to you as if they're your ma or pa but they aren't".

(c) miscommunication: in some cases there is a mismatch between what children say and how this is interpreted by panel members. A child might, for example, explain that s/he does not attend school because of being bullied. This explanation may be treated as an excuse, or even where accepted, be met with the response that non-attendance at school is not an option, even although the circumstances are such that school authorities and social workers can do little to alter the realities that such children face.

In the light of these difficulties children adopt various strategies for dealing with the panel which may range from outright defiance to saying nothing or keeping comments to a minimum, through to playing the game or participating as best they can.

Case 1 Sue (13) came before the panel because she was outwith parental control. She was staying out all night at weekends without letting her parents (who were separated) know where she was. She refused to co-operate with the Panel expressing the view "I hate people telling me what to do." Discussion got so heated that she stormed out of the hearing shouting "Fuck off the lot of youse".

Case 2 Tom (14) came before the panel because he had not been to school for months and had serious health problems (anorexia according to the reporter). His mother had a drug problem and had difficulty in caring for him. He failed to attend one hearing because he was afraid that he would be taken into care and when he came before the panel he sat with his head bowed throughout and gave monosyllabic answers when questioned by panel members.

Case 3 Sam (12) initially came before the panel as a victim of sexual abuse by his father but was also a truant. He was placed on supervision and went to live with his uncle and aunt. He appeared to have settled into his new home and to be going to school regularly. He came back to the panel for a decision on whether his supervision order should be continued. Sam plainly stated that he did not want the order to be continued or "to come back here". As he was about to start secondary school the panel decided that supervision should be continued while he was adjusting to this change in his life and he finally agreed to this when he was told that a review could be called for in three months' time. In this case he appeared to be participating as best he could as well as accepting that he had to bow to the panel members' wishes.

Thus the Scottish ethnography, like that of Canal County, highlights the need for a more in-depth analysis of concepts such as "participation" and "voice" and of the relationship that exists between them when it comes to state forums for dealing with children.

III. CONCLUSION

The Scottish system of informal children's hearings with lay decision-makers differs from the more formal New York Family Court with its judge. Yet, in looking ethnographically at the two systems, it becomes evident that similar problems emerge in implementing the child's voice in children's proceedings (where children either commit offences or are victims of offences by family members). These are (1) an ongoing tension and conflict between rights-based and welfare-based approaches; (2) social difficulty for children in speaking "directly" in court-either because of the formalities of the situation itself or the anxieties about speaking out to and about family members in a public forum. In part, this is something that children actually experience. In part, it is something that the legal system recoils from in an attempt to "protect" children; and (3) the transfer of the child's "voice" from the child's "direct" speech to the "indirect" speech of a representative. Interestingly, although the two systems have taken very different approaches to the representative's role (law guardians in New York State and safeguarders in Scotland) the people who purport to "speak" for the children find that they themselves must continually negotiate the tension among rights-based and welfare-based approaches to this representation and, yet a third possible role, as independent investigator, reporter and analyst.

Despite the differences between the two systems, both concern proceedings where children have either done wrong, and hence are quasi-defendants, or have had wrong done to them, and hence are victims and/or objects of solicitude. Whatever their position, neither forum provides an independent assertive role for children. Indeed, what the two systems lack, and what may be very difficult or even undesirable to provide, are forums in which children can advocate for their interests, and strategically present their narratives to achieve desired ends through legal means. To allow for this, however, would involve resolving the tensions that currently exist as a result of the way in which society perceives the legal person-hood and social agency of children. This is something which is beyond the scope of Article 12. It is here that socio-legal research can inform the question of drafting implementing legislation for Article 12 of the UNCRC, and the sub-questions which must be addressed, (to supply clarity, specificity and teeth) by providing an opportunity for renewed and informed debate on the legal meaning and status of children and childhood at the dawn of the twenty-first century.

REFERENCES

Alfieri, A. (1996). "Welfare stories", in G. Bellow and M. Minow (eds.) *Law Stories* (Ann Arbor: University of Michigan Press), 31–50.
Appell, A. (1996) "Responses to the Conference: Decontextualising the child client: the efficacy of the attorney-client model for very young children", *Fordham Law Review* 64:1955.

Bakhtin, M. (1981). *The Dialogic Imagination: Four Essays* (trans. C. Emerson and M. Holquist, ed. M. Holquist) (Austin: University of Texas Press).

Bellow, G. and M. Minow (1996) "Introduction: Rita's case and other law stories", in G. Bellow and M. Minow (eds) *Law Stories* (Ann Arbor: University of Michigan Press), 1–30.

Boyden, J. (1990) "Childhood and policy makers: a comparative perspective on the globalisation of childhood", in A. James and A. Prout (eds) *Constructing and Reconstructing Childhood* (London: Falmer Press), 184–216.

Buss, E. (1996). "You're my what?' The problem of children's misperceptions of their lawyers' roles", *Fordham Law Review* 64:1699.

Caputo, V. (1995) "Anthropology's silent 'others'. A consideration of some conceptual and methodological issues for the study of youth and children's cultures", in V. Amit-Talai and H. Wulff (eds) *Youth Cultures: A Cross Cultural Perspective* (London and New York: Routledge).

Clelland, A. (1996) "The Child's right to be heard and represented in legal proceedings", in A. Clelland and E. Sutherland (eds) *Children's Rights in Scotland* (Edinburgh: W. Green/Sweet & Maxwell).

Cobb, S. (1993) "Empowerment and mediation: a narrative perspective", *Negotiation Journal* 9, 245.

—— (1994). "A narrative perspective on mediation: toward the materialisation of the 'storytelling' metaphor in new directions mediation", in J. Folger and T. Jones (eds) *Special Issue of Communication Research and Perspectives*, 48.

Cobb, S. and J. Rifkin (1991) "Practice and paradox: deconstructing neutrality in mediation", *Law and Social Inquiry*, 16, 35.

Cohen, C. (1997) "An introduction to the developing jurisprudence of the rights of the child", 3 ISLA *Journal of International and Comparative Law*, 659.

Cohen, C. and S. Kilbourne (1998) "Jurisprudence of the Committee on the Rights of the Child: a guide for research and analysis", *Michigan Journal of International Law*, 19, 633.

Conley, J. and W. O'Barr (1990). *Rules v Relationships: the Ethnography of Legal Discourse.* (Chicago: University of Chicago Press).

Cover, R. (1983) "The Supreme Court 1982 term—foreword: nomos and narrative", *Harvard Law Review*, 97, 4.

Detrick, S. (1992) *The United Nations Convention on the Rights of the Child: a Guide to the Travaux Préparatoires.* (Netherlands: Martinus Nijoff Publishers).

Dolgin, J. (1997a) "Suffer the children", in J. Dolgin (ed.) *Defining the Family: Law, Technology and Reproduction in an Uneasy* (New York: New York University Press).

—— (1997b) "The fate of childhood: legal models of children and the parent-child relationship", *Albany Law Review*, 61, 345.

Duquette, D. and S. Ramsay (1987) "Representation of children in child abuse and neglect cases: an empirical look at what constitutes effective representation", *University of Michigan Journal of Law Reform*, 20, 341.

Edwards, L. and A. Griffiths (1997) *Family Law* (Edinburgh: W. Green/Sweet & Maxwell).

Federele, K. (1996) "The ethic of empowerment: rethinking the role of lawyers in interviewing and counselling the child client", *Fordham Law Review*, 64, 1655.

Gallagher, R. (1998) *Children and Young People's Voices on the Law, Legal Services, and Systems in Scotland* (Glasgow: Scottish Child Law Centre).

Guggenheim, M. (1996) A paradigm for determining the role of counsel for children", *Fordham Law Review*, 64, 1399.

Hafen, B. and J. Hafen (1996) "Abandoning children to their autonomy: the United Nation Convention on the Rights of the Child", *Harvard Journal of International Law*, 37, 449.

Hallett, C. and C. Murray (1998) *The Evaluation of Children's Hearings in Scotland*, Vols I and II (Edinburgh: The Scottish Office Central Research Unit).

Haralambie, A. (1995) "The role of the child's attorney in protecting the child throughout the litigation process", *North Dakota Law Review*, 71, 939.

Hill, J. and J. Irvine (1993) "Introduction" in J.H. Hill and J.T. Irvine (eds) *Responsibility and Evidence in Oral Discourse* (Cambridge: Cambridge University Press), 1–23.

Hill, J. and O. Zepeda (1993) "Mrs Patricio's trouble: the distribution of responsibility in an account of personal experience", in J.H. Hill and J.T. Irvine (eds) *Responsibility and Evidence in Oral Discourseupra* (Cambridge: Cambridge University Press), 197–225.

Jackson, B. (1988). *Law, Fact, and Narrative Coherence*. (Liverpool: Deborah Charles Press).

Kandel, R. (1994) "Power plays: a socio-linguistic study of inequality in child custody mediation and hearsay analog solution", *Arizona Law Review*, 36, 879.

Kelly, R. and S. Ramsay (1982–83) "Do attorneys for children in Protection Proceedings make a difference? A study of the impact of representation under conditions of high judicial intervention", *Journal of Family Law*, 21, 405–55.

Kelly, R. and S. Ramsay (1985) "Legal and other determinants of effective court intervention in child protection proceedings: a policy analysis", *Journal of Social Research* (2), 25–48.

Kilbrandon, Lord (1964) *Report of the Committee on Children and Young Persons, Scotland*. (Kilbrandon Report), Cmnd 2306 (Edinburgh: , HMSO).

Knitzer, J. and M. Sobie (1984) *Law Gguardians in New York State: a Study of the Legal Representation of Children* (New York: New York State Bar Association).

Lockyer, A. and F. Stone (1998). *Juvenile Justice in Scotland: Ttwenty-five Years of the Welfare Approach* (Edinburgh: T & T Clark).

Mandelbaum, R. (1996) "Responses to the conference: rules of confidentiality when representing children: the need for a 'Bright Line' test", *Fordham Law Review*, 64, 2053.

Margulies, P. (1966) "The lawyer as caregiver: child client's competence in context", *Fordham Law Review*, 64, 1473.

Masson, J. and M. Oakley (1999) *Out of Hearing: Representing Children in Care Proceedings* (Chichester: John Wiley & Sons).

Miller, B. (1994) "Give them back their lives: recognising client's narrative in case theory", *Michigan Law Review*, 93, 485.

Moore, N. (1996) "Conflict of interest in the representation of children", *Fordham Law Review*, 64, 1819.

New York State Bar Association, Committee on Children and the Law (1966) *Law Guardian Representation Standards*.

New York State Bar Association (1991) *Report and Recommendations of the Task Force on the Law Guardian System*.

Norrie, K. (1997) *Children's Hearings in Scotland* (Edinburgh: W. Green/Sweet & Maxwell).

O'Barr, W. (1982) *Linguistic Evidence: Language, Power and Strategy in the Courtroom.*

Ogletree, C. (1966) "Public defender, public friend: searching for the 'best interests' of juvenile offenders", in G. Bellow and M. Minow (eds) Law Stories (Ann Arbor: University of Michigan Press) 131–48.

Peters, J. (1996) "The roles and content of best interest in client-directed lawyering for children in child protective proceedings", *Fordham Law Review,* 64, 1507.

Renteln, A. (1997) "United States Ratification of Human Rights Treaties: who's afraid of the CRC; objections to the Convention on the Rights of the Child", 3 ILSA *Journal of International and Comparative Law,* 629.

Scheppele, K. (1992) "Just the facts ma'am: sexualised violence, evidentiary habits, and the revision of truth", *New York Law School Law Review,* 37, 123.

Shepherd Jr., R. and S. England (1996) "I know the child is my client but who am I?", *Fordham Law Review,* 64, 1917.

Stevens, S. (1995) "Introduction: children and the politics of culture in 'late capitalism', in S. Stevens (ed.) *Children and the Politics of Culture* (Princeton: Princeton University Press).

Sutherland, E. (1996) "The role of the safeguarder", in *Representing Children: Listening to the Voice of the Child* (Glasgow: BBC Children in Need).

Tannen, D. (1989) *Talking Voices: Repetition, Dialogue and Imagery in Conversational Discourse* (Cambridge: Cambridge University Press).

White, L. (1991) "Subordination, rhetorical survival skills, and Sunday shoes: notes on the hearing of Mrs G."*Buffalo Law Review,* 1.

Wu, C. (1996) "Conflicts of interest in the representation of children in dependency cases", *Fordham Llaw Review,* 64, 1857.

10

Family Law-Making and Human Rights in the United Kingdom

CLAIRE ARCHBOLD

INTRODUCTION

U NTIL RECENTLY IN the United Kingdom, the average family lawyer, and especially those who looked at the regulation of adult relationships rather than child law, could survive reasonably well without a detailed knowledge of human rights law. True, there were occasional references to Strasbourg from the "far reaches" of family law; such as in relation to transsexuals' right to marry.[1] However, the average divorce practitioner, family law teacher or policymaker could, most of the time, comfort themselves by assuming that human rights law was something someone else did. When the English Law Commission said in 1989 that "Family law is now largely a law of remedies not rights",[2] few voices were raised in contradiction.

However, increasingly things have changed. In particular, the Human Rights Act 1998 makes the discussion of human rights central to every area of law. The Act, due to come into force in 2000, brings the European Convention on Human Rights into United Kingdom domestic law for the first time, and imposes wide duties on courts and public authorities. However, the European Convention alone does not represent the sum total of human rights law relevant to courts and policy-makers in the UK. For example, the UN Convention on the Rights of the Child, and the Convention on the Elimination of all forms of Discrimination Against Women have both been taken into account in government policy for over a decade. In Northern Ireland, the Belfast Agreement of 1998 and the Northern Ireland Act 1998 place a strong emphasis on human rights and equality as part of the peace-building process, and impose further rights obligations on the institutions of the new devolved administration.

This chapter is not written by a human rights lawyer, but by a family lawyer contemplating the implications of human rights law for her field of work. In line

---

[1] See for example *Rees* v. *UK*, Series A No. 106, 9 EHRR 56; *Cossey* v. *UK*, Series A No. 184, 13 EHRR 622; *B* v. *France*, Series A No. 232–C, 16 EHRR 1; *Sheffield and Horsham* v. *UK*, Case No 31–32/1997/815–816/1106–1019 [1998] 2 FLR 928.

[2] Law Commission No.172, *Family Law: Review of Child Law, Guardianship and Custody* (HMSO, 1988), para. 1.8.

with the theme of this book, it asks what new approaches this increased focus on human rights will require of family law policy-makers in the United Kingdom. The family lawyer seeking to use human rights law can feel a little like someone playing tennis with a baseball bat. There isn't anything wrong with the tool. The problem is rather that it has not been developed for the job for which it is being used. This chapter will explore the possible causes of this perceived poor fit, and ask whether and how it might be possible for family law-makers in the United Kingdom to meaningfully incorporate rights-thinking into their deliberations.

EFFECT OF THE HUMAN RIGHTS ACT 1998 ON DOMESTIC LAW

Although the rights set out in the European Convention on Human Rights and Fundamental Freedoms (hereafter called the Convention Rights) have increasingly been discussed and occasionally applied in the United Kingdom, they have not, until now, formed part of domestic law. The United Kingdom has a dualist constitution,[3] thus treaties ratified by the Government bind only the Government, and a domestic statute must be passed before a treaty can confer rights on individual citizens. Although the United Kingdom was one of the first countries to ratify the European Convention, in 1951,[4] the Convention and its jurisprudence have not been directly enforceable in domestic courts until now. The Convention has been used by the courts as, for example, an aid to interpretation where a statute is ambiguous, but where there is a direct contradiction between the statute and the Convention, national law must prevail, so that even a clear breach of a Convention right might find no remedy in the domestic courts.[5] Courts in the UK are increasingly looking to the Convention as they develop the common law,[6] but the Human Rights Act will require more than this.

The Human Rights Act incorporates the Convention Rights into domestic law, and imposes duties on the executive, legislature and judiciary. Much of the analysis of the Act to date has involved consideration of the shift in constitutional power which it may signal,[7] from the executive (and/or legislature) to the judiciary. The courts are made the arbiters of whether or not existing and new statutes and secondary legislation comply with the Convention Rights, and are required to interpret them to comply where possible.[8] If this is not possible, they may declare a statute incompatible with the Convention, although if Parliament

---

[3] See Wade and Bradley (1985), pp. 00.

[4] 1951, Cmnd 8969.

[5] See for example statements in R v. *Secretary of State for the Home Department, ex parte Bhajan Singh* [1976] QB 198; R v. *Secretary of State for the Home Department, ex parte Phansopkar* [1976] QB 606; *Re Lohrho plc* [1990] AC 154.

[6] See Clapham (1993), p. 4.

[7] See for example, Ewing (1999); Laws (1998).

[8] Human Rights Act 1998, s. 3.

chooses not to reform it, it will remain law.[9] The courts are also given the task of developing the common law in compliance with the Convention Rights.[10] They may declare the actions of public bodies *ultra vires* and unlawful if they contravene the Convention Rights.[11]

However, the Human Rights Act also places new duties directly on the executive. Ministers must make a statement in Parliament that any new statute being introduced complies with the Convention Rights,[12] and have power to use expedited procedures to amend existing or newly made legislation which a court has declared incompatible.[13] Public authorities[14] may not act in a way incompatible with the Convention Rights,[15] and the victim of any resulting unlawful act of a public authority can bring legal proceedings for a remedy, including damages, or rely on the right in any proceedings brought by someone else.[16] Policy-makers will therefore have to assess the human rights implications of policy reforms, both to enable the initial Ministerial statement to be made, and to protect legislative and policy initiatives from later judicial attack.[17] The judicial aspect of the Human Rights Act is likely to be the more public and high profile one, and judicial pronouncements will be key to the successful engrafting of the Convention Rights into domestic law. However, explicit consideration of the Convention Rights by policy-makers and administrators at every stage of policy formulation and execution could have an equally profound, if less public, effect on the law-making process in the United Kingdom.[18] Furthermore, policy-makers will have no time to see how the courts react, but will have to develop their own strategies for incorporating human rights thinking into their work from the outset.

EFFECT OF THE HUMAN RIGHTS ACT ON FAMILY LAW— A CRISIS-MANAGEMENT APPROACH

One way for policy-makers to approach the Act might be to ask simply whether any aspects of United Kingdom family law at present breach the Convention

[9] Ibid., s. 4.
[10] Human Rights Act 1998, s. 2. This is achieved by requiring the courts to take the Convention Rights into account when coming to a decision (see comment by the Lord Chancellor, Lord Irvine of Lairg that "we believe that it is right as a matter of principle for the courts to have the duty of acting compatibly with the Convention . . . in developing the common law in deciding cases between individuals" Hansard, HL Deb. 24th November 1997, Col. 771). It means that the Convention Rights will be relevant not only in relation to actions by State bodies, but in every legal dispute, including those between private individuals. Hunt (1998a) describes this as "indirect horizontal effect" of the Convention Rights.
[11] Human Rights Act 1998, ss. 7–9.
[12] Ibid., s. 19.
[13] Ibid., s. 10.
[14] Defined in s.6(3) to include a court or tribunal and any person "certain of whose functions are of a public nature".
[15] Human Rights Act 1998, s. 6.
[16] Ibid., ss. 7, 8.
[17] Ryle (1994).
[18] As it is said to have had in New Zealand. See Taggart (1998).

Rights. The Government White Paper *Rights Brought Home*,[19] which preceded the introduction of the Human Rights Act 1998 acknowledged that United Kingdom law in relation to the equal rights of spouses within marriage breaches Article 5 of Protocol 7 to the Convention, which the UK is therefore unable to ratify. Rights Brought Home proclaims the Government's intention of bringing the law into line with the Protocol and ratifying it.[20]

Three technical rules of family property law breach the Protocol.[21] The first is the husband's common law duty to maintain his wife,[22] the second is the law relating to ownership of housekeeping money, which differs according to whether the money was provided by the husband or the wife,[23] and the third is the presumption of advancement, which infers that a transfer of property by a man to his wife or child is intended as a gift.[24] Transfers by a woman to her husband or child are not presumed to be a gift,[25] the presumption of resulting trust,[26] which applies in all cases but that of husband to wife or child, infers that she intends to retain an interest in the property.

This example of identifying narrow, technical rules, which expressly contradict the Convention, illustrates that the exercise is necessary, but alone is inadequate to meet the challenge of the Human Rights Act. A narrow "crisis management" approach which responded only by making specific, narrow reforms when existing or proposed law was found to be in direct conflict with the Convention Rights would not encourage thinking throughout the field of family law to become human rights-sensitive. Such an approach is also likely to take a legalistic view of the Convention Rights, construing them as if they are

[19] Cmnd 3782 (HMSO, 1997).

[20] Ibid., at paras. 4.14–4.17.

[21] Parliamentary Question, Lord Lester of Herne Hill, *Hamsard*, HL Debs, 31 March 1999, Col. WA 71.

[22] The rule is essentially rendered obsolete by subsequent reciprocal statutory duties to maintain (Domestic Proceedings and Magistrates' Courts Act 1978, s.1, Matrimonial Causes Act 1973, s. 27), but still exists. See comments of Ward J. in *Re C (A Minor) (Contribution Notice)* [1994] 1 FLR 111, at 116 that "there may be a so-called common law duty to maintain, but when one analyses what that duty is it seems effectively to come to nothing . . . [there is] no remedy", quoted in Cretney and Masson (1997), p. 83.

[23] Savings from an allowance made by a husband to a wife and any proceeds of them, such as lottery winnings, belong jointly to both spouses (Married Women's Property Act 1964, s. 1). The statute does not extend to Northern Ireland, where the common law rule giving ownership of the savings and proceeds to the husband alone still applies (see *Blackwell* v. *Blackwell* [1943] 2 All ER 579; *Hoddinott* v. Hoddinott [1949] 2 KB 406). In both jurisdictions, where the allowance is paid by a wife to a husband, the rebuttable presumption of resulting trust means that the savings or their proceeds will be inferred to belong solely to the wife.

[24] *Silver* v. *Silver* [1958] 1 WLR 259. Even in 1958, Lord Evershed felt it possible to say that the rule subsisted "even though in this day and age one may feel that the presumption is more easily capable of rebuttal" (at p. 261).

[25] Cretney and Masson (1997) note that the presumption has never been applied to a wife-to-husband or mother-to-child transfer (n. 33, p. 130).

[26] As a result of the equitable doctrine of resulting trust, a rebuttable presumption that where one person provides all or part of the money to purchase something in the name of someone else, he or she will be entitled in equity to a share in the property proportionate to the amount of the contribution (see Cretney and Masson (1997), pp. 128–9).

statutory provisions with exact, fixed meanings. This legalistic approach is anti-
thetical to the way in which lawyers reason in the civil law world, in which the
Convention jurisprudence has its roots, and in the common law world too, judicial authorities have counselled against it. The Privy Council, in *Terence
Thornhill v. Attorney General of Trinidad and Tobago*[27] warned against construing statements of broad general principles protecting rights and freedoms as
if they were statutes, whether in Commonwealth Constitutions or in the
European Convention.

Such a narrow, legalistic approach does not do justice to either the difficulties
or the opportunities inherent in really looking at how the principles, as well as
the substance, of United Kingdom family law might be affected by the spirit and
the letter of human rights law. Before considering whether, and how the in-
depth incorporation of human rights thinking into the family law-making
process might occur, it will be useful to consider some aspects of each in turn.

WHAT RIGHTS ARE UNDER DISCUSSION?

To step into the debate about rights is to confront "a bewildering disarray of
issues and opinions",[28] which could easily overwhelm the lesser concerns of this
chapter. However, the views which family lawyers take of rights discourse more
generally is one factor which contributes to the tensions between the operation
of the jurisprudence of the European Convention on Human Rights and the
thinking of family lawyers and policy-makers in the United Kingdom.

The word "right" may refer to one of a number of categories of claim. At the
highest level of generalisation, a right may be described as a justified claim to the
protection of a person's important interests.[29] The justification may come from
law, morals, rules or other norms. Legal rights are claims which are legally
enforceable because they are accepted as law. Advocates of natural rights hold
that they exist independently of any human institution, but arise from basic reasons for action and basic human goods.[30] The categories of rights overlap, and
human rights may be seen to be both natural rights and legal rights. They are
generally interpreted as deriving their imperative nature from the inherent dignity of every human being,[31] although positivists might see them as deriving it
from the fact that they have been identified and set out in national or international documents having legal effect.

---

[27] [1980] 2 WLR 510.
[28] Halpin (1997), p. 105.
[29] Honderich (1995), p. 777.
[30] Ibid., pp. 606–7.
[31] The Preamble to the Universal Declaration of Human Rights (1948) states that " . . . recognition of the inherent dignity and the equal and inalienable rights of all members of the human family is the foundation of freedom, justice and peace in the world". Article 1 goes on to state that "All
human beings are born free and equal in dignity and rights".

The European Convention on Human Rights is far from the full sum of human rights law. It contains mainly first-generation human rights; the civil and political liberties which it was felt important to protect after the grave human rights abuses of World War II. Civil and political rights are usually phrased in negative ways—the State is to refrain from interfering with the liberty of the individual. More recent developments in international human rights law have involved rights which place a positive obligation on the State, for example to provide basic education and health care to its citizens,[32] rights commonly referred to as second- and third-generation rights. Some of the Convention rights are expressed in terms of positive obligation on the State,[33] and the Strasbourg jurisprudence has developed others to include a duty to act,[34] but the primary obligation remains negative.

Another important characteristic of the Convention is that it is primarily concerned with the protection of the individual against abuse of his or her rights by the State. In the language of the Convention, the rights have vertical effect, but not horizontal effect; they produce no actionable obligations on individuals in their dealings with others.[35] This feature is carried through into the Human Rights Act, which imposes its duties on "public authorities".

Criticism of the European Convention is well-summarised in the words of the Irish poet Justin Quinn, who writes, of human rights more generally:

> ". . . you associate [it] with the 1940s and 50s,
> When the world was a better place, and Ma
> was not your Da in drag (like now)
> and men in suits met in high-ceilinged rooms to
> say that there are rights, that there are
> human rights . . ."[36]

Quinn's poem in its entirety deals with nostalgia for the black-and-white certainties of the post-war era which yet cannot provide answers to the complexities and inhumanities of modern life. Legal scholars voice their criticisms in sometimes more prosaic terms. The beneficiary of the Convention may be imagined as an individual standing alone against the State, protected by his or her rights in the exercise of his or her free choices. It has been argued that thinking primarily in terms of liberal first-generation rights can result in the citizen being seen as a contextless, atomised individual.[37] Glendon argues that the "intemperate rhetoric of personal liberty" in the United States has led to the creation of

---

[32] International Covenant on Economic, Social and Cultural Rights, UN 1965, Arts. 12–14.

[33] For example, the right to respect for private and family life in Article 8(1) ECHR.

[34] For example, in the *Belgian Linguistics (No. 2) case* [1979–80] 1 EHRR 252, the European Court held that the citizen's right not to be denied an education in Protocol 1, Article 1 ECHR in some circumstances includes a duty on the State to provide an education.

[35] Although the fact that all laws must be compatible with the Convention Rights does give it an "indirect horizontal effect", as described by Hunt (1998).

[36] From Quinn (1998).

[37] Cossman (1990).

"a generation of lone rights-bearers",[38] and feminist critics have identified the rights holder of first-generation rights and the mechanisms for enforcing those rights as confrontational, hierarchical and distinctively male concepts.[39]

As already mentioned, the Convention is not the total of human rights law, nor did it stop developing in 1951. It is a theme of the Strasbourg jurisprudence, and of commentary on it, that the Convention is a living instrument, and must be interpreted in the light of modern conditions.[40] Other Conventions to which the UK is a signatory also bring into the debate second- and third-generation human rights, such as the rights to be fed, clothed, housed and educated,[41] which feminist scholars argue reflect a female way of seeing oneself within a web of community to which one has responsibilities, rather than in contradistinction to a society against which one has rights.[42] Some critics doubt the achievability of these rights, including Freeman, who, speaking in relation to children's rights, says that "many references to . . . rights turn out on inspection to be aspirations for the accomplishment of particular social or moral goals".[43] Steiner is one of many who argue that the late twentieth century has seen an over-extensive invocation of rights,[44] which can lead to a devaluation in their currency.

THE EUROPEAN CONVENTION AND THE FAMILY

Before asking how family lawyers see the Convention, it is worth asking how the European Convention sees the family. Article 8(1) protects the individual's right to respect for his or her family and private life, home and correspondence. The close linkage between family life and privacy[45] is reinforced by the fact that Article 8(2) forbids the State to interfere without justification with the four protected spheres. Furthermore, respect will itself often consist of non-interference, although it may occasionally require positive action.[46] The definition of the family in the European Convention is autonomous and freestanding, and the right to family life of both de jure and de facto families is protected.[47] The range

---

[38] Glendon (1991).

[39] Binion (1995).

[40] Jacobs (1975), p. 18 says that "The Convention must be interpreted in the light of developments in society and political attitudes. Its effects cannot be confined to the concepts of the period when it was drafted."

[41] International Covenant on Economic, Social and Cultural Rights 1965, Arts. 11–14.

[42] Binion (1995), p.525 credits Gilligan (1982) with this insight. See also Stark (1996); Brems (1997); Higgins (1996); Bunting (1993).

[43] Freeman (1983), p. 37.

[44] Steiner (1998), p. 233.

[45] O'Donnell (1995).

[46] For example, in effectively enforcing the right of an estranged parent to access in *Hokkanen* v. *Finland* Series A No. 299–A, 19 EHRR 139.

[47] *Keegan* v. *Ireland*, Series A No. 290, 18 EHRR 342 (unmarried father no longer living with mother has family life with his child); *Marckx* v. *Belgium*, Series A No. 31, [1979] 2 EHRR 330 (unmarried mother and her child); *Kroon* v. *Netherlands*, Series A No. 297–C 19 EHRR 263 (father of child conceived during extra-marital affair with the mother).

of relationships regarded as familial is increasing; the family life of a female-to-male transsexual living with a woman and children conceived by artificial insemination to whom he was the social father has been recognised.[48]

However, the Strasbourg institutions seem to base their conception of family very much on relationships which are distinctively marriage-like or capable of leading to marriage. Homosexual relationships do not fall within the Strasbourg definitions of family life, although they are protected as "private life",[49] and nor do transsexuals have a right to marry[50] under the Convention. More generally, like other international conventions, the European Convention leaves signatories a wide margin of appreciation as regards which family forms are accepted as legitimate. Although the Court did undertake some "trail-blazing" work in relation to homosexuality,[51] Feldman suggests that it has recently "been rather too tender towards the claims of States to institutionalise dominant moralities",[52] and it is possible that rather than providing a coherent, rights-based focus for developments at the boundaries of family law in the United Kingdom in the near future, the Court and Commission may simply reflect back the status quo of national law.

Family Law and the Language of Rights

The chapter has already alluded to the tensions between the Convention and family lawyers in the United Kingdom in the late 1990s, and the time has come to explore the elements of family law which give rise to these.[53] First and most obvious is the fact that, more perhaps than in any other area of law, modern family lawyers sees themselves as applying "people law". Atkin and Austin, writing in New Zealand, suggest that family lawyers claim their subject to be free of ideology, and that the subject is dominated by "the theme that it is a peculiarly human branch of the law which responds humanely to individual human problems".[54] This is an attractive insight, encompassing both the claims of family judges that what they are doing is just "common sense", and the extent of "multiculturalism" in family law, where the legal system has either subsumed or been colonised by extra-legal forms of thought and practice, particularly from the social and "psy" sciences.

---

[48] *X, Y and Z* v. *United Kingdom*, Application No. 21522/93, [1997] 2 FLR 892.

[49] *X and Y* v. *United Kingdom*, Application No. 9369.81, 32 D and R 220 (1981).

[50] *Rees* v. *UK*, Series A No. 106, 9 EHRR 56.

[51] Notably refusing to accept the blanket criminalisation of homosexual acts as necessary to protect public morality in Northern Ireland in *Dudgeon* v. *United Kingdom*, Series A No. 59 5 EHRR 573; in the Republic of Ireland in *Norris* v. *Ireland*, Series A No. 142, 13 EHRR 186.

[52] Feldman (1997).

[53] The tensions perhaps arise primarily in the common law world. As Encarna Roca has kindly reminded me, lawyers in civil law jurisdictions start from rights and argue towards remedies, not the other way around.

[54] Atkin and Austin (1998); p. 305.

Gibson has contrasted "family law thinking" with the closed-off formalism of equity or land law. She expresses the characteristics of family law thinking well when she says:

"When all is said and done, we are simply not willing to hear that a judge has narrowed his or her consideration of a child's domestic welfare down to the one or two telling facts which would allow comparison of one case with another by juridical analogy . . . We don't want them to because this is the kind of problem about which we expect them to think purposively, not juridically."[55]

Dealing with the chaotic lives of individuals, the law claims to be driven by concrete policy objectives rather than by legal doctrine or overt ideology. This "therapeutic liberalism" of United Kingdom family law wavers uneasily between the liberal desire to allow the family to be self-governing and the belief that therapeutic interventions by third parties, such as mediators, health visitors, counsellors and educators, can make things better for families in crisis.[56]

Clearly, no law is without ideology; but the non-ideological claims and mixed influences of modern family law mean that its philosophical underpinnings are hidden, and often confused. Dewar's richly descriptive phrase "the normal chaos of family law" describes the result:

"Family law . . . is contradictory, disordered, incoherent, and in part at least, antinomic. In saying this, I am not diagnosing a crisis of any sort. Indeed, I want to suggest that this is a perfectly normal state of affairs; normal, because family law engages with areas of social life and feeling . . . that are themselves riven with contradiction or paradox . . ."[57]

Parker[58] identifies two themes running through developments in United Kingdom and Australian family law which are useful in identifying the tensions in policy-making. He suggests that until the advent of the era of mass divorce, after World War II, family law was a relatively traditional legal subject, based on rights of individuals enforced through an adversarial system. The system which replaced it, based largely on judicial discretion, was oriented towards questions of welfare and the allocation of scarce-resources, rather than the enforcing of rights. Parker suggests that the rights-based approach he describes[59] will give priority to the liberty of individuals to pursue their own conception of the good life and will give their pre-existing rights priority over the good of the community. The ethic which replaced it[60] is a utilitarian, welfare-based one which primarily has regard to the consequences of legal decisions, and which may tend to judge cases according to a particular conception

[55] Gibson (1994), p. 218.
[56] As exemplified by the Government Consultation Paper *Supporting Families* (The Stationery Office, November 1998).
[57] Dewar (1998).
[58] Parker (1992).
[59] Described by Parker (1992) as deontological liberalism.
[60] Described by Parker (1992) as teleological liberalism.

of the good life. He argues persuasively that from the late 1980s, a "normative anarchy"[61] can be seen in family policy in England and Australia, with both rights and utility being given some scope. The tension is very clear in the Children Act 1989, which draws heavily on the idea of children's rights and the UN Convention on the Rights of the Child, but draws back from unequivocal statements of rights, for example the child's right to be heard in proceedings concerning him or her,[62] where that might prejudice the principle that the child's welfare is to be paramount.[63]

The arguments as to if and when the liberal state should intervene in the family are inevitably bound up in the public/private dichotomy. Family law in liberal states exists at, defines, and is defined by the boundaries between privacy of the family unit and interference with it by a public power. The classical opposition in liberal societies between the altruistic, relational, yet patriarchal Gemeinschaft of the private family sphere, wherein law has no place and the contract-based, self-interested, arms-length dealing of the Gesellschaft public sphere,[64] which is law's domain, are too well-known to require further exposition. The accuracy of the distinction and the location of the boundaries have been questioned,[65] and the pre-legal nature of the private sphere has been called into question by feminist and other critical scholars, who point out that the private sphere is defined by the very laws which refuse to enter its domain.[66] These critics also emphasise the fact that the private sphere can be for many, particularly women and children, a place of oppression and injustice, out of law's reach.[67] For present purposes, however, the importance of the public/private divide is its central place in family law discourse rather than its accuracy. It is particularly significant given the oft-cited theme of "privatising the family" seen in Britain and elsewhere over the past twenty-five years,[68] by encouraging family members themselves[69] to take responsibility for each other and for managing transitional moments in their relationships.

The pertinent characteristics of family law debate identified so far are that it characterises itself as pragmatic, purposive and non-ideological. Behind this smokescreen, one of the major trends in modern family law, at least in the common law world, is that policies have been driven by a welfarist, consequential-

---

[61] Described by Parker (1992) as teleological liberalism, p. 325.

[62] UN Convention on the Rights of the Child, Article 12.

[63] The principle states that any judicial decision about the child must make his or her welfare the paramount consideration. Children Act 1989, s. 1.

[64] See Olsen (1983) and O'Donovan (1993)

[65] Eekelaar (1989).

[66] As Romany (1993) points out "The public/private dichotomy, by ignoring the political character of power unequally distributed in family life, obscures the political nature of so-called private life. The dichotomy clouds the fact that the domestic arena is itself created by the political realm where the state reserves the right to intervene" (p. 101).

[67] Dingwall (1994), p. 57.

[68] See Maclean and Kurczewski (1994).

[69] Diduck (1995) makes the useful comment that the State finds it easiest to intervene in "deviant" families, leaving those which adhere to the norm without encouragement to manage their own affairs.

ist ethic. However, the welfarist drive is held in check by a liberal belief in the privacy of the family, and a reluctance to interfere without justification in this private sphere, whether by individual therapeutic intervention or by the ascription of legal rights to family members. The language of rights is sometimes used, in both historic and modern family law, particularly in recent "privatising" reforms, but increasingly creates tension and confusion with what may still be seen as the dominant welfare discourses.

The reluctance to impose strongly-worded legal rights within the "black box" of the family may contain another element in addition to a disinclination at the level of theory. The grant of a right infers the imposition of a duty on someone, and duties on family members, especially while the family is intact, will be difficult to enforce. Furthermore, the imposition of rights, especially strongly-worded, emotive human rights, in complex family situations may give rise to situations where rights conflict, and render difficult decisions even more complex. These considerations, whether justified or not, may fuel a gut-feeling of squeamishness on the part of many common law family lawyers when discussing rights. Justice Albie Sachs puts it thus:

"I find increasingly the concept of rights in relation to family law incongruous. If rights are understood as that little bit of space and it is my space, whether in relation to property or in relation to a person, they just do not correspond to and describe what is going on. We are dealing with relationships . . . and these relationships are constantly in flux in a way that rights based on a property concept or defensible space are not."[70]

The argument so far has been at perhaps an unduly theoretical level. In ascertaining whether or not it is reasonable, as well as in order to find a way forward, it will be necessary to consider some concrete examples.

The European Convention and Corporal Punishment of Children

Corporal punishment of children has been the subject of progressive reforms over the past twenty years in the United Kingdom, impelled each time by critical decisions in Strasbourg. Flogging as a criminal punishment was abolished in the United Kingdom in 1967, except for the Isle of Man, where youths could be sentenced to be "birched", a form of caning, for minor criminal offences. In *Tyrer* v. *United Kingdom*,[71] the European Court held that this constituted degrading treatment within Article 3 of the Convention, and the practice of birching as part of the State criminal justice system was stopped. Cases followed regarding corporal punishment in State schools,[72] and in private schools to

---

[70] Sachs (1998), p.xviii.
[71] Series A No. 26 (1978) 2 EHRR 1
[72] *Campbell and Cosens* v. *UK*, Series A No. 48 (1982) 4 EHRR 293 held that the exclusion of their children from school, because the parents would not permit them to receive corporal punishment, with which they disagreed, was a breach of the parents rights to have their children educated in conformity with their philosophical convictions under Article 1(2) of Protocol 1.

which the State had delegated its duty to educate the children under the school's care.[73]

In all these cases, the message from Europe was clear; corporal punishment was contrary to the Convention. This European case law was a direct cause of the prohibition of corporal punishment in the Education (No.2) Act 1986,[74] which applied both to State schools and to independent schools which received an element of public funding and provided government assisted places. Purely independent schools were forbidden to administer punishment which could be described as "inhuman or degrading treatment" in 1993,[75] and the complete abolition of corporal punishment in all schools was finally achieved in 1998.[76] A State-registered childminder may now only smack a child if the parent has given their consent.[77] The State or its agents cannot be involved in a practice which breaches the child's or parents' rights under the Convention. Within the private sphere of the home, however, it is a different matter, and corporal punishment which does not go beyond "reasonable chastisement" can still be administered to a child.

Thus far, the case law illustrates clearly the doctrine that the Convention Rights impose duties on the State but not on individuals. However, the most recent European case, in which the UK was held in breach of its obligations to protect a boy who had been subject to a series of beatings with a cane by his stepfather,[78] begins to make inroads into corporal punishment within the family. The jury in the domestic criminal prosecution of the stepfather had acquitted him, accepting his defence of lawful chastisement, and none of the public bodies who had been aware of the beatings (including the boy's school and local social workers) had intervened successfully. The case is important firstly because it imposes a positive duty on the State to protect the individual from violation of his or her rights by another private person, and secondly because in so doing it indirectly imposes duties to respect at least some human rights on private individuals.

Public opinion on corporal punishment is divided in the United Kingdom, and Government press releases at the time of the European Court's judgment recognised this, emphasising the excessiveness of the stepfather's response in the *A* case, and stating that "reasonable" chastisement such as a slap with an open hand were not covered by the ruling.[79]

---

[73] In *Costello-Roberts* v. *UK*, Series A No. 247–C (1994) 19 EHRR 112 the European Court did not find the practice of "slippering" a pupil at a private school to breach the boy's rights under Article 3, but was concerned that corporal punishment continued in British schools. See also *Warwick* v. *UK* (1986) 60 D and R 5 and *Y* v. *UK*, Series A No. 247–A, (1992) 17 EHRR 238.

[74] Education (No.2) Act 1986, ss. 47 and 48.

[75] Education Act 1993, re-enacted as Education Act 1996, ss. 548–9.

[76] School Standards and Framework Act 1998.

[77] Guidelines to this effect were issued in December 1994 (*The Times*, 3rd December 1994), following the case of *London Borough of Sutton* v. *Davis* [1994] 1 FLR 737. See Fortin (1999).

[78] *A* v. *UK* (human rights: punishment of child) [1998] 2 FLR 959.

[79] Department of Health press release, 23 September 1998, quoted in Fortin (1999) at p. 361.

On one reading, the effect of the European litigation on corporal punishment is a good news story.[80] Intervention from Strasbourg led to incremental law reform, and may be leading to changes in how corporal punishment is viewed (at least by the chattering classes). Politically, however, the case and its aftermath show the difficulty of imposing human rights norms which may be seen as contrary to the community norms of a given society.[81] Views on corporal punishment in the UK are not uniform. For example, although 91 percent of interviewees in a 1992 survey by the Scottish Law Commission thought that beating a nine-year-old child with a belt or stick was wrong, 87 percent believed that it was right to smack the same child with an open hand.[82]

The UN Committee on the Rights of the Child[83] has criticised the ongoing failure to prohibit corporal punishment of children in the UK, which it found to be in breach not only of the European Convention, but also of Article 19 of the UN Convention on the Rights of the Child.[84] This criticism was dwelt on by the European Commission on Human Rights in *A v. UK*. The matter is said to be the subject of a forthcoming government Consultation Paper, which both Barton[85] and Fortin[86] predict will result in partial reform, perhaps in terms of a defined standard of reasonable chastisement, and in subsequent confusion, but not in abolition.

The issue provides a good example of some of the theoretical tensions discussed above, particularly in contrasting the position in relation to corporal punishment in the home and by public bodies such as schools. Although corporal punishment by the State and its agents is outlawed, it is much harder, both practically and theoretically to prohibit it within the family. In practical terms, the boy in *A v. UK* may in part have been able to bring his case only because his natural father, who was estranged from his mother, knew and disapproved of the beatings administered by his stepfather. Otherwise his right would have been effectively nugatory. In theoretical terms, the unwillingness of policy-makers to prohibit corporal punishment in the home against the wishes of many in the country, despite its prohibition in schools, illustrates a queasiness explicable in terms of the public/private divide.

---

[80] Although Barton (1999) notes that the almost exclusively British contribution to the jurisprudence would be a source of shame to some.

[81] Bainham (1995).

[82] Scottish Law Commission Report on Family Law (SLC No. 135) (1992), para.2.101.

[83] Concluding Observations of the Committee on the Rights of the Child; United Kingdom of Great Britain and Northern Ireland CRC/C/15/Add 34 Centre for Human Rights, Geneva, January 1995, para. 16, quoted by Fortin (1999).

[84] Article 19(1) states that "States parties shall take all appropriate legislative, administrative, social and educational measures to protect the child from all forms of physical . . . violence . . . while in the care of parents, legal guardians or any other person who has care of the child".

[85] Op. cit., n. 38.

[86] Op. cit., n. 34.

The European Convention and Unmarried Parents

The other difficulties, that of the conflict between rights and welfare, and that of conflicting human rights of family members, are illustrated by another current policy issue; the position of unmarried fathers. When considering the ending of illegitimacy in 1979,[87] the Law Commission argued that the only way to end discrimination against illegitimate children was to end the discrimination against their fathers. The Children Order 1989 provided that unmarried fathers could for the first time obtain parental responsibility for their children, by agreement with the mother or by application to the court.[88] In 1998, the Lord Chancellor's Department proposed[89] a further step; that unmarried fathers in England and Wales whose names appear on the child's birth certificate should have automatic parental responsibility. This would create a statutory presumption of paternity for (inter alia) Child Support purposes. The Scottish Law Commission considered the matter in its 1992 *Report on Family Law*,[90] and recommended that both parents should have parental responsibility whether or not they are married, subject to a court order to the opposite effect. The matter is being considered in Northern Ireland at present.

In relation to England and Wales, the Lord Chancellor's Department took the view that the current law complies with Articles 8 and 14. It said:

> "The wide range of types of relationship outside marriage means that the interests of the child and mother have to be protected. The law gives this protection while still permitting the unmarried father to acquire parental responsibility by agreement or court order."[91]

Article 8 of the Convention requires the State to respect (inter alia) the family life of individuals. The term "family life" has an autonomous meaning within the Convention. It will be presumed to exist in the case of the married family, but people in other situations may proceed if they can prove the existence of family life. In the case of *X, Y and Z* v. *United Kingdom*,[92] in which one party was a transsexual, the European Court set down a useful test for its existence:

> "When deciding whether a relationship can be said to amount to 'family life', a number of factors may be relevant, including whether the couple live together, the length of their relationship, and whether they have demonstrated their commitment to each other by having children together or by any other means."

---

[87] Working Paper No. 74, *Family Law and Illegitimacy* (HMSO, 1979).

[88] Children Act 1989, s. 4.

[89] Lord Chancellor's Department Consultation Paper, *Procedures for the Determination of Paternity and on the Law on Parental Responsibility for Unmarried Fathers* (1998).

[90] Scottish Law Commission No.135 (The Stationery Office, Edinburgh, 1992).

[91] Lord Chancellor's Department Consultation Paper, *Procedures for the Determination of Paternity and on the Law on Parental Responsibility for Unmarried Fathers* (1998), para. 62.

[92] Application No.21830/93, 24 EHRR 143.

The Court has also held that an unmarried couple who are no longer together, or who may not have lived together, may still have or have had a family life with their children.[93] In *Keegan* v. *Ireland*,[94] an unmarried father had lived with the child's mother before the birth, and planned to marry her. The relationship ended before the birth and the father paid one visit to see the child at the hospital. Although he had no further contact with the child, the European Court found that he had a family life with the child, and that the State had failed to respect it when it failed to require his consent to the child's adoption.

Family life exists for unmarried fathers. The fact that they do not have parental responsibility discriminates against them within Article 14, as compared to married fathers, or to unmarried mothers. However, this discrimination will not contravene the Convention if the difference in treatment has an objective and reasonable justification. The questions asked by the Court in *Geillustreede Pers NV* v. *The Netherlands*[95] provide a useful framework for discussion of the relevant concepts of legitimacy of purpose and proportionality. The court in *Geillustreerde Pers* suggested that in ascertaining whether there was discrimination, the following questions should be asked:

1. Do the facts disclose a differential treatment?
2. Does the distinction have an aim—an objective and reasonable justification having regard to the aim and the effects of the measure under consideration?
3. Is there reasonable proportionality between the means employed and the aim sought to be realised?

In a recent domestic case, *Re W: Re B (Child Abduction: Unmarried Father)*[96] Hale J. reviewed the human rights case law on this topic, and concluded:

"no case has yet held that all the differences between mothers and fathers, or between married and unmarried fathers, are contrary to the Convention. There may come a time when the Parliament of this country, having considered the policy matters further, decides to eliminate those differences . . . But in my view that time has not yet come."

The two most relevant cases from Europe are *Marckx* v. *Belgium*[97] and *McMichael* v. *United Kingdom*.[98] In the former case, an unmarried Belgian mother and her infant daughter claimed that the State had breached their rights under Articles 8 and 14 because, unlike a married mother, she had no automatic legal bond with her daughter, but had to execute a formal deed of recognition. Even with this deed, her daughter was still disadvantaged in terms of inheritance rights on intestacy from her mother's side. The Court reiterated that the right to respect for family life applied to "illegitimate" as well as "legitimate" families.

---

[93] *Kroon* v. *Netherlands* Series A No. 297–C (1995) 19 EHRR 263.
[94] Series A No. 290, 18 EHRR 342.
[95] Commission Decision of 6/7/76, D and R 8/1977.
[96] [1998] 2 FLR 146.
[97] Series A No. 31 [1979] 2 EHRR 330.
[98] Series A No. 308, 20 EHRR 205.

The duty of respect imposed on the State could be more than a mere duty not to interfere—it could require the State to take positive steps. The fact that the act of recognition was not especially onerous did not detract from the fact that it was the State's failure to recognise the maternal relationship which made it necessary. Finally, and importantly in this context, the Court said:

> "In the court's judgement, the fact that some unmarried mothers, unlike Paula Marckx, do not wish to take care of their child cannot justify the rule of Belgian law whereby the establishment of their maternity is conditional on voluntary recognition or a court declaration . . . As the Commission points out, it may happen that also a married mother might not wish to bring up her child, and yet, as far as she is concerned, the birth alone will have created the bond of affiliation."[99]

The case of *McMichael* deals with the position of the unmarried father. The main issue in the case was in relation to the disclosure of documents in proceedings to free the applicant's child for adoption. However, the father also complained that his rights had been violated by reason of his initial lack of rights[100] in respect either of custody or of standing in the care proceedings preceding the adoption proceedings. The court unanimously found that there had been no violation of Articles 8 and 14 in this regard. The justification is the same as that for the proposed new English reform:

> . . . the aim of the relevant legislation, which was enacted in 1986, is to provide a mechanism for identifying meritorious fathers who might be accorded parental rights, thereby protecting the interests of the child and the mother."[101]

Branchflower has criticised the decision in *McMichael* on several grounds.[102] The Court did not carry out a full analysis of the justification for the clear differential position of unmarried fathers. There is a bald statement[103] that "The conditions . . . respect the principle of proportionality", but this is not expanded upon. In addition to seeming to say that the Convention Rights are only available to those who deserve them, the judgment is at odds with the finding in *Marckx* that there should be no discrimination between married and unmarried mothers on the ground of "unmeritoriousness". Finally, the case does not test whether the rights of the child were breached under the Convention. Marckx found that the fact that she was legally motherless for a period of thirteen days, until the declaration was made was a breach of the child's rights under Article 8, and the requirement of a declaration also violated her rights under Articles 8 and 14.

These arguments, especially the incompatibility with *Marckx*,[104] are persuasive. It is certainly arguable that the question of whether the mother is prepared

---

[99] [1979] 2 EHRR 330, para. 39.
[100] The statute governing the situation was the Law Reform (Parent and Child)(Scotland) Act 1986.
[101] [1995] 20 EHRR 205, para. 98.
[102] Branchflower (1999).
[103] [1995] 20 EHRR 205, para. 98.
[104] Although there is no system of binding precedent in civil law jurisdictions, and the Convention follows this tradition.

to allow the father to put his name on the birth certificate is not a failsafe method of testing his merit as a father. It particularly disadvantages those men whose relationship with the child's mother has ended acrimoniously, but who want to remain part of their child's life out of love for him or her.

Three classes of difficult case spring to mind. The first is the mother who wishes her child to live free from the shadow of a father who is a rapist, or a violent and vengeful former partner. The second is the father kept from a relationship with his child by an implacably and unreasonably hostile mother. The third is the child, whose right to know both parents, and to be safe from harm, may be in opposition to their parents' rights.

This is the key to the dilemma of the paternity proposals. Articles 8 and 14 do not give immediate answers as to what is to happen where family members' rights conflict. The solution in Strasbourg is to return to a welfare rationale. The European Court,[105] like the English courts[106] gives priority to the best interests of the child over the rights of the parents, illustrating perhaps that any analysis of an individual case solely in rights terms must be only partial, if the debate is not to degenerate into the unreasoning brawling of two opposed litigants, each shouting "I know my rights!". Eekelaar puts it more elegantly when he says:

". . . within families, the idea of justice is particularly complex . . . [it was and is] difficult to apply principles within families which are usually associated with justice between individuals such as giving each person his or her due, or treating each person on a basis of equality. This is because wider interests are seen to be at stake."[107]

BEYOND THE HUMAN RIGHTS ACT—EQUALITY AND
HUMAN RIGHTS

So far, this chapter has explored some of the possible reasons for the tensions perceived between family law and human rights law. Family law claims to be ideology-free, yet the "therapeutic liberalism" of modern family law may be seen to have strong welfarist presumptions, as well as sometimes using the language of rights, as the State tries to determine how far it is proper to intrude into what is seen as the privileged private sphere of the family. For family law-makers trying to navigate between these competing priorities, as well as those of cost and resources, the addition of the Convention Rights to the list of matters to which they are to have regard may seem an onerous duty. This chapter has considered some of the difficulties inherent in a serious attempt to come to terms with the implications of the Convention rights for family law. However, it may be easier to develop a way forward for family law-makers by taking a step back from the Human Rights Act and considering another recent United Kingdom statute, in relation to Northern Ireland.

[105] *Johanssen* v. *Norway*, Application No. 17383/90, 23 EHRR 33.
[106] *Re KD (A Minor)(Ward: Termination of Access)* [1988] AC 806.
[107] Eekelaar (1994).

The Belfast Agreement of Good Friday 1998 placed strong emphasis on human rights, in particular as a way of ensuring parity of esteem, cultural and group rights for the various communities represented in the negotiations. The Northern Ireland Act 1998 brings into effect the main planks of the Belfast Agreement. In addition to providing for the usual institutions of government, it also provides for the setting up of a Human Rights Commission[108] and an Equality Commission,[109] and sets out the human rights parameters within which the institutions of the new Northern Ireland will have to work. The Assembly can only pass legislation which is compatible with the Convention rights,[110] but the Human Rights Commission has the power to comment on pending legislation from a wider human rights perspective,[111] and furthermore has the duty to advise the Secretary of State as to the development of a Bill of Rights for Northern Ireland,[112] to be enshrined in Westminster legislation, which will be additional to the Convention Rights.[113] This is likely to include second and third-generation rights, and will bring new dimensions of human rights considerations in law reform and policy-making discussions in the jurisdiction.

More particularly, public authorities in Northern Ireland (including family law-makers[114]) have imposed on them by the Northern Ireland Act a strong equality duty. They are required, in carrying out their functions to[115]

"(1) . . . have due regard to the need to promote equality of opportunity:
   (a) between persons of different religious belief, political opinion, racial group, age, marital status or sexual orientation;
   (b) between men and women generally;
   (c) between persons with a disability and persons without; and
   (d) between persons with dependants and persons without.
(2) Without prejudice to its obligations under subsection (1), a public authority shall in carrying out its functions relating to Northern Ireland have regard to the desirability of promoting good relations between persons of different religious belief, political opinion or racial group."

---

[108] Northern Ireland Act 1998 ss.68–70 and Schedule 7.

[109] Ibid., ss. 73–74 and Schedules 8 and 9.

[110] Ibid., s. 6(2)(c).

[111] Ibid., s. 69(4). The fact that the Commission will base its advice on the full range of international human rights law was confirmed by the Chief Commissioner, Professor Brice Dickson, in a speech at the Institute of Advanced Legal Studies, London, on 8 May 1999.

[112] Ibid., s.69(7) and Belfast Agreement, p. 25, para. 4.

[113] The Human Rights Act 1998 extends to Northern Ireland, and the Convention Rights are also mentioned in the Northern Ireland Act.

[114] Northern Ireland Act 1998 s.75(3). In Northern Ireland, aspects of family law are at present within the remit of the Office of Law Reform, the Law Reform Advisory Committee, the Department of Health and Social Services for Northern Ireland and the Northern Ireland Court Service. Family law is a "transferred matter" within the Northern Ireland Act 1998 s. 4(1) and will therefore be within the legislative competence of the Northern Ireland Assembly.

[115] Northern Ireland Act 1998, s. 75.

The equality duty is extremely widely drawn in the range of persons whom it protects.[116] However, the extent of the duty is arguably quite limited, requiring bodies only to give a reasonable amount of consideration ("due regard")[117] to the "need" to promote "equality of opportunity". It seems likely that this last phrase refers to formal equality rather than to equality of outcomes, but even such a limited interpretation could require new considerations of the rights to marriage of transsexual[118] and homosexual people,[119] and of the development of property rights for cohabitees on separation analogous to those of married people,[120] as well as of the equality of spouses within marriage as required by Protocol 7 of the European Convention and Article 16 of the UN Convention on the elimination of all forms of Discrimination Against Women.[121]

What is the significance of an equality clause? Both the Preamble and the first Article of the Universal Declaration of Human Rights commence with a statement that all human beings are free and equal in dignity and in rights. Canada[122] and South Africa,[123] to take two not-quite-random examples, included in their Bills of Rights comprehensive equality clauses. Dworkin bases his argument for human rights on the concept of equality, saying:

> "The concept of an individual political right . . . is a response to the philosophical defects of . . . utilitarianism. . . It allows us to enjoy the institutions of political democracy, which enforce overall or unrefined utilitarianism and yet protects the fundamental right of citizens to equal concern and respect by prohibiting decisions that seem, antecedently, likely to have been reached by virtue of the external components of the preferences democracy reveals. . ."[124]

In a pluralist society, the explicit introduction of human rights into the law-making process is one way of ensuring that the competing interests of everyone,

[116] By contrast, Article 14 of the ECHR provides a right to non-discrimination only within the subject matter of the Convention Rights.

[117] The issue of the distinction or similarity between the United Kingdom concept of irrationality (*Associated Provincial Picture Houses Ltd* v. *Wednesbury Corporation* [1948] 1 KB 223) and the EU and ECHR concepts of proportionality will be of relevance here. See Hunt (1998b), pp. 207–61 and Beatty (1997).

[118] See Khaliq (1998).

[119] *Fitzpatrick* v. *Sterling Housing Association Ltd* [1998] 1 FLR 6, and the comment on it by Wikely (1998). See also Griffin (1997), Broberg (1996), Butler (1998).

[120] Despite rumours that it might be imminent (*The Independent* 17 May 1999), the Law Commission's long-anticipated discussion paper on homesharers, which may deal with the issue, has yet to be released. The Law Reform Advisory Committee for Northern Ireland is presently carrying out a separate consideration of rights in the family home.

[121] See Bailey-Harris (1998), p. 263.

[122] Section 15(1) of the Canadian Charter of Rights and Freedoms sets out the right that "Every individual is equal before and under the law and has the right to the equal protection and equal benefit of the law without discrimination and, in particular, without discrimination based on race, national or ethnic origin, colour, religion, sex, age or mental or physical disability."

[123] Article 9 of the South African Constitution of 1996 states that: "(1) Everyone is equal before the law and has the right to equal protection and benefit of the law . . . (3) The State (and individuals, Clause (4) may not unfairly discriminate directly or indirectly against anyone on one or more grounds including race, gender, sex, pregnancy, marital status, ethnic or social origin, colour, sexual orientation, age, disability, religion, conscience, belief, culture, language or birth".

[124] Dworkin (1977), p. 277.

especially minority groups and those without significant lobbying power, are taken into account as fully as possible.

This is particularly significant for family law, an area dramatically affected by the development of a plurality of family forms in the late twentieth century. Obviously, any policy, no matter how restrictive, can be dressed up in rights language. Alone, rights discourse does not feel as if it permits a full debate of all matters relevant to a given family law reform. However, it protects both against leaving family members vulnerable in an unregulated private sphere, and against the tyranny of "unrefined utilitarianism". Modern democracy is decreasingly a matter of pure majority rule, but can be seen[125] as a process of dialogue which can create an agreed social space in which individuals may hold mutually incompatible views or live incompatible lives. In a multicultural society, an inquiry into human rights based on equality may be one way of allowing this dialogue to enter the family law reform process; a way of ensuring that everyone's voice is heard in the dialogue.

A PRACTICAL SOLUTION—STRIKING A BALANCE

Philosophically, it makes little sense to speak of balancing human rights; a human right is either respected or breached. However, the structure of the Convention Rights themselves, as well as the way in which the European Court has interpreted them does involve a balancing act. The rights in the Convention are not stated as absolutes, but are for the most part followed by a list of exceptions, and occasions on which the State is permitted to interfere with the rights in question. It seems not unreasonable to suggest that policy-makers could develop a checklist, balancing the public interest in a reform which would curtail an individual's human rights, with the disadvantage to that person. Such a development would bring a structured and deliberate consideration of human rights to the very centre of United Kingdom family law-making. Such a checklist might be developed from the considerations set out in Article 8 ECHR and the tests in *Geillustreerde Pers NV* v. *The Netherlands*[126] and *Silver* v. *UK*,[127] and could include questions such as the following:

1. Does the case in question interfere with the human rights (under the Convention or any other relevant document) of any individual?
2. Is the interference authorised/going to be authorised by law?
3. Is the interference necessary (in a democratic society) for the protection of a legitimate objective or the rights of others?
4. Is the interference proportionate both to the legitimate objective and the effect on the rights of the individual?

---

[125] Explored in relation to Northern Ireland in Morison and Livingstone (1995).
[126] Commission Decision of 6 July 1979, D&R 8/1977.
[127] Series A No. 61, 5 EHRR 347.

5. Does the case in question disclose a differential treatment between persons affected by it (or persons affected by it and those who are not)?
6. Does the differential treatment have an aim?
7. Is that aim objectively and reasonably justifiable having regard to both the aim and the effects of the practice?
8. Is there reasonable proportionality between the means employed and the aim sought to be realised?

Bringing these explicit considerations into the balancing act; requiring the overt discussion of principle in relation to the competing demands of private and public interests, the needs of different family members[128] and cost, would be a positive factor. It may help to strike a balance between the competing demands of lobbying groups, whose voices were heard clearly in, for example, the Child Support debate which led to the 1995 amendments.[129]

CONCLUSIONS

Lord Slynn has suggested[130] that it will take fifty years for the full impact of the Human Rights Act to be felt in the United Kingdom. To simply ask what overt breaches of the Convention Rights exist in our law at present and to specifically reform them would be a limited, "crisis management" approach far-removed from the spirit of either family law or human rights law.

Family law policy in the United Kingdom contains a strong thread of "therapeutic liberalism", and tends to deal with difficult issues in a pragmatic, welfare-based, utilitarian way. However, it is riven with tensions and conflicts. Perhaps chief among these is that between the welfarist desire to intervene, and the liberal desire to allow the "private sphere" of the family to govern itself. This latter aim was in the ascendant in Britain during the privatisation of the Conservative years, and this privatisation has been seen in the United Kingdom and elsewhere as involving an increased, but sometimes confused invocation of rights-based arguments. For these reasons and because of the practical difficulties attendant on ascribing rights to individuals within families, family lawyers may be reluctant to discuss family law-making in human rights terms.

The European Convention on Human Rights may be of limited use to the family law-maker. It emphasises the "vertical" protection of individual rights against State abuses, rather than "horizontal" protection against abuse by other private individuals. The duties imposed on the State tend to be negative rather than positive, although the latter is a developing trend. It contains mainly first-generation civil and political rights. In relation to family law, the rights it grants

---

[128] Fortin (1998), p. 14.

[129] See 5th Report of the Social Services Select Committee (1994–5 Hansard HC 470) and the White Paper *Improving Child Support* (Cmnd 2745, 1995).

[130] In a speech to the Society of Advanced Legal Studies at Middle Temple Hall, London on 30 October 1998.

and the protection offered to the liberal "lone rights-bearer" may be criticised by feminists as unduly masculine.

However, thinking in more general terms about the role of human rights discourse in policy-making, it is clear that it contains potent ideas. Alone, human rights discourse does not feel as if it permits a full debate of all matters relevant to a given family law reform. However, the inclusion of discussion of human rights in family law and policy-making protects both against leaving family members vulnerable in an unregulated private sphere, and against the tyranny of "unrefined utilitarianism".

Ultimately, the family policy-maker is a juggler. Already, he or she has to deal with many competing priorities. The existing law, the welfare of children, the needs of adult parties, efficiency, cost, the public interest, those unprotected by the law, must all be taken into account. A half-hearted nod to the Human Rights Act will make little difference to the way in which family law is made in the United Kingdom. A serious attempt to include discussion of human rights in family law-making means that the juggler has to keep another ball in the air. However, a rights discourse is not just another factor to be balanced. At a time when the competing claims of different groups and policies are becoming ever more complex, it may also be a mechanism for regulating and prioritising those claims, allowing difficult decisions to be taken with due regard to both welfare and justice.

REFERENCES

Atkin, W.R and G.W. Austin (1999) "Family law in Aotearoa/New Zealand: facing ideologies", in J. Eekelaar and T. Nhlapo (eds) *The Changing Family: Family Forms and Family Law* (Oxford: Hart Publishing).

Bailey-Harris, R. (1998) "Equality or inequality within the family", in J. Eekelaar and T. Nhlapo (eds) *The Changing Family: Family Forms and Family Law* (Oxford: Hart Publishing).

Bainham, A. (1995) "Family law in a pluralistic society", 22 *Journal of Law and Society* 234.

Barton, C. (1999) "*A v. UK*—the 30,00 Caning—an 'English vice' in Europe", 11 *Child and Family Law Quarterly* 63.

Beatty, J. (1997) "The Canadian Charter of Rights: lessons and laments", 60 *Modern Law Review* 481.

Binion, (1995) "Human rights: a feminist perspective", 17 *Human Rights Quarterly* 509.

Branchflower, (1999) "Parental responsibility and human rights", *Family Law* 34–7.

Brems, E. (1997) "Enemies or allies? Feminism and cultural relativism in human rights discourses", 19 *Human Rights Quarterly* 136.

Broberg, (1996) "The registered partnership for same—sex couples in Denmark", 8 *Child and Family Law Quarterly* 149.

Bunting, A. (1993) "Theorising women's cultural diversity in feminist international human rights strategies", 20 *Journal of Law and Society* 6.

Butler, (1998) "Same-sex marriage and freedom from discrimination in New Zealand", *Public Law* 316.

Clapham, (1993) *Human Rights in the Private Sphere* (Oxford: Clarendon Press).

Cossman, (1990) "A matter of difference: domestic contracts and gender equality", 28 *Osgoode Hall Law Journal* 303.

Cretney, S. and J. Masson (1997) *Principles of Family Law*, 6th edn. (London: Sweet and Maxwell).

Department of Social Security (1995) *Improving Child Support Cmnd.* 2745 (London: Stationery Office).

Dewar, J. (1998) "The normal chaos of family law", 61 *Modern Law Review* 467.

Diduck, A. (1995) "The unmodified family: the Child Support Act and the construction of legal subjects", 22 *Journal of Law and Society* 527.

Dingwall, R. (1994) "Dilemmas of family policy in liberal states", in M. Maclean and J. Kurczewski (eds) *Families, Politics and the Law* (Oxford: Clarendon Press).

Dworkin, R. (1977) *Taking Rights Seriously* (London: Duckworth).

Eekelaar, J. (1989) "What is 'critical family law'?", 105 *Law Quarterly Review* 244.

—— (1994) "A jurisdiction in search of a mission: family proceedings in England and Wales" 57 *Modern Law Review* 839.

Ewing, (1999) "The Human Rights Act and parliamentary democracy", 62 *Modern Law Review* 79.

Feldman, D. (1997) "The developing scope of Article 8 of the European Convention on Human Rights", *European Human Rights Law Review* 265.

Fortin, J. (1998) *Children's Rights and the Developing Law* (Butterworths).

—— (1999) "Rights Brought Home for Children", 62 *Modern Law Review* 350.

Freeman, M. (1983) *The Rights and Wrongs of Children* (Francis Pinter).

Gibson, S. (1994) "Social Work, Law-Jobs and Modern Law", in M. Maclean and J. Kurczewski (eds) *Families, Politics and the Law* (Oxford: Clarendon Press).

Gilligan, C. (1982) *In a Different Voice: Psychological Theory and Women's Development* (   ).

Glendon, M. (1991) *Rights Talk—The Impoverishment of Political Discourse* (New York: The Free Press).

Griffin, A. (1997) "Another case, another clause—same-sex marriage, full faith and credit and the US Supreme Court's evolving gay rights agenda", *Public Law* 315.

Halpin, A. (1997) *Rights and Law, Analysis and Theory* (Oxford: Hart Publishing).

Higgins, T.E. (1996) "Anti-essentialism, relativism and human rights", 19 *Harvard Women's Law Journal* 89.

Home Office (1998) Supporting families: A Consultation Paper (London: The Stationery Office).

Honderich, T. (1995) (ed.) *The Oxford Companion to Philosophy* (Oxford: Clarendon Press).

Hunt, M. (1998a) "The horizontal effect of the Human Rights Act 1998", *Public Law* 423.

—— (1998b) *Using Human Rights Law in English Courts* (Oxford: Hart Publishing).

Jacobs, F. G. (1975) *The European Convention on Human Rights* (Oxford: Clarendon Press).

Khaliq, U. (1998) "Transsexuals in the European Court of Human Rights", *Northern Ireland Legal Quarterly* 191.

Kramer, M., N. Simmonds and H. Steiner (eds.) *A Debate Over Rights* (Oxford: Clarendon Press).

Law Commission (1979) *Family Law and Illegitimacy: a Consultation Paper* (London, HMS).

Law Commission (1988) *Family Law: Review of Child Law, Guardianship and Custody*, No. 172 (London: HMS).

Laws, J. (1998) "The limitations of human rights", *Public Law* 255.

Lord Chanceller's Department (1998) Procedures for the Determination of Parenting and on the Law on Parental Responsibilty for Ummarried Fathers: a Consultation Paper (London: Stationery Office).

Maclean, M. and J. Kurczewski (1994) "Introduction", in M. Maclean and J. Kurczewski (eds) *Families, Politics and the Law* (Oxford: Clarendon Press).

Morison, J. and S. Livingstone (1995) *Reshaping Public Power: Northern Ireland and the British Constitutional Crisis* (London: Sweet and Maxwell, Modern Legal Studies Series).

O'Donnell, K. (1995) "Protection of family life: positive approaches and the ECHR", 17 *Journal of Social Welfare and Family Law* 261.

O'Donovan, K. (1993) *Family Law Matters* (London: Pluto Press).

Olsen, F. (1983) "The family and the market: a study of ideology and legal reform", 96 *Harvard Law Review* 1497.

Parker, S. (1992) "Rights and utility in Anglo-Australian family law", 55 *Modern Law Review* 311.

Quinn, J. (1998) "Manumission", in K. Morgan and A. Schlepper (eds.) *Human Rights have no Borders: Voices of Irish Poets* (Dublin: Marino Books/Amnesty International).

Romany, C. (1993) "Women as aliens: a feminist critique of the public/private distinction in international human rights law", 6 *Harvard Human Rights Journal* 87.

Ryle, M. (1994) "Pre-legislative scrutiny: a prophylactic approach to the protection of human rights", *Public Law* 192.

Sachs, A. (1998) "Introduction", in J. Eekelaar and T. Nhlapo (eds.) *The Changing Family: Family Forms and Family Law* (Oxford: Hart Publishing).

Scottish Law Commission (1992) Report on Family Law no. 135 (Edinburgh: Scottish Office).

Stark, B. (1996) "International human rights law, feminist jurisprudence and Nietzsche's 'Eternal Return': turning the wheel", 19 *Harvard Women's Law Journal* 169.

Taggart, M. (1998) "Tugging on Superman's cape: lessons from experience with the New Zealand Bill of Rights Act 1990", *Public Law* 266.

Wade, E.C.S. and A.W. Bradley (1985) *Constitutional and Administrative Law*, 10th edn. (London: Longmans).

Wikely, N. (1998) "*Fitzpatrick v. Sterling Housing Association Limited: Same sex partners and succession to Rent Act tenencies*", 10 *Child and Family Law Quarterly* 191.

Index